The Obama Files
Chronicles of an Award Winning War Criminal

Cindy Sheehan

"The writer must earn money in order to be able to live and to write, but he must by no means live and write for the purpose of making money."

Karl Marx

Donald

Love & Peace

Cindy Sheehan

"Cindy's voice—righteous, outraged, and uncompromising, rises from these pages like a messenger from the future compelled by a deep knowledge of our past transgressions to sound an alarm. One can heed her warning and follow her call or remain silent, and in doing so, remain violent."

– Dennis Trainor, Jr. | writer, filmmaker, activist

"The Clash once sang about that opportunistic breed of rebel that inevitably 'joins the church.' Cindy Sheehan, however, has never and will never tow the company line. As *The Obama Files* passionately articulates, the work of a true dissident requires one to avoid easy compromises and comfortable alliances. This book—and all of Cindy's work—is a testament to the long term vision of collective liberation."

– Mickey Z. | author of *Occupy this Book*

"Cindy Sheehan's many books document her transformation from a woman whose 'entire world was my family and this suburban intellectually challenged sinkhole' to an international activist with humanity and the whole planet in her thoughts and big heart. In *The Obama Files* she excoriates the world of presidential assassination programs; pre-emptive indefinite detention; spreading government surveillance, police brutalizing and killing people of color in the Obama years. Even as I share much of her critique and experience in calling out crimes of the Democrats, I am choked up at Cindy's deep outrage. She continues to call us to resist the crimes done in our name, and to join in creating a world where people will be free."

– Debra Sweet | National Coordinator of World Can't Wait

"As far as I'm concerned, Obama has continued and expanded on all of Bush's worst policies. I never supported him. Like Cindy, I knew better. After my years of activism, I learned that the system does NOT work for the people. I have been very fortunate to work alongside Cindy throughout most of Obama's presidency. Because of that, I've read most of her articles, and listened to most of her podcasts. The corporate media would lead you to believe that Cindy went away after Obama came into office. If you want to see how wrong they were, and how consistent Cindy has been, read this book. If you want to see how much of a war criminal Obama has been, read this book."

– Jon Gold | 9/11 Truth Activist and author

The Obama Files: Chronicles of an Award-Winning War Criminal

ISBN-13: 978-1508436713
ISBN-10: 1508436711

Published by:
Cindy Sheehan
Vacaville, CA USA

Also by Cindy Sheehan:

Not One More Mother's Child

Peace Mom: A Mother's Journey through Heartache to Activism (Atria)

The Vigil: 26 Days in Crawford, Texas (All Access)

Dear President Bush (City Lights Open Media)

Myth America: 20 Greatest Myths of the Robber Class and the Case for Revolution

Revolution, A Love Story

I Left My Marbles in San Francisco: The Scandal of Federal Electoral Politricks

Dedication

This book is dedicated to my friends and colleagues (you know who you are) who never bought the Madison Avenue hype of the "new and improved" POTUS; the struggle has been hard and lonely at times, but the dedication and persistence you have shown have been my motivation and inspiration.

Acknowledgements

Without the help and support of the following people, this book would not have been possible:

Michele Fergus: Editorial Services Plus

Brother Larry Pinkney

Dede Miller: My sister/assistant

Barack Obama, whose unfettered War Crimes have unfortunately made this book possible.

David Keenan

Keith Baker

Dan Scanlan

Jill Estensen

Harvey Smith

Sue Chan

Dave Jensen

Jolie De Pauw

Dave Bartram

Paul Castaldi

Woods Elliott

Joshua Pritchett

Sarah Roche-Mahdi

Mike Powers

Dan Yasseen

Greg Fernandez, Jr.

Rhonda Neugebauer

PF Soto

Paul Abram

Carol Holland

Shellie Frisina

Clifton Buck-Kauffman

Jeff and Susan Roughgarden

Michael Kuzma

Dennis Trainor, Jr.

Joanna Folino

Mark Truppner

Ed Stengel

Robert and Jesse Turner

Grace Richardson

Jon Phillips

Dan Myers

Gary Roberts

Riva Enteen

Stuart Simon

Martin Gugino

Table of Contents

Foreword

by Larry Pinkney

Though often hidden or distorted, human history is replete with examples of courage and sacrifice by a relatively few political dissenters sounding the alarm and speaking truth to power. These dissenters are scorned and ridiculed by those who control the corporate mass media and its concomitant systemic machine of perpetual war, death, and destruction. Yet, US society in particular, and Mother Earth as a whole, are in dire need of these principled dissenters whose stories represent the very best of struggling humanity. This is the essence of Cindy Sheehan and why her actions and writings over many years are of such invaluable and enduring significance. She has repeatedly *actualized* the words of the late Dr. Martin Luther King Jr., when he said, "Our lives begin to end the day we become silent about things that matter."

After suffering the terrible loss of her son Casey, in the US war on Iraq, in 2004, Cindy Sheehan demonstrated an unshakable commitment to raise awareness nationally and internationally about 1) the underlying and unacceptable causes of war; 2) who the *real* purveyors of war actually are; and 3) the inextricable connection of—militarism and war—to poverty, corporate hegemony, the obliteration of human rights, 'racism,' and the de facto state sponsored 'terrorism' against humanity carried out as an integral part of the national and global surveillance police-state.

In the stalwart tradition of Rosa Luxemburg, Lucy Parsons, Fannie Lou Hamer, and so many other courageous women and men of all colors, Cindy Sheehan has taken her message directly to everyday ordinary people. In plain language she urges people to critically think, and to link the issues *together* in order to bring about an end to the insane militarism, corporate greed, and environmental ravaging of our Mother Earth.

Well before the conclusion of the eight years of G.W. Bush's disastrous rule of perpetual war and unspeakable horrors abroad and at home, the tiny US corporate/military power elite was preparing and grooming a successor who would *continue and substantively exacerbate* the same Bush policies, while insidiously and effectively masquerading as someone who would bring about genuine change on behalf of the suffering masses in the US and globally. This successor and articulate political conjurer was Barack Obama—Mr. 'hope and change,' whose second largest 2008 Obama campaign contributor was none other than Wall Street's notorious corporate blood-sucking Goldman Sachs. Thus, in 2008, the handwriting was in fact already on the wall, but with the complicity of the US corporate-stream mass media and numerous so-called 'progressives,' etc., the majority of everyday struggling people were thoroughly and cynically bamboozled to their own detriment. Indeed, on the *third day* of his first term as US President, Barack Obama mercilessly droned the sovereign nation of Pakistan, murdering children, women, and men non-combatants. Subsequently, Obama has gone on to *massively increase* the use of deadly US drone attacks upon many *other* sovereign nations in Africa, Asia, and the so-called 'Middle East.' It is estimated that at least 90 percent of the victims murdered and/or maimed by US killer drone attacks are non-combatant children, women, and men. Thus, Obama spawns more rage and hatred as a result of these ongoing killer drone attacks, and with it, the concomitant spiral of terror and perpetual war.

Prior to 2009, when Barack Obama was officially installed as the nominally 'black' designated standard-bearer for the US system of global Empire at home and abroad, there were precious few who had the principled courage to sound the alarm. Fortunately for us all, Cindy Sheehan and a relative handful of other dissenters, refused to be complicit with, or silenced by, the nauseating and deafening chorus in those days by the supporters of corporate brand Obama's euphoria of madness on the US Democrat/Republican plantation of the damned.

Not satisfied with his war crimes abroad, the wily corporate-controlled Drone Man Barack Obama, in service to the corporate/military elite, has bestowed upon himself his very own 'kill list'—empowering him to target and have killed at will, individuals of any nationality (including US citizens) in the US, or anywhere else in the world, whom he, as judge, jury, and executioner, decides must die. This is Barack Obama's so-called 'hope and change.' Whatever happened to international law and the US Constitution?

Barack Obama's repeated annual signing of the so-called National Defense Authorization Act (NDAA), which includes an outrageous unconstitutional provision authorizing the indefinite *detention* of any person or persons in the US without the due process of a legal defense attorney, a jury of one's peers, or even an open trial is—onerous and utterly unacceptable—and is yet another indication of Obama's hypocritical and arrogant disdain for the US Constitution, the Universal Declaration of Human Rights, and the International Covenant On Civil and Political Rights.

Cindy Sheehan has long made the *connection* between US militarism abroad and political repression, including the militarization of the police, at home. Thanks to her courage and diligence, an increasing number of people are becoming aware of just how relevant and extremely important making these connections are to our very survival as human beings on this precious planet of Mother Earth.

It is with a sense of urgency that this book containing the writings of Cindy Sheehan—particularly as they pertain to Barack Obama and the current US political system—need to be read *and re-read* with a view towards making a critical analysis of the recent past, in order to bring about a seismic political change in the US and *avert an even larger* pending political, economic, and social future disaster in the year 2015 and beyond.

May you be inspired to creative action by the clarity and cutting-edge honesty of Cindy Sheehan's writings in this book!

Larry Pinkney is a veteran of the Black Panther Party, the former Minister of Interior of the Republic of New Africa, a former political prisoner and the only American to have successfully self-authored his civil/political rights case to the United Nations under the International Covenant on Civil and Political Rights. In connection with his political organizing activities, Pinkney was interviewed in 1988 on the nationally televised PBS News Hour, formerly known as The MacNeil/Lehrer News Hour, and more recently on the nationally syndicated Alex Jones Show, and RT (formerly known as Russia Today). He is currently founder and curator of the Black Activist Writers Guild (BAWG) BlackActivistwg.org). Pinkney is a former university instructor of political science and international relations, and his writings have been published in various places, including The Boston Globe, San Francisco BayView newspaper, Black Commentator, Intrepid Report, Global Research (Canada), LINKE ZEITUNG (Germany), 107 Cowgate (Ireland and Scotland), and Mayihlome News (Azania/South Africa). He is in the archives of Dr. Huey P. Newton (Stanford University, CA), cofounder of the Black Panther Party. For more about Larry Pinkney see the book, Saying No to Power: Autobiography of a 20th Century Activist and Thinker, by William Mandel [Introduction by Howard Zinn]

Introduction

Even though I lost to Nancy Pelosi (D-Fraud) in 2008, I came in second and we ran a damn good campaign. Consequently, on election night, you'd think I would get a lot of communications from people congratulating me on that victory.

Not so much—I got dozens of emails and phone calls congratulating me on Obama's victory!

There were a few things that were completely misguided about those well wishes: A) I didn't support Obama; and B) I supported Cynthia McKinney of the Green Party; and C) I had a campaign of my own that year.

I always try to answer all my emails and after I pointed out those facts to people, I got the first inkling of how my future in political/social activism was going to proceed from the pat responses:

"Who did YOU want, McCain?"

"I used to like you, but now you're just angry and bitter."

"What, are you a tea-bagger, now?"

"How dare you, you racist!" (Interesting since I supported a black female for president).

The last six-plus years have been very difficult ones for me (and those like me) who have principles that transcend the "two" party scam that the elite have been running on us for years.

While I was in the process of collecting my numerous essays for this book, an interesting item appeared on the US Corporate Propaganda Mill (aka media) for a relative few minutes: *The US Senate Torture Report.* Predictably, the Obama regime is bending over backwards to protect the Bush regime. Why? Because Obama would appreciate the same "professional courtesy" from the next US regime.

This book may seem premature to some since Obama still has almost two years remaining, but let's face it: He has now made himself one of the lamest ducks the US has ever seen with an overwhelming Republican majority in both Houses of Congress, and an aggressive and progressive legislative agenda he proposed in his 2015 State of the Union speech. Why didn't Obama propose those wonderful reforms (free college tuition; raising minimum wage) in his first SOTU speech in 2009?

WAKE UP!

Obama, and his puppeteers, don't really want those things that would help the rest of us. We the people who live in this hostile Empire of death must not be involved in, or even fall for, the destructive games. The only way wars will end and Capitalism will collapse is if we go on a dedicated effort to educate others and ourselves about the true nature of the United States of America.

I hope this book can be a valuable addition to this effort.

Cindy Sheehan
Vacaville, CA
January 27, 2015

Part One
2009

History repeats itself, first as tragedy, second as farce.

Karl Marx

February 17, 2009

Open Letter to Barack Obama from Cindy Sheehan Re: Flag-draped coffins

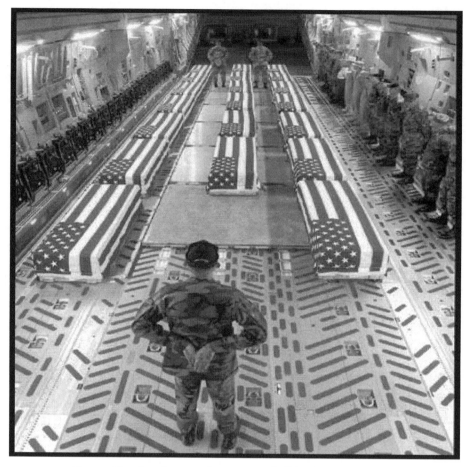

Casey Sheehan's remains are probably in one of these
Photo by Tami Silicio

Dear President Obama:

Recently, your Secretary of Defense Robert Gates said that the DOD would be "re-evaluating" the blockade on the press taking photos of the returning flag-draped coffins from the illegal and immoral occupations of Iraq and Afghanistan.

In 1991, George H.W. Bush signed an executive order banning those photos and early on in George W. Bush's War OF Terror, his mother, and the wife of the 41st president, Barbara, agreed with that order saying that she did not want to "bother her pretty mind" with the images.

President Obama, first of all, you do not need to have the DOD "re-evaluate" that order. In the transparent Republic that you claim to seek, the Department of War should never get to pick and choose what the members of that transparent Republic see. That seems like military tyranny to me. You can sign an Executive Order reversing the one that the first President Bush signed during the First Gulf War.

Secondly, as a mother whose pretty mind was not only "bothered" but whose heart was torn to pieces on April 4, 2004, by the news that my family would be receiving our dear Casey in one of those flag-draped coffins, I implore you to lift the ban on the images.

The order was put in place 18 years ago to remove the costs of war as far away from the average American as possible. Only a relative few American families have had to bear the burden of these fiascoes in the 21st century (although 100 percent of Iraqi families have) and if there are conflicts going on where American flesh and blood is being slaughtered (with which I wholeheartedly disagree), then the entire country should be required to share that sacrifice.

I think there should be a "war tax" levied against every American when there is a conflict to help pay for it. In my opinion, if there is a valid, constitutionally declared, war for defensive purposes, there should be a universal draft (no exemptions or exceptions) with the children of Congress-members and Presidents being the first to be drafted. I think CEOs and other executives of companies that profit off of war should have their salaries reduced to that of the Infantry during times of war and their children should be second in line for a draft. My proposals are designed to make war obsolete, but at the very least, Americans should be able to see the devastating images of the flag-draped coffins.

Taking photographs of the coffins does not violate any kind of privacy, because when the coffins are at Dover AFB the remains are anonymous. If the families wish privacy when their loved one returns home, that is the family's prerogative.

President Obama, I have a shirt with my son's picture on it and the dates of his birth and death. When he was first killed in April 2004, I would wear it and many strangers would ask me who that was in the picture and what happened to him.

I would say: "This is my son Casey, and he was killed in the war." I cannot tell you how many times the next question was, "What war?" The occupations of Iraq and Afghanistan are waged on lies, but that there is little to no shared sacrifice is a national disgrace. Yes, removing the ban is a political ploy, but so was instituting it. If more Americans shared in the grief, then maybe more Americans would protest the cause for that grief.

Bringing our needlessly dead children home under the shadow of secrecy exploits their sense of honor, even if the wars and the reasons for secrecy are ignoble.

Bring our troops home immediately and/or lift the ban.

Sincerely,

Cindy Sheehan
Gold Star Mother and President of Gold Star Families for Peace

CINDY NOTE: *Of course, I do not believe today (if I ever did) that Congress has the moral tools to declare war. That institution is bought and paid for by the War Machine, as is the president.*

Saturday, February 21, 2009
Could You Do It?

Yes, they are getting ready for another war.
Why shouldn't they? It pays high dividends.
But what does it profit the men who are killed?
What does it profit their mothers and sisters, their wives and their sweethearts?
What does it profit their children?

3

What does it profit anyone except the very few to whom war means huge profits?
War is a Racket by Major General Smedley Butler

Could you plunge a knife into the heart of a sleeping baby or into the stomach of a pregnant woman?

Could you shoot an entire family while they slept cozily in their beds at night?

Could you pick off students with a sniper's rifle one-by-one as they skipped out of school while viewing their innocent faces clearly through the scope?

"No!" Why not? "Because I am not a psychopath," you smugly tell yourself.

What if you could murder these people long distance by either ordering their killings, or pressing a button from hundreds, even thousands of miles away that would drop a deadly bomb on their innocent heads? Could you, would you do it?

I still get a lot of flak from a part in a book I wrote called *Peace Mom* where I talk about seeing an episode of "The Twilight Zone." In this episode a woman is sent back into time to kill Hitler when he is a baby, but she could not do it, even though she knows that she will prevent millions of innocent people from dying. I was in such indescribable pain at the time, I wondered if I could go back in time to kill a baby George Bush before he could grow up to murder my own son and thousands of others. However, as I recounted in my book, I decided that I could never kill a baby. How many people besides Bush, Hitler, Obama, etc., are able to slaughter innocent people by the boatload?

President Obama is inheriting two occupations and continuing many other crimes from the Bush regime. The cross-border drone raids into Pakistan murder innocent people with the press of a button here in the states. In an historically incomprehensible move (one can practically hear a pin drop from the antiwar movement), Obama will send more troops to Afghanistan, which will do nothing but kill more innocent Afghans and troops, and further destabilize a region that is already teetering on the brink of oblivion.

I originally wanted to title this piece: *Obama are you Effing stupid*? But he is not stupid, so his continued Bushian trajectory can only be intentional and he needs willing foot soldiers, trigger pullers, bomb droppers and snipers to wage his war of terror on the world, as did Bush.

Obama is turning out to be a Chickenhawk a la Clinton, Bush (II) and Cheney who have never worn the uniform of this country (well, Bush did in the Air National Guard before he went AWOL to avoid drug testing), but send our children off to war to die or kill innocent babies with nary a tweak in their consciences.

If you cannot kill innocent people in close quarters, or even at a distance, then the US military is not the job for you. If you don't want to be shuffled around the world stage to be used as a paid assassin for yet another Chickenhawk, this is definitely not the job for you.

My son Casey was told by his recruiter that even if there were a war he "would not see combat," as he would be going in a support role. In time of war there is no such thing as a military "non-combatant" and even I knew this nine years ago when Casey enlisted. Casey, a HUMVEE mechanic, was killed five days into his deployment in Iraq, in COMBAT, on a mission for which he was forced to go.

There is no such thing as a "good war" or a "smart war."

The mis-leadership of our country is as out of control as a bloodthirsty serial killer and will keep committing its crimes as long as it has the personnel to carry out its murders. The Robber Class (or the children of the Robber Class) would never do the dirty work for itself!

Could you kill for the Robber Class?

Could you die for the Robber Class?

Could you do it?

CINDY NOTE: I have gone past the worn out term of "Chickenhawk." I think the only good things the past few presidents have done is not go to war. However, it's despicable that they send others to fight and die. How about we just call them all "Murderhawks?"

Thursday, March 5, 2009
For What Noble Cause, Mr. Obama?

I am not opposed to all wars. I'm opposed to dumb wars.
Barack Obama: October 2002

For the record, I did not support Barack Obama for president of this country. Of course the above quote was from his famous "antiwar" speech, that was not an antiwar speech, but an anti-Iraq war speech and this is just a sound bite from a mostly nationalistic and pro-war speech.

I opposed Obama because I actually listened to what he said about foreign policy when he was Candidate Obama. He never, ever said that he was going to withdraw all troops from Iraq and he always said that he was going to increase troop levels, not only in Afghanistan, but also in the military over-all. His budget increases military spending at a time when education, health care, wages, and jobs are declining. Obama is a militarist-corporatist and haven't we had enough of this kind of "leadership" in the past three decades?

Gaza is dumb. Afghanistan is dumb. Pakistan is dumb. Iran will be dumb, etc. Any use of violence in geo-political strategy or problem solving is DUMB! Remember, though, that Obama specifically called Iraq a "dumb war." Then why is he extending the withdrawal time past even his too long original timetable? How many more of America's sons and daughters and Iraqi civilians will die in this "dumb war?" My son died in that "dumb war" nearly five years ago and my heart re-breaks with every death; for lives cut short and other lives ruined everyday while the US prolongs the "dumb war" so the war profiteers can wring every last dollar and every drop of oil out of that unfortunate country.

Former President George Bush (I like saying that) was fond of saying that our troops were in Iraq for a "Noble Cause." I even spent a lot of time in Crawford, TX and Washington, DC trying to ask George what that "Noble Cause" was. Now I want to ask the new Oval Office denizen this same question:

Mr. Obama: For what "Noble Cause" are you extending the occupation of Iraq?

For what "Noble Cause" are you compromising the life of even one more soldier? Over 4200 have died, when a single one was too many for this "dumb war."

Mr. Obama, for what "Noble Cause" will you ruin the life of even one more mother— here or in Iraq. Are you willing to be the cause of such bottomless pain? What is this "Noble Cause" that insulates the Robber class from the agony, but pumps up their bank accounts?

Can you visit the bedside of one of our young people who has limbs blown off and tell him/her why you felt compelled to continue that "dumb war," and give that soldier a "Noble Cause" that will justify a life of physical handicap and mental horror?

5

How can you look to a future in America (and indeed, the world) where The Empire has collapsed on the heads of our children and grandchildren and know that you had a chance to reverse that disastrous path and voluntarily reduce The Empire, but instead you chose to continue the policies that guaranteed economic and environmental doom?

Mr. Obama, like George Bush, you cannot look me in the face and tell me that my son died for a "Noble Cause" in the "dumb war," but I will look you right in your face and tell you that all wars are "dumb," and if you think that you can "win" a "smart war" in Afghanistan, then you are far dumber than you appear.

The Noble Cause is peace and a foreign policy that is free from murder and belligerence.

Mr. Obama, be the change that you promised us you were: bring our children home from Iraq AND Afghanistan.

CINDY NOTE: Now the US Empire has invented a new regime and Obama has expanded the war machine to at least seven countries and is supporting the Neo-Nazi fascist regime in Kiev, Ukraine.

Wednesday, March 18, 2009
Our Shame

I remember sitting in my living room, six years ago, watching the "Leader of the Free World" announcing that the United States military had just embarked in "shock and awe" against the country of Iraq.

The images made me physically ill, as they had 12 years before when the criminal's criminal father was bombarding Iraq.

I was also personally sick with fear, as my family had "skin in the game"— our son and brother Casey. On that night, Casey's life clock starting ticking down: He had exactly one year and 15 days to live from "shocking and awful."

Six years and over a million lives later, our military is still shamefully in Iraq. Our "Peace President" has created no positive change there and is in fact extending the length of the deployment of "combat troops." The country has been ethnically cleansed. Violence is down because everyone there is either dead, displaced, or too poor, wounded, or frightened to move or continue fighting. Violence is down, but not out, and you can bet there will be a strong US military presence in Iraq until every last drop of oil has fallen into the hands of foreign oil companies.

What about Afghanistan? When will the "peace movement" begin to protest the anniversary (Octtober 7, 2001) of the invasion of that war-torn country? When will we begin saying "illegal and immoral" in connection with Afghanistan and start mourning the dead there? Maybe when US casualties begin to ratchet up as Obama surges US troop presence there? Obama is sending incursions farther and farther into Pakistan every day. From one "dumb war" to another "dumb war," and the cycle of death will never end for we in the Robbed Class or the poor innocents of that region.

The economic collapse is a very worrisome and immediate problem to so many of us, but we need to remember that the Military Industrial Robber Class Complex is the reason we are in this current crisis, and the economic costs of the occupations cannot and must not be separated from the human cost. Whose life clock is ticking away today? How can we allow yet another year to pass?

Every year I say that this will be our last. I don't believe that anymore. I believe that a very few of us will be demonstrating against these "wars" for years and every year that goes by, fewer of us will be out.

It is our shame that we as a nation complacently sit by and allow the audacity of the atrocities of empire to continue in our names.

Our demands must be the same with the Obama regime as it was with the Bush regime: *Troops home completely and immediately.* Leave cowardice and compromise to the politicians—we in the movement must never compromise or sell out the values of peace with justice. Or if we have already sold-out, we must buy-back. We need everyone!

Many have already given up or have been co-opted by the Democratic Party or the false specter of "hope." Most have never even protested other than bitching on blogs or yelling at the TV when Bush or Cheney came on spewing their lies (Cheney is still at it).

Some will never give up. Here's to you! I honor your commitment to peace, no matter who the current warmonger is occupying the Evil Office (oops, I sorta meant "Oval Office.")

Hasta la victoria, siempre!

CINDY NOTE: Sadly, I was correct. Our antiwar protests have diminished almost to extinction.

Monday, March 30, 2009
Five Years

This Saturday on April 4, my son Casey (and at least 11 other Americans and hundreds of Iraqis) will have been dead for five years. Casey, a Humvee mechanic, was killed on 04/04/04 in Sadr City, Baghdad in combat after he had been there for only five days.

Five years have passed in the blink of an eye and, besides missing Casey so much, our lives have changed about as dramatically as they could have, as has the life of our country.

We just passed the anniversary of the invasion of Iraq with very tepid opposition and President "Change You Can Believe In" is following the path in the Middle East that was blazed by his predecessor, George Bush. Obama's surge in Afghanistan and on the Afghan/Pakistan border guaran-damn-tees that there will be many more "Caseys" and the people of Afghanistan should not be made subject to more "help" from The Empire.

I collaborated with Bay Area CODEPINK today to call for a protest of Obama's Afghan Plan and (although an emergency prohibited me from attending) there were not so many people there and no press at all. To be sure, noon on Monday is not the best time, but when I sent out the Emergency Action alert, I was attacked vehemently.

One person wrote: "Opposing such a thoughtful and smart president smacks of grandstanding" and another person wrote: "You want Obama to fail, shame on you." You're damn right that I want Obama to fail in killing more people and if Obama was so "thoughtful and smart" he would be withdrawing troops from Afghanistan before more of our troops and civilians are slaughtered and the US of A is crushed like many other Empires that crumbled trying to subdue the people of that region.

My family and I made a horrible, horrible (understatement) mistake when Casey joined the military. I will regret until my last breath here on earth that I did not run him over with the car, just enough to wound him, so he couldn't go to Iraq. Our mistake cost the life of a priceless and irreplaceable family member—Obama is making another mistake (for our class, not his) of historic proportions and I implore you who are reading this: DO NOT ALLOW YOUR SON/DAUGHTER; HUSBAND/WIFE; BROTHER/SISTER, friend or other relation to be killed by the Obama Administration. Dead is dead whether the occupant of the White House has an "R" or a "D" behind his name.

I am ashamed that I gave a son to the Robber Class War Machine, but I am not ashamed to oppose Obama on his foreign policy. Anyone who supports Obama's adherence to BushCo's scheme of "More War for More Profit" should be ashamed of themselves.

I know how it feels to bury a child for the greed and unrepentant sins of The Empire. I also know how it feels to try and live one's life with an un-fillable vacuum and I will continue to do everything I can to oppose Obama's foreign policy, with or without help, and even though people who previously thought wars for profit were wrong until Obama became president attack me as passionately as Bush supporters did and still do.

Whether war supporter, or not, my heart goes out to everyone who has had a loved one killed in US wars of aggression and, as always, my heart and apologies go out to people in foreign lands who have unfortunately been born in the way of the trajectory of Empire.

As Martin Luther King, Jr., with whom Casey shares a death date with, said: "The greatest purveyor of violence in the world today is my own government."

Dr. King said this during the height of the Vietnam War and not one thing has "changed." Nothing has changed for the better, but things have become far worse. This was over 40 years ago.

No matter what we in the Robbed Classes do, we cannot make the Robber Class less ravenous for blood and coin, but we can change ourselves and quit allowing our children to be its cannon fodder and paid assassins.

Do it for Casey and his comrades who are unnecessarily dead. Make their deaths "Noble" by not allowing yourself or your child to become another corpse in a long line of victims of the US of A.

For Casey: May 29, 1979 to April 04, 2004

Love,

Mom

CINDY NOTE: I fully stand by everything I wrote here . . . except the use of ellipses, LOL. I am seeing my writing style "mature" and "improve" over the years, but one thing that hasn't changed, I write from my head, via my heart.

Sunday, April 19, 2009
"Hope" less in the "Two" Party System

Since November of 2006 when the Democrats regained majorities in both Houses of Congress, I began my gradual awakening to the fact that the "Two"-Party Robber Class political system is a fraud.

Nancy Pelosi ran for her Congressional seat in 2006 (which would for certain transform her into the House Speakership if the Dems became the majority) promising "No more blank checks for war." She broke that promise, but kept her treasonous "impeachment is off the table" promise. What Nancy Pelosi really meant was the opposite: "I will give George Bush EVERY blank check for war that he asks of me! Why wouldn't I? I am protecting him from accountability—billions of dollars for war is nothing!"

You have to understand that Nancy Pelosi's district is PRO-Impeachment and ANTI-war. If she refused to fund the wars and impeach George Bush, she would be following the will of her constituency. However, the "Two"-Party Robber Class political system protects and preserves itself no matter what party the criminal belongs to.

Now, after 89 days of an Obama administration that is also protecting the torturing murderers of BushCo and has broken its marginal promise to bring (some) troops home from Iraq by the end of 2011 and is escalating hostilities in Afghanistan and Pakistan, some so-called progressives are finally seeing the error in supporting Obama during the elections.

I left the Democratic Party in May of 2007 because of the continued war funding and the continued lack of accountability and I was roundly, thoroughly, and viciously attacked by the same "progressives" who are beginning to doubt the "hope" that they bought into, or allowed themselves to be co-opted by. Some are even calling for an "independent third party" movement here in the US to challenge the corrupt two parties!

Really? Where were these "progressives" when I was running as an independent against the Queen of the Robber Class here in SF? Their heads were buried in the sand, or they were wearing the Rose Colored Glasses of denial, and now we are mired in a situation that cannot be remedied— once the Genie is out of the bottle, she can't be easily put back in. Do you think the Democrats will hold Obama to account when they failed to hold Bush to account? I doubt it. We will continue to see the Obama-Summers-Geithner-Bernanke collapse of the economy and the continued war crimes of the Obama-Clinton-Gates occupations for profit.

It is way past time to stop giving the "Two"-Party Robber Class system "a chance." It's time to stop the "inside" part of an "inside-outside" strategy. We have virtually nobody on the inside that will speak for us besides a token bone thrown out of those marble cesspools. We have to stand up for our class.

Warren Buffet, a famous Robber Class businessman, who loves to dabble in the Democratic part of the One-Robber Class party said: "It is a class war, and my class is winning." They are only winning because we allow them to.

We have been beaten down for so long by the Robber Class we actually believe that we should send our sons and daughters to their wars to die and kill other sons and daughters to make the Robber Class wealthier!

We actually believe that we are not entitled to the same health care that the Robbers in Congress receive (110%).

We actually believe that we should work our asses off and go into insurmountable debt to be able to send our children to college.

We actually believe that we are not entitled to our shacks while the Robbers have numerous mansions (John McCain doesn't even know how many he owns) that sit empty, except for servants most of the time. Some people don't even have a roof over their heads and many tent cities are popping up over the country. The obscenity of a horrible homeless problem makes it difficult for me to sleep at night, knowing so many have no homes!

Now are you ready for an independent third party that is pro-worker; pro-peace; pro-the rule of law for everybody (especially the Robber Class); pro-environment; pro-prosperity for all; and above all Pro-Us?

Please order a copy of my new eBooklet: *Myth America: 10 Greatest Myths of the Robber Class and the Case for Revolution* and let's begin the Revolution today!

CINDY NOTE: After I wrote "Myth America" I rewrote it to have "20 Greatest Myths of the Robber Class." After my campaign against Nancy Pelosi I did my own honest, heartfelt, and humble class analysis where I broke the world up into two parts: Robber Class and Robbed Class. You will find a free PDF file at the link above.

You know, Mr. Randolph, I've heard everything you've said tonight, and I couldn't agree with you more. I agree with everything that you've said, including my capacity to be able to right many of these wrongs and to use my power and the bully pulpit. But I would ask one thing of you, Mr. Randolph, and that is go out and make me do it.
FDR to Labor Activist A. Philip Randolph

President Obama and his followers are fond of quoting this little historical vignette. President Obama has told his followers if they want him to do anything then they have to "Make him."

How is that working out so far?

The biggest rebellion against Obama from his supporters came during the campaign when he made it known that he would vote to authorize the Bush regime to spy on us and immunize telecom companies from releasing our phone records without warrants.

The uprising was immediate and huge. The outcry was without teeth, though. Very few Obama voters threatened him with vote withholding. They wrote to him, blogged on his site threatening to withhold donations, but nothing worked and he eventually did vote for the FISA Modernization Act (FMA) against his supporters' wishes and against the will of his liberal base. Obama obviously did not care because he knew that these people would vote for him anyway and that Goldman-Sachs, et al, would continue funding his campaign.

Since he has been president his behavior has been consistent with being a tool of the Empire (Military-Industrial-Wall Street- Robber Class-Complex) and not with the will of the people.

The most recent issue has been "health care reform." I receive the most mail and requests to sign petitions and call Congress or the White House to make sure that single-payer health care, or Medicare for all, is on the table. This issue has been called the "litmus test" for the progressives on the Obama regime. Again, how's that working out for we the people so far? Obama has again fallen in lockstep with corporations and has ensured that only health insurance companies, HMOs, and big pharma have a voice in health care reform and the "promise" that he extracted from the health insurance companies is just another smokescreen to appease his gullible followers.

He has flip-flopped on important issues like not releasing torture photos and reinstating military commissions after adamantly opposing military commission during the campaign and he also promised to repeal the illegal and inhumane program.

I don't think Obama voters, in fact I am positive they do not, support torture or military commissions, but the silence from the left is certainly and crashingly deafening, as are the accolades about these policies from the right.

On other issues he is doing exactly as he promised, from the agonizingly slow and partial, at best, withdrawal in Iraq to surging, against all reason, troops and violence to what Obama and his War Hawks call Af/Pak.

Flying under the radar because of the "they-said, she-said, he-knew, she-knew, they all knew" torture brouhaha is the fact that Congress passed another 94 BILLION dollar supplemental funding package for Obama's so called Overseas Contingency Operations and the fact his EPA—which stands for Environmental Protection Agency (what an Orwellian name)—has approved 42 new sites for West Virginia mountaintop removal to extract coal. Obama loves to promote the myth of "clean coal" which Robert Kennedy, Jr. calls a "dirty lie." The Sierra Club is rightfully distressed over this, but the group endorsed "clean coal" nuclear power supporting Obama during the election.

What did the Sierra Club expect?

Where is the outcry? Where were the protests demanding that Congress not fund Obama's occupations? Where are the huge marches protesting the occupations that regularly occurred during the Bush Administration?

Don't forget, Obama wants you to "Make him."

His voters and supporters tried in vain to make him vote no on the FMA. Apparently the attempt failed because they are only against warrantless wiretapping when Republicans are doing it and refused to go the extra mile to withhold votes from the PINO (Progressive In Name Only).

Single payer advocates tried and it didn't work.

The ACLU is trying and, so far, Obama's DOJ is blocking their efforts.

Bush left office as the most unpopular president in American history—he wasn't only loathed by Democrats. Profound disgust with Bush helped to usher in this Age of Obama which holds much resemblance to the Age of Bush.

If you are not in an organized and persistent way taking up Obama's challenge of "making him" do the right thing, then one of three things may be happening:

1) You think it will be a waste of time because you have seen that the pressure does not work;

2) You agree with his neo-con and neo-liberal global domination policies; or

3) You are only against violence, suppression, oppression, and economic scandals and impoverishment only when Republicans are in the Oval Office.

Do not let the right accuse the left of hypocrisy. Let's show everyone that we are consistent with our integrity and progressive, peaceful platform.

"Making him" means having the integrity and courage that is so lacking in DC, to withhold your support from someone who doesn't deserve it.

CINDY NOTE: Just about every day I read that some knee-jerk conservative is accusing me of my "hypocrisy" in not supporting Obama. I hope they buy this book (yeah, right)!

Friday, June 5, 2009
Right or Left Wing Media Bias

I am sort of confused?

When I was protesting George Bush, his administration, and the wars, I received a fair amount of media attention, especially when we were in Crawford the first summer. As time wore on and the novelty of having a mother speak out against the atrocities wore off, the coverage dwindled, but never down to practically zippo until I ran for Congress against a "liberal," Nancy Pelosi.

After the Summer of Camp Casey and Katrina, it became really popular to protest and hate George Bush. George Bush slunk out of office as the most detested president in American history. However, from the time Casey died until today, my focus has shifted from blaming George Bush only, to blaming the entire system: The Military-Industrial-

Congressional-Prison-Media-Banker Complex—or whatever you want to call it.

I have integrity. I oppose war, torture, economic oppression, and environmental degradation no matter who is in the White House or what political party they belong to. I have been one of President Obama's earliest and most ardent critics, but where's the media coverage when I protest the carnage now that Obama is president? Where's Air America calling me to comment on the war crimes that Obama has already committed? Why won't most "progressive" online sites print my articles anymore (except AfterDowningStreet.org, OpEd News and MichaelMoore.com)?

One time when Bill O'Reilly heard that I criticized Obama he criticized me!

What is the bias? Is it always towards the Robber Class?

I will do what I think is right, no matter if anyone pays attention, or not.

I just think it's weird.

CINDY NOTE: *This is why I started Cindy Sheehan's Soapbox and I am pleased with the Indy media we still have. Air America is gone, but Cindy Sheehan's Soapbox remains!*

Friday, June 19, 2009
The War Party and its Faux-gressive Minions

For years now, I have been writing about the duplicity of the Democrats and the shocking similarity between the two parties when it comes to the use of state-sanctioned terrorism against innocent populations.

This past week, after the betrayal of every American who elected Democrats to end the occupations of Iraq and Afghanistan, I am wondering if there is anyone still in this nation who thinks that there's any significant difference between the war ideologies of Democrats and Republicans.

I know many faux-gressive entities on the "left" whose silence on this matter is so loud it's hurting my eardrums. Where was MoveOn.org over these past few weeks when the Dems were bludgeoning their caucus to vote "Aye" to extend the war crimes in the Middle East? Where were Markos Moulitsas (Daily Kos) and his bloggers that day? The day the funding bill passed, I wandered over to The Daily Kos and saw that it was all a-twitter about Senator Ensign (R) having an extra-marital affair. Nancy Pelosi, Steny Hoyer, and Harry Reid may, or may not, be loyal spouses, but their calumny will kill, maim, torture, or displace thousands of people over the next 4–8 years. I am not so interested in what happens in bedrooms as what happens in Democratic war zones.

Faux-gressives MoveOn.org and The Daily Kos supported me, and my work, as long as it solely focused on the Bush regime and the Republicans. However, when I had a late-in-life epiphany and figured out that the Democrats were abusing the energy of the antiwar movement to regain power, and I started to speak out against the entire War Party, not just one-half of it, I was kicked off blogging for The Daily Kos and ostracized by the fully co-opted MoveOn.org. To add insult to injury, Nathan Diebenow of the Lonestar Iconoclast then accused me of "alienating" my friends.

I think that I have unfortunately been vindicated by almost every single action that the Democratic Party has taken since 2006 when impeachment was taken "off the table," but "blank-check" war funding was served up to the Military Industrial Complex on a bloody platter dripping with the flesh and blood of real human beings.

Our politicians have no integrity partly because the organizations in the movements that have the largest emailing lists have no integrity. Wars that were wrong under Bush become acceptable under Obama and the stain of torture fades into the woodwork or is hidden from sight like a demented relation because a Senator has an affair. As I understand it, MoveOn.org was founded to oppose the impeachment of Bill Clinton for the same thing Ensign did. (***CINDY NOTE:*** *Senator John Ensign from Nevada who had to resign under the scandal of an extramarital affair.*) Now the gatekeepers of the War Party are going to crucify Ensign to distract their subscribers from real issues?

MoveOn.org sent this out in April 2008 in a fundraising email to its five million subscribers: ***No matter what happens in Iraq, the Bush Administration and John McCain always have the same answer: six more months. They're at it again this week, asking for six more months. But six months won't change anything—except the body count and the price tag.***

They were not talking about the Democratic war funding this week. Apparently it's fine to fund wars if we have a Democratic Despotism, but dangerous for our troops if we have a Republican Regime.

Hey, MoveOn.org: ComeBack.org. Come back from the dark side of partisan politics. You look like Move America Forward, now: (a reich-wing organization that irrationally and blindly supports Republicans and unquestioningly supported BushCo). CODEPINK supported Barack Obama, but at least CODEPINK is over in Gaza trying to call attention to that crime, while MoveOn.org ignores the situation, and most of the bloggers at The Daily Kos just like to sit behind their computer screens and snarkily criticize anyone who is actually on the streets doing the work.

What Pelosi and her Wrecking Crew did last week was disgraceful, but it's shameful that people who opposed the exact same policies under BushCo support the same crimes of ObamaCo.

Saturday, July 4, 2009
Happy Co-Dependence Day

> *The ultimate end of all revolutionary social change is*
> *to establish the sanctity of human life, the dignity of man,*
> *the right of every human being to liberty and well-being.*
> **Emma Goldman**

One of the reasons, in my opinion, that so many people are ready, willing, able, and yes, eager to succumb to "hope" is because most of us believe that true change is not possible.

In our heart of hearts, do we really think that Obama is an agent of change for the people? Have we not been fooled, yet again? So, we lay all of our hopes and dreams for a better life on one person and allow the inevitable heartache of betrayal to wash over us and, once again, drown us in disappointment when that person turns out to be just another politician. Politicians just act like politicians because we always let them.

I just returned home from a 28-day, 18-city (multiple event) trip from California to New Hampshire and back where I talked about the need for us to recognize the fact that we cannot, must not, place false hopes in any politician. Yet, even people who know that the Dalai Bama is not what the gurus on Madison Avenue sold to us don't think they have any power.

"We need a leader, we need a leader," a Russian woman cried to me during a talk I gave in Philly last week. We "consumers" (remember when we used to be "citizens?") here in America have been sold another bill of goods—that one person cannot make a difference so why should we even try? We want "leaders" to do all the work and take all of the heat so we don't have to. That is an absolute myth. If you can fog a mirror, you can make a relevant and profound difference. If you sit around waiting for a politician to lead you to a better life, you will sit around forever.

I just had a heartbreaking conversation with a veteran who struggles on a daily basis with suicide issues. He wants to hang on so he can tell his story of betrayal and try to stop what happened to him from happening to others. He has been so thoroughly traumatized by this Empire that he must make a daily choice to either work to make things better or to physically or mentally check out. Unfortunately, this story is not rare, so I ask myself, why are people so mesmerized by a system that is so harmful to 98 percent of the people of this country, and by extension, the world?

We are Co-Dependent with a Robber Class that expects us to keep it in the style to which it has been accustomed and unfortunately we are accustomed to doing so. When AIG needs billions of dollars in bailouts, it gets all the money that is asked for with no strings attached. Does that money ever trickle down to us in the steroidal capitalism of Obamanomics? Heck no! My state needs a bailout of 24 billion to save tens of thousands of jobs and public services. When the Governator asks DC for the money, he is told: "No, if we bailed out your state, we would have to bail out all the states!" So what? Bailout all the states; save jobs and services, and fix the economy from the ground up, instead of supporting a cancerous capitalism that sucks the life out of the Robbed Class.

Two hundred thirty-three years ago, some of the colonists here rose up to say that they would no longer be bound to a system that hurt them, not helped them. It must have taken a fair amount of courage to do so. I am sure there were some colonists who were too afraid to stand up to the Empire of the day and say: "enough is enough," and were grateful that some did have the courage to resist.

Well, after these 233 years, the USA has become the dominant military empire of today and we need the courage to stand up to it and say: "enough is enough!"

Enough bankster bailouts.

Enough of the unitary executive when even a one-party dictatorship still necessitates illegal presidential signing statements. (Which Obama promised he wouldn't do, but does).

Enough "pre-emptive" indefinite detention.

Enough torture.

Enough war.

Enough environmental plunder.

Enough economic pillage.

Enough of our Co-Dependence with the Robber Class.

Declare your Independence from the Robber Class today!

CINDY NOTE: *Since this post the Governator (Schwarzenegger) has changed to Jerry Brown who is a rabid supporter of Big Oil, Big Ag, Big Prisons and Privatized Education. I ran against him in the California June primary this year on a platform that would totally transform this state. I came in 7th out of 15. Two members of the bourgeois political parties vied for Governor in November: Brown and another Republican. I wrote in: "None of the Above!"*

Tuesday, July 21, 2009
George W. Bush, Part III

> *When a government lies to you, it no longer has any authority over you.*
>
> **Cindy Sheehan, Dallas, TX, 2005**

Okay, so the United States of America has had a new puppet regime for six months now. I was never so much into giving Obama a "chance" and I think it is way past time to call out Obama and his supporters, like we called out Bush and his supporters. Our presidents are merely puppets for the Robber Class and Obama is no exception.

I am observing very little "change" in actual policy, or even rhetoric, from an Obama regime. Granted, his style and delivery are more polished than the last puppet, but, especially in foreign policy, little has changed. Evidently, we elect presidents based on empty rhetoric, and if we can find someone who can say as little as possible with using as many words as he can, that's better. I knew a year ago when Obama and his ilk were blathering on about "change" that they didn't mean positive "change" for us, but it's a shame Obama's voters didn't ask him to be a little more specific or demand some good "change."

Besides foreign policy, where he is a complete disaster, it appears Obama's jobs program is little more than adding tens of thousands of troops to an already bloated military, instead of bringing troops home from anywhere. Billions will go to the money trap of the Pentagon to invest in recruiting our innocent, young, jobless, and hopeless youth, when the budgets of peace groups that do counter recruitment are tanking. This is the third week in July and already it's the deadliest month for US and coalition troop deaths in Af/Pak. Who would ever have thought when violence is surged that deaths would also surge? I think I've seen this movie before.

The blueprint for this disastrous administration came early when O appointed nothing but neocons to his foreign policy team. The Secretary of State and the National Security advisor have even both admitted that the Council on Foreign Relations/Henry Kissinger are calling the shots.

Secretary Clinton at a speech at the new HQ for the Council on Foreign Relations:

I have been often to, I guess, the mother ship in New York City, but it's good to have an outpost of the Council right here down the street from the State Department. We get a lot of advice from the Council (Council of Foreign Relations), so this will mean I won't have as far to go to be told what we should be doing and how we should think about the future.

National Security Advisor, James Jones, who also VERY coincidentally, I'm sure, was on the boards of directors of Chevron and Boeing, had this to say earlier this year:

As the most recent National Security Advisor of the United States, I take my daily orders from Dr. Kissinger. Jones was also giving a speech to the Council on Foreign relations at the time. Kissinger is a fabulous role model for war, don't you think?

How many deaths will Kissinger be forced to atone for when he goes to the same place as McNamara? If there is an afterlife for war-mongering, murderous bastards, I hope it's truly hellish!

As an early, ardent, and unapologetic supporter of the Bush Pre-emptive Wars of Aggression Doctrine, Secretary Clinton showed her true colors early on in her tenure as an elected official and, of course, Jones is a war profiteer. Added to this mix is George Bush's SecDef, Robert Gates, and these are just the main players. Contrary to his "promise" Obama has appointed former lobbyists to key positions in the Pentagon.

We all know all of these things, but the more things "change" the more they stay the same. Apparently the OBots are co-opting the excuses of the BushBots to justify their savior's surge in Afghanistan and Pakistan and broken promise after broken promise in Iraq.

The other day Howard Dean on Democracy Now! told Amy Goodman that although Iraq was bad, we need to stay in Afghanistan because (first and foremost), for the women:

And if we leave, women will experience the most extraordinary depredations of any population on the face of the earth. I think we have some obligation to try and see if we can make this work, not just for America and our security interests, but for the sake of women in Afghanistan and all around the globe. Is this acceptable to treat women like this? I think not.

Laura Bush earlier this year:

There's still a risk to women in Afghanistan. I hope the people of the United States will stay committed. We don't want to see Afghanistan go back to what it was before.

I have been on my *Myth America* book tour for three months now and almost everywhere I go an older white male will stand up and say: "Cindy, we really need to stop allowing Iraq to distract us. Afghanistan always was the place we needed to focus our attentions!" And besides the other neocon reasons given for why US troops need to decimate that country further and kill more innocent women and children is: you guessed it—For the women!

So, we are literally sending in the cavalry to rescue the poor women of Afghanistan, and the patriarchal state apparatus and its zombie adherents don't care how many women we have to kill to save them.

Disgusting.

I give Obama an "F" for his first six months. There has been nothing to like from his continuing the Bush failed economic policies to excluding single-payer advocates from the table. Not to mention reinforcing and protecting Bush Crimes.

The good news is: He's got plenty of room for improvement!

CINDY NOTE: The bad news is, Obama only got worse.

Wednesday, August 5, 2009
Peace, Finally: Reflections on the Fourth Anniversary of Camp

So much has happened in the last four years since about seven dozen of us marched down Prairie Chapel Road on August 5, 2005, in Crawford, TX to confront the now disgraced President George W. Bush!

Our little protest of a few people grew to tens of thousands of people all over the world who resonated with my simple question: "What Noble Cause?" What was a little spark on a hot and dusty small road in Texas turned into a blazing inferno of peace and justice that I never even imagined would happen. From Camp Casey to Peace has been a long road, but after much toil, we have finally arrived.

During that summer in August of 2005, sweltering in constant 100+ degree days (and nights), our country also experienced the tragedy of Hurricane Katrina. With our protest on the literal doorstep of the Idiot Emperor, George Bush, his inept handling of both situations killed his regime.

The part that Camp Casey had in bringing the Bush Regime down is particularly satisfying to me, since Camp Casey was named after my son Casey Sheehan, aged 24, who was killed in Iraq on April 4, 2004. I believed even before Casey was killed that the war was wrong and I tried unsuccessfully to talk him out of going—even telling him, only half in jest, that I would run over his legs with the car before he left. Since Casey was killed, I worked overtime to expose George Bush for the liar he was/is and in the summer of '05, many people caught on.

As a matter of fact, we caught on so well that the Democrats were swept to victory in 2006, and despite my skepticism at first, they really started to "clean house" in DC. The end for Dick and George was hastened when, under Democratic leadership, the very first war funding bill that George Bush tried to get passed was rejected by a narrow vote, but miraculously, the Democrats stuck together and Bush's two wars of his choice for profit began to unravel and with it the presidency of George Bush.

Buoyed by the success of the battle for control of the Nation's purse strings, Chairman of the House Judiciary Committee John Conyers, intrepid Democrat from Michigan, incredibly followed through with his promise to hold George Bush and Dick Cheney accountable and began impeachment proceedings.

The Chairman, who is the hero of about 75 percent of everyone here in America, and 99 percent of world citizens, was supported by such organizations as The World Can't Wait, Drive Out the Bush Regime; ImpeachBush.org, and After Downing Street. Of course I joined all of these organizations in working for accountability.

Once the hearings got rolling it was the revelation of one despicable crime after the other that began to really put the hubris and greed of the ruling class in sharp focus for everyone that didn't have a stone for a brain. The rest is history! The ruling class began to turn on BushCo, and in one of the finest moments in our Republic's relatively short history, Bush and Cheney were forced to resign in disgrace in an unprecedented double-dutch treat for the world! We all remember that day —if you weren't drunk on champagne, that is, like me!

House Speaker Nancy Pelosi ably stepped up to her constitutionally mandated roll as second in line to the president and bravely never pardoned George and Dick! Wasn't that a fine day when we all watched George, Dick, and many other members of BushCo reporting to duty at Ft. Leavenworth to serve their imprisonments for life for high crimes and misdemeanors and treason? What a glorious time to be alive!

(Note: Click here to contribute to the Pelosi/Conyers' Monument in DC Fund)

Now that BushCo have been held accountable, our current president is fearful of the power of the people, and rightfully so, because a sleeping giant was awakened, first on Prairie Chapel Road and now throughout this great nation of ours.

Even though, by default, Nancy Pelosi became our first female president, she never wanted the job and gladly handed it over to Barack Obama on January 20, 2009 and then she went back to San Francisco to be a grandmother and community servant.

No one was happier than I when Barack Obama did not turn out to be yet another puppet of the Military Industrial Complex and in his first 100 days our collective heads spun as he signed executive orders to: immediately close Guantanamo, Bagram (in Afghanistan), and all other torture prisons; repeal the USA PATRIOT ACT (which we progressives feared that he supported because he voted to extend it as a Senator); repeal the FISA Modernization Act and, in fact, repealed FISA, since we have a Bill of Rights, anyway; repeal the Military Commissions' Act, and restored Habeas Corpus! What less did we expect when he appointed mavericks and wise elders (male and female) to his Cabinet and not war mongers and Wall Street mavens as all prior administrations were wont to do?

President Obama's bold leadership put the final nail in the coffin of the occupations and during the second hundred days, now, our troops are returning home to, not hero's welcomes, but sober welcomes befitting the terrible way they were used.

The money being saved on the Death and Destruction of Empire is not only being put to good use, but is healing our economy as untold countless billions (if not trillions) are staying here in America to support good jobs, health care, education, and renewable and sustainable forms of energy.

Just think where this nation would be if instead of taking profound action on August 6, 2005, I had stayed in my safe home for fear of failure or worse?

Then I woke up and realized that none of these things happened and we are still in the Imperial Dog House, but now its roof is leaking and the steps are sagging.

I see signs of this country coming out of the "Hope"-nosis of Obama as positive change is not even in the forecast, but the reawakening is not happening fast enough. We really need everyone to walk towards the light of truth and peace if we ever want to see any of my dreams become reality!

Stay tuned to Cindy Sheehan's Soapbox for exciting ways we can also hold Obama and the Robber Class accountable as we did Bush—coming up in the fall!

CINDY NOTE: *Jeez, smartass much?*

August 14, 2009
Warnography

We'll know it when we see it.
Richard Holbrooke, Special US Envoy to Afghanistan and Pakistan
on defining victory in Af/Pak

I shall not today attempt further to define the kinds of material I understand to be embraced . . . [b]ut I know it when I see it . . .
Supreme Court Justice Potter Stewart defining pornography in 1964

Well, there you go—Richard Holbrooke has defined the US's demented mission in Af/Pak as an indefinite proposition and when I say, "define" I am joking, because what kind of definition is "we'll know it when we see it?"

Oh yeah, I know what kind of definition that is. It's a Bush era definition, which is totally appropriate because it seems like in so many ways that we are still in the Bush/Cheney era—or error.

In a related article, Bush/Obama Secretary of Defense Robert Gates spells success in Af/Pak even more ephemerally than Holbrooke when he said: "Mysteries were those where there were too many variables to predict. And I think that how long US forces will be in Afghanistan is in that area." I know I had to read that last sentence a few times before it even began to make sense to me.

Does this inspire confidence in anyone that A) high-ranking officials in the Obama Administration are either profoundly stupid, or deliberately obfuscating on the length of the "mission;" and that B) as in Iraq, the US is never leaving that beleaguered region unless our ass gets deservedly handed to us like the USSR's was.

What is a "mystery" to me is where the antiwar movement is.

There has been no significant removal of troops from Iraq and there has been a very significant increase of troops to Af/Pak, with the unfortunate commensurate increase in casualties on all sides. Yet, there is very little movement in the "movement."

McCain would be doing the exact same thing that Obama is doing in Iraq/Af/Pak—the EXACT same thing. There is no difference between what Obama is doing and what McCain would be doing, except Obama has a (D) behind his name.

The profound difference to us here in the grassroots would be that if McCain were president, faux-gressives would still be up in arms about the wars and, even though our protests wouldn't change McCain's mind, at least we could retain our moral high-ground that has been sold out to the Democrats for absolutely nothing in return.

War always has been and always will be the most obscene slasher-porn ever invented by deeply sick minds and perpetuated in the 21st century by even sicker minds that kill indiscriminately for power and profit.

I know evil when I see it.

War is evil and the US Empire that is the "greatest purveyor of violence in the world today" (MLK, Jr.), is the greatest evil no matter who is at the helm of the ship of state.

CINDY NOTE: *Yes, what I said!*

Monday, August 17, 2009
Cindy Sheehan Heads to Martha's Vineyard to Confront Obama on the War

For immediate release:

Next week, Cindy Sheehan will join other like-minded peace activists to have a presence near the expensive resort on Martha's Vineyard where President Obama will be vacationing the week of August 23–30.

From her home in California, Ms. Sheehan released this statement:

"There are several things that we wish to accomplish with this protest on Martha's Vineyard.

First of all, no good social or economic change will come about with the continuation or escalation of the wars in Iraq, Afghanistan, and Pakistan. We simply can't afford to continue this tragically expensive foreign policy.

Secondly, we as a movement need to continue calling for an immediate end to the occupations even when there is a Democrat in the Oval Office. There is still no Noble Cause no matter how we examine the policies.

Thirdly, the body bags aren't taking a vacation and as the US-led violence surges in Afghanistan and Pakistan, so are the needless deaths on every side.

And, finally, if the right-wing can force the government to drop any kind of public option or government supported health care, then we need to exert the same kind of pressure to force a speedy end to the occupations."

Cindy Sheehan will arrive on the Vineyard on Tuesday, August 25th.

CINDY NOTE: *This was the thing that curtailed my entire month of August off. Wowzers, I got a ton of crap from the "liberals" about "bothering Obama" on his "vacation."*

August 30, 2009
Cindy Sheehan: Alone at Martha's Vineyard
The Silence of the Antiwar Movement is Deafening
Cindy Sheehan's Lonely Vigil in Obamaland

By John V. Walsh / August 26, 2009

Cindy Sheehan will be at Martha's Vineyard beginning August 25 a short way from Obama's vacation paradise of the celebrity elite but very far from Afghanistan and Pakistan and Iraq where the body bags and cemeteries fill up each day as Obama's wars rage on. She will remain there from August 25 through August 29 and has issued a call for all peace activists to join her there. For those of us close by in the New England states and in New York City, there would seem to be a special obligation to get to Martha's Vineyard as soon as we can.

A funny thing has happened on Cindy Sheehan's long road from Crawford, Texas, to Martha's Vineyard. Many of those who claim to lead the peace movement and who so volubly praised her actions in Crawford, TX, are not to be seen. Nor heard. The silence in fact is deafening, or as Cindy put it in an email to this writer, "crashingly deafening." Where are the email appeals to join Cindy from The Nation or from AFSC or Peace Action or "Progressive" Democrats of America (PDA) or even Code Pink? Or United for Peace and Justice. (No wonder UFPJ is essentially closing shop, bereft of most of their contributions and shriveling up following the thinly veiled protest behind the "retirement" of Leslie Cagan.) And what about MoveOn although it was long ago thoroughly discredited as principled opponents of war or principled in any way shape or form except slavish loyalty to the "other" War Party. And of course sundry "socialist" organizations are also missing in action since their particular dogma will not be front and center. These worthies and many others have vanished into the fog of Obama's wars.

Just to be sure, this writer contacted several of the "leaders" of the "official" peace movement in the Boston area—AFSC, Peace Action, Green Party of MA (aka Green Rainbow Party), and some others. Not so much as the courtesy of a reply resulted from this effort—although the GRP at least posted a notice of the action. (It is entirely possible that some of these organizations might mention Cindy's action late enough and quickly enough so as to cover their derrieres while ensuring that Obama will not be embarrassed by protesting crowds.) We here in the vicinity of Beantown are but a hop, skip and cheap ferry ride from Martha's Vineyard. Same for NYC. So we have a special obligation to respond to Cindy's call.

However, not everyone has failed to publicize the event. The Libertarians at Antiwar.com are on the job, and its editor-in-chief Justin Raimondo wrote a superb column Monday on the hypocritical treatment of Sheehan by the "liberal" establishment. (1) As Raimondo pointed out, Rush Limbaugh captured the hypocrisy of the liberal left in his commentary, thus:

"Now that she's headed to Martha's Vineyard, the State-Controlled Media, Charlie Gibson, State-Controlled Anchor, ABC: 'Enough already.' Cindy, leave it alone, get out, we're not interested, we're not going to cover you going to Martha's Vineyard because our guy is president now and you're just a hassle. You're just a problem. To these people, they never had any true, genuine emotional interest in her. She was just a pawn. She was just a woman to be used and then thrown overboard once they're through with her and they're through with her. They don't want any part of Cindy Sheehan protesting against any war when Obama happens to be president."

Limbaugh has their number, just as they have his. Sometimes it is quite amazing how well each of the war parties can spot the other's hypocrisy. But Cindy Sheehan is no one's dupe; she is a very smart and very determined woman who no doubt is giving a lot of White House operatives some very sleepless nights out there on the Vineyard. Good for her."

Obama is an enormous gift to the Empire. Just as he has silenced most of the single-payer movement, an effort characterized by its superb scholarship exceeded only by its timidity, Obama has shut down the antiwar movement, completely in thrall as it is to the Democrat

Party and Identity Politics. Why exactly the peace movement has caved to Obama is not entirely clear. Like the single-payer movement, it is wracked by spinelessness, brimming with reverence for authority and a near insatiable appetite to be "part of the crowd." Those taken in by Obama's arguments that the increasingly bloody and brutal Af/Pak war is actually a "war of necessity," should read Steven Walt's easy demolition of that "argument." (2) Basically Obama's logic is the same as Bush's moronic rationale that "We are fighting them over there so we do not have to fight them over here." There is a potential for "safe havens for terrorists," as the Obamalogues and neocons like to call them, all over the world; and no one can possibly believe the US can invade them all. However, the ones that Israel detests or which allow control of oil pipelines or permit encirclement of China and Russia will see US troops sooner or later.

The bottom line is that everyone in New England and NYC who is a genuine anti-warrior should join the imaginative effort of Cindy Sheehan in Obamaland this week and weekend. We owe it to the many who will otherwise perish at the hands of the war parties of Bush and Obama.

Tuesday, August 18, 2009
The President Exhibits Crazy Speech Patterns

As I listened to clips of Obama's speech to the VFW on August 17, 2009, I was wondering if his speechwriters were on vacation and they just recycled an old Bush/Cheney/Rumsfeld/Rice speech.

While the so-called left is focused on the health care debacle and is allowing the so-called right to define the debate when it should be: Medicare for all, and all for Medicare; Obama and his neocon foreign policy team are preparing for a decades long, bloody foray in Af/Pak.

As Yael T. Abouhalkah, an editorial writer for the *Kansas City Star* put it:

President Barack Obama did his best imitation of former President George Bush Monday at the VFW national convention in Phoenix.

Obama sounded downright hawkish—and, yes, presidential—when he addressed the issue of terrorism in front of the veteran-laden crowd . . . Dick Cheney could not have said it better.

This is one of the reasons I am leading protests next week on Martha's Vineyard where President Obama will be vacationing. The antiwar movement cannot allow itself to be co-opted by the Democratic Party any longer.

We cannot allow the War Party and other elites to define the terms of the War Debate.

Obama actually had this to say in his speech in front of the Veterans of Foreign Wars (VFW):

We must never forget. This is not a war of choice. This is a war of necessity. Those who attacked America on 9/11 are plotting to do so again. If left unchecked, the Taliban insurgency will mean an even larger safe haven from which al Qaeda would plot to kill more Americans. So this is not only a war worth fighting. This is fundamental to the defense of our people.

He also made a lot of other crazy Bushian statements, but this one has to take the cake and lead the charge for peace!

One thing that we must NEVER forget is that the Taliban, and especially the people of Afghanistan (26 members of a WEDDING party, not WAR party, but WEDDING party were bombed and killed yesterday) DID NOT attack us on 9/11. Even if Osama did plan the attacks from some place in Afghanistan (not likely) this war of choice is not about defending America.

Remember: profit is not a consequence of war; it is the reason for war. And how can we as a nation allow the War Party to sacrifice innocent babies for the illusion of safety? Afghanistan is just as much a war of choice as Iraq is, and Obama is choosing to continue it by exploiting the lies.

What is fundamental to the defense of our people is a sane foreign policy, not more war crimes brought to the world by the War Criminals in DC. What is fundamental to our health and prosperity is to bring the troops home from Iraq/Af/Pak and reduce the Pentagon budget so we can afford such basic human rights as health care, housing, and education.

Besides Afghans and Pakistanis being killed and displaced at a Bushian clip, these days, our troops are increasingly being killed and wounded so the War Profiteers can squeeze more bucks out of violence. More of our families will be harmed while most of the antiwar movement stands down for Obama.

This is unconscionable.

I don't care if you love Obama, or hate him, or something in between (he has the lowest approval ratings of any president after seven months in office), we must loathe his wars and his crazy hate speech directed at our brothers and sisters in war torn regions.

Please join us on Martha's Vineyard from August 26–30 to demonstrate to the world that there are still some people here in America who want peace no matter who inhabits the Oval Office.

Wednesday, August 19, 2009
We Have the Moral High Ground

Hate begets hate; violence begets violence; toughness begets a greater toughness.
We must meet the forces of hate with the power of love . . . .
Dr. Martin Luther King, Jr. 1958

There comes a time when silence is betrayal . . . .
Dr. King, 1967

I remember back in the good ol' days of 2005 and 2006 when being against the wars was not only politically correct, but it was very popular. I remember receiving dozens of awards, uncountable accolades and I was even nominated for the Nobel Peace Prize.

Those were the halcyon days of the antiwar movement before the Democrats took over the government (off of the backs of the antiwar movement) and it became anathema to be against the wars and I became unpopular on all sides. I guess at that point, I could have gone with the flow and pretended to support the violence so I could remain popular, but I think I have to fiercely hold on to my core values whether I am "liked" or not.

Killing is wrong no matter if it is state-sanctioned murder or otherwise. Period. Not too much more to say on that subject, except what I quote above from Dr. King.

However, while the so-called left is obsessed over supporting a very crappy Democratic health care plan, people in far-away countries are being deprived of their health and very lives by the Obama Regime's continuation of Bush's ruinous foreign policy.

I was never dismayed when the so-called right attacked me and called me names for protesting Bush. However, something inside me gets a little sick when I hear people who claim to be peace activists supporting the Obama Administration's foreign policy; a policy that is not like Bush's—in the fact that it's much worse.

I have been called a "racist" from the so-called left. In these people's opinion, I was totally justified in protesting Bush, but I am a racist for protesting the same policies under Obama. When I opposed Bush's policies, I was called traitor, anti-American, anti-Semitic, and other names I cannot print. Name-calling is a great way to shut down critical thinking and discussion. And, not to mention, I think the murder of innocent life in the Iraq/Af/Pak regions is racist and morally corrupt.

There are many people in this country who oppose Obama because they're racist, but I am not one of them. I oppose Obama's policies because they are wrong—again, period!

One cannot obfuscate when innocent lives are being destroyed, here and abroad. We cannot allow "political reality" to get in the way of morality. Human sacrifice is not worth the political reality. Violence, killing, war and more war are NEVER the solution to any problem. Period.

If Obama has violent shadow forces around him pulling him in the direction of violence, which begets more violence and more resistance; then we, especially people in the peace or antiwar movements need to gather and organize to pull him in the direction towards peaceful conflict resolution and solutions that aren't based on exploiting people's fears, anxieties, or ignorance.

I am going to Martha's Vineyard because we have the moral high ground. The war supporters aren't going to protest Obama's wars. They are strangely silent over his foreign policy, unless they are praising it.

I am going to Martha's Vineyard because someone has to speak for the babies of Iraq, Afghanistan, and Pakistan that do not deserve the horrible fate that has been handed to them by the US Military Industrial Complex.

The voiceless need a voice, and even if I am called every name in the book by all sides, I will speak up for them.

I am going to Martha's Vineyard because so many people have been blinded to the fact that the system has momentum that rolls on and over and around no matter who is the titular head of the system.

Let's just pretend that elections are fair in this country and my candidate, Cynthia McKinney, won for president. If she wasn't able to rein in the systemic violence, then I would be going wherever she vacationed to protest her policies, too. I guess at that point, I would not only be called "racist," but I would be called a "self-hating female."

In a recent conversation someone was trying to convince me that I should not be so stridently opposed to Obama's policies and I responded that today 75 people were killed and 300 people were wounded in a bomb blast in Iraq and 26, mostly women and children, were killed in a wedding party in Afghanistan this week and she said: "Oh, that wouldn't be acceptable if it happened here."

And that's the problem: it's not acceptable if it happens anywhere, to anybody, no matter who is president of the USA.

Not only is the death toll mounting for innocent civilians but also is once again climbing for our troops.

While the "festivities" are occurring on Martha's Vineyard next week, there are families all over the world who will never again be able to fully feel festive. Ahhhh—everyone should just stand down, relax, and sip an Obamarita on the beach. Hope reigns once again in The Empire.

And, yes, we are going to Martha's Vineyard to get attention. We vehemently want to call attention to all of the points I have made above.

Even though there is a small antiwar, peace movement in this country, there still is one and this movement has the moral high ground and punditry, personal attacks, glitzy marketing, or "political realities" won't drown us out.

Members of Dr. King's own caucus tried to convince him not to publicly speak out against the Vietnam War, and that's when he delivered his brilliant Beyond Vietnam speech at the Riverside Church in NYC exactly one year before he was assassinated. That speech was in response to the critics. Dr. King took the moral high ground when he said: "There comes a time when silence is betrayal."

That time has now come, once again. By our silence we are betraying humanity.

Love the president or hate him, or anywhere in between, but we must speak out loudly and without any timidity against the institutional violence of the US Empire.

CINDY NOTE: I think a very convincing argument to rally around, but apparently it didn't sway many.

Thursday, August 20, 2009
"Enough Already"

And you look at somebody like that (note: me) and you think here's somebody who's just trying to find some meaning in her son's death.

And you have to be sympathetic to her. Anybody who has given a son to this country has made an enormous sacrifice, and you have to be sympathetic.

But enough already.

ABC Nightly News Anchor, Charles Gibson August 18, 2009

"Enough already?" Hmmm . . . I don't know Charlie Gibson and I don't pay any attention to his career, but I seem to agree with him on this one: "Enough already."

Enough with the killing, torturing, wounding, and profiting off the backs of our troops and off of the lives of the people of Iraq/Af/Pak—as our brothers and sisters in Latin America say: "Basta!"

Somehow, I don't think this is what Charlie Gibson meant, though. I am sure that he just wants me to go away like most of the rest of the antiwar movement has done under the Obama presidency.

One of the things I hear quite often from people from all over the political spectrum is: "Why don't you just go away, you've had your 15 minutes of fame."

Yes, that's exactly what I thought as soon as I heard that my son was killed in the US's illegal and immoral war in Iraq: "This is a perfect opportunity to get my 15 minutes of fame." Actually, after I slowly recovered from the shock and horror, the pain always remains, I thought that I had to do everything I could to end this nightmare so other mothers and families wouldn't have to go through what I was going through and what I am still going through.

I certainly am not the anchor of a major network news show, but last time I checked people are still dying at a heartrending clip in Iraq/Af/Pak.

If my goal was "15 minutes of fame," I could have gone quietly away a long time ago. I started because I wanted the wars to end, and I will figure I can go away when the wars end—but when is that going to be? In my lifetime, probably not.

I am cutting my writing-staycation short to head to Martha's Vineyard because I think the new titular head of the empire needs to know that his policies are devastating people as much as the same policies did when Bush was president.

I would rather be able to go away and spend the rest of my life worshipping my grandchildren, writing, reading, resting, and doing humanitarian work where I am needed.

I wish the wars would go away, but they aren't going away if we the people don't get more militantly insistent.

CINDY NOTE: I wonder what Gibson thinks of me now? Oh, wait, I don't give a poop what he thinks of me!

Monday, August 24, 2009
Activities on Martha's Vineyard this Week—Protesting the wars and creating Peace!

—FOR IMMEDIATE RELEASE—

MARTHA'S VINEYARD—CINDY SHEEHAN, Peace Activist, Gold Star Mother, Organizer of 'Camp Casey' memorials and a nominee for the 2005 Nobel Peace Prize, will be arriving on Martha's Vineyard on Tuesday August 25, to confront President Obama on his engagement in the wars in Iraq, Afghanistan, and Pakistan. She will issue a challenge to Obama on his escalation of troop presence in the Middle East and his continuation of war policies around the globe.

Her schedule of public events is as follows:

Wednesday, Aug. 26, 11am, Press Conference at Oak Bluffs Elementary School.

Wednesday, Aug. 26, 8pm, Peace Vigil, Ocean Park Bandstand, Oak Bluffs.

Thursday, Aug. 27, Friday, Aug. 28 and Saturday, Aug. 29: Boat trips with Cindy for peace movement leaders, press and public. These 'shipboard peace summit' meetings will leave Vineyard Haven twice daily on the 105 foot sloop 'SS Camp Casey' in the afternoons.

Saturday Aug. 29, 9 to 5 Peace Vigil Ocean Park, Oak Bluffs and Walkabout around the Island.

Saturday, Aug. 29, 8pm Cindy Sheehan speaking event "Peace Now, Again" Katharine Cornell Theater, 54 Spring St., Vineyard Haven.

In addition to these planned events, there will be impromptu gatherings during the week. A memorial site will be present on the island with an outdoor area designated as 'Camp Casey,' a living tribute to her son Casey Sheehan, who died in the Iraq War, as well as honoring others who were war casualties.

The SS Camp Casey will welcome all those who wish to come to meet Cindy; She will also be available on the Vineyard for gatherings of visitors, which will be open to the public, the press, and anyone desiring to connect with those for whom the costs of war are a daily reality in their lives.

No Vacations for Body Bags!

CINDY NOTE: *So, if she holds a protest and no one sees it, did it really happen? We did get some wonderful help on the Vineyard from residents who housed us and the few that supported us and came to our events. However, Obama never met with us.*

Tuesday, September 1, 2009
The New Face of the Antiwar Movement

I resigned as the "Face" of the antiwar movement a couple of years ago when I was attacked for trying to hold Democrats to the same standards as I held Republicans. Democrats are obviously not the "Peace Party" and now I also believe it has been proven that Obama is not a "Peace President."

Since the Democrats have taken back the majority (off the backs of its antiwar base), the situation in our nations' misbegotten wars have deteriorated measurably. Unfortunately, the anti-Bush movement is betraying the children of the world as the Democrats have betrayed it.

Who will speak for the baby in the picture? That baby is as beautiful and as worthy of life and peace as my beautiful grandson Jonah who is about the same age.

This baby is the new "Face" of the antiwar movement and should be the rallying image to personalize the politics of peace.

The establishment peace groups should rip down their posters of the war criminal, Obama, with its message of "Hope," because that "Hope" is only a new wrapping for the violent policies of the Empire and what it represents to most people around the world.

I became the "Face" of the antiwar movement because I represented the personal cost of war.

While US troops and families are still suffering, the new "Face" should be the children of the world who are suffering for the imperial greed of the War Party's violence.

September 15, 2009
"You Have to Learn Lessons from History"

I was just watching a report on CNN and after the commentator said that support for Afghanistan is rapidly dwindling (58 percent now think it's not worth fighting), an interview with Obama was shown.

The interviewer asked the president if he was afraid that because war-weary America is growing impatient with the wars, that failing to withdraw and, in fact, sending more troops would look like what Johnson did in Vietnam, and therefore make Obama a "One-term president."

Well, I have been saying that whoever won in 2008 would not do the right thing and would send the USA even farther down the path to ruin (because every president has to follow orders from his masters, the corporations) and be a one-term president.

But, Obama incredibly answered the interviewer with: "You have to learn lessons from history." Somehow, Obama believes he's going to stain his hands darker with blood, but he's not going to pay any political consequences.

That Obama is talking about "history" in relation to trying to subdue Afghanistan is fraught with irony. First of all, the Afghanistan that was invaded in 2001 has very little resemblance to the Afghanistan of today. Many analysts say that our rationale for being there—al Qaeda—has long ago moved on. What about the history that Jimmy Carter's administration was responsible for arming, training, and otherwise supporting (and creating) al Qaeda in the first place and that Jimmy Carter signed an order supporting the Mujahadeen against the USSR in 1979, which spurred the Soviet Union's invasion that resulted in a decade long bloody war that defeated the USSR's military empire.

Let's go back to Genghis Kahn and Alexander the Great and Great Britain. No empire has ever been "successful" in Afghanistan and it really makes me wonder what "history" Barack Obama is learning from. Not the "history" where Afghanistan has been the burial place for empire, that's for sure.

Obviously, our "leaders" are out of control and there is no mass movement of Americans who will be able to get out in the streets to stop the homicidal maniacs.

We need to stop allowing ourselves to be used as weapons of mass destruction against each other, and that is by refusing to join the Army of the Empire or by refusing to be deployed to the messes in the Middle East

All of this excess of the War Machine is getting fundamentally ridiculous. The cannon fodder of the US military should refuse to be used as these pawns for idiotic and ignorant Commanders in Chief. Why die or kill innocent Afghans for the arrogance of Emperors?

Bloody hands are bloody hands. Our president, love him or hate him, is a reflection of us. So long as we quietly sit by and allow him to murder in our names, our hands get bloodier, too!

I will be one that stands up and is counted against Obama and his policies as adamantly as I was against Bush and his—because they are the same and they are wrong.

CINDY NOTE: Well, this is near the end of 2014 and the much-touted timeline for withdrawal from Afghanistan. The USA just signed a Status of Forces agreement with the new puppet in

Wednesday, September 30, 2009
President Obama: Give Peace a Meeting

President Obama:

I know that you are only fulfilling your campaign promises to increase the violence in Afghanistan and Pakistan, and I notice that not a significant amount of troops have been withdrawn from Iraq. However, even with your hostile rhetoric and promises to escalate the violence, many people voted for you because they believed you were the peace candidate.

Since the election, you have betrayed the progressive base that gave you victory on many occasions already, but the cause that keeps many of us motivated is the continued carnage in the Middle East. What bothers me even more, especially, is the fact that the so-called antiwar movement has given you a nine-month free pass and thousands of people have died, including hundreds of our own troops.

Since you took office, 125 of our irreplaceable young have been killed in what you called a "dumb war" in Iraq, and 223 in what I call the "other dumb war," Afghanistan. I have been waiting for a mother of one of those needlessly killed troops to demand a meeting with you to ask you: For "What Noble Cause?" her child was sacrificed.

No such mother has come forward and since your rhetoric is eerily similar to the Bush regime and you are reportedly considering strategies for Afghanistan before you condemn more than the 21,000 troops you have already condemned, I am requesting that you meet with a contingent of the true Peace Movement that will be assembling outside your house this Monday, October 5th at noon.

You are listening to your "Afghan War Council," McChrystal, Clinton, Gates, Mullens, and Petraeus, who have all fully demonstrated their Hawk credentials, and what do you really think they will tell you? It is a *War* Council after all and will inevitably lead our country further down the path to ruin.

Many people supported you because they say you are "smarter than Bush." Bush would never meet with voices of reason and it appears that the voices you are listening to are extremely unreasonable, also.

President Obama, meet with us and show the country and the world that you are at least willing to listen to opposing view-points.

Give Peace a Meeting.

Peace is the only logical solution to the human made diseases that plague our planet and Peace never gets a seat at the table.

Peace will heal the economy.

Peace will heal the environment.

Peace will heal the geo-political tensions.

Peace is the only way out.

Our Peace Contingent will be ready to meet with you any time on Monday the 5th. Just say the word, we'll clear our calendars!

Cindy Sheehan
Peace Contingent Representative

Saturday, October 10, 2009
"Visions"

Today, a president of the largest, violently military empire in the world won the Nobel Peace Prize while his nation is mired in wars in three countries where his actions have oftentimes made things worse.

Let's also make this clear that the Nobel prizes are supposed to be awarded for work done the previous year (2008), so that means Obama was awarded the prize for campaigning for the presidency of the USA, where his "vision" (platform) was consistently pro-more war. The nominations are also due by February 1st. Ten days after the inauguration and about a week after a drone in Pakistan killed over three-dozen innocent people.

He was awarded the prize partly for his "vision" for a "nuclear free world."

Let's examine this. Probably at least a few billion people on this planet have that same "vision" and I know thousands have been working on this "vision" for decades, beginning right around the time the USA dropped two of its WMD on Japan.

I also have this "vision," but my vision extends to include "conventional" WMD like bunker buster bombs, drone bombers, and white phosphorous, depleted uranium—WMD that are being used in the Middle East right now.

I have the "vision" of a nuclear free world, but there are many of us savvy people who know that the USA has been waging a nuclear war in the Middle East for a couple of decades now, at least with the low-grade WMD of depleted uranium. The USA used DU in Kosovo and the Balkans, also.

We billions of us have the "vision" but only one person in this world has his finger on the triggers of almost 10,000 active nuclear weapons, and that is Barack Obama. You know, the one who was just awarded the Nobel Peace Prize and the one who has threatened Iran with military nuclear power if the leaders of that country even dare to get one atomic bomb.

Obama has the power, but his "vision" has not reduced the world's nuclear arsenal by one bomb. However, his "vision" has so far been responsible for killing 300 US service members and thousands of the unfortunate inhabitants of the countries we are occupying and destroying.

Former Premier of the USSR Mikhail Gorbachev and former President Jimmy Carter were awarded the tainted Prize after Gorbachev bombed the Holy Crap out of Afghanistan and the Carter regime's covert support of the freedom fighters in Afghanistan gave rise to: Taliban, al Qaeda, War Lords, and the Northern Alliance.

So the Nobel Peace Prize Committee is sending the message to Afghanistan, that if anyone is responsible for killing mass amounts of them, then he will be awarded a Prize.

It's true, Obama did not begin the wars, but he is sending more troops to all theaters. That doesn't sound too peaceful to me. Torture, indefinite detention, "crippling sanctions," threats towards Venezuela and Iran; silent support of a military coup that overthrew a democratically elected President in Honduras and so on, ad nauseam, are all the "accomplishments" of this Nobel Laureate.

I was tear-gassed and chased down by US Stormtroopers in Pittsburgh for wanting to express my opinion when the leaders of the G20 were assembled a couple of weeks ago. I saw those same imperial Stormtroopers shoot children with rubber bullets or beanbags filled with steel BBs in the Empire's new game of, not protest suppression, but protester attack.

Are these the actions of a country that is "led" by a Nobel Laureate?

I chained myself to the White House fence last Monday and was arrested, along with 61 others, protesting the Laureate's war polices, as he met with his "War Council." Five hundred more of us were there. We were and still all are adamantly opposed to the war policies of The Laureate.

What does that make us candidates for?

The Bizzarro World Peace Prize?

The only "vision" that has come true today is George Orwell's *1984*: War is Peace; Ignorance is Strength, and Freedom is Slavery.

We can't allow the fact that Obama has been awarded a prize—that oftentimes goes to mass murderers anyway—be the final nail in the coffin of the US antiwar movement.

As far as I am concerned, this Prize that was a slap in the face to true peace workers around the world, changes nothing.

Peace of the Action will still go down in DC this spring unless The Laureate signs orders to bring our troops home from the Middle East.

Period.

Peace!

CINDY NOTE: *Peace of the Action was an organization I formed with another person and is now defunct. But you will see in the following pages that we did many actions before it became defunct.*

Saturday, October 10, 2009
Travels of a Dedicated Peace Monger

I am up late in Sweden after spending five days here speaking at seminars and doing interviews. I am heading back to the US tomorrow and after a stop in Albuquerque, I will head back to my home in California on Monday.

I have been gone from the beautiful, yet broke, state of my birth for over three weeks now. This trip hasn't been the longest one, or even most grueling one, but it has been eventful!

I left Sacramento Airport on Friday, September 18th early in the morning to fly to Dallas. There I once again, for the umpteenth time, protested George Bush at his Dallas home, with dozens of others; spoke at my radio station's (Rational Radio) progressive forum (with Thom Hartmann and David Swanson); and snuck into an event at Texas Stadium where George Bush was speaking to young, impressionable students and barely missed confronting him, but got my pic taken with war-supporter Roger Staubach. Yep, that's a pic of Roger and Me! I think he looks a little stunned, myself!

After Dallas, I headed to the G20 protest, where I was hit by an LRAD (LONG RANGE ACOUSTIC DEVICE), teargased, and chased around Pittsburgh by US Stormtroopers there to protect the globalists meeting at the Convention Center from We the Peaceful. Pittsburgh showed me the actual and potential brutality of the Police State.

I was getting ready to go to Nevada to protest at the air force base, from where many drone bombing missions are controlled, when I came down with some kind of yucky flu and had to go to the ER in Pittsburgh because I was having trouble breathing—yes, I have no health insurance—and I was trapped in a hotel room for three days before I felt strong enough to head down and over to our nation's capital to participate in an anti-economic sanctions conference.

In my opinion, sanctions are a WMD, and our Secretary of State has been threatening "crippling" ones against Iran. Sort of like the sanctions against Iraq that killed over one million children and were "worth it" to Madam Madeline Albright.

On to St. Louis for a book event (*Myth America*), then back to the capital for an antiwar rally where I joined hundreds of others and read the International People's Declaration of Peace in front of the White House. Oh, by the way, I also got arrested (after I chained myself to the fence) with activist Janine Boneparth from the Bay Area.

So, hundreds of us protested the future Nobel Peace Laureate and that makes me wonder what that makes us? Anti-peace?

Anyway, here I am in Sweden, late Saturday night missing my grandson and my children and my dog and my cat and my own bed and looking forward to the birth of my granddaughter at the end of this month (an event that I will be present for).

Thank you for your love and support. My supporters help me get through the tough times and rejoice with me in the victories and the good times.

Now, we are planning the most ambitious and bold peace action ever in Washington, DC beginning as soon as we have 5000 people sign up.

With a Nobel Peace Laureate as our president, I think it's time to strike while the iron is smoking hot!

CINDY NOTE: I was actually in Stockholm when the Nobel Peace Prize committee announced that Obama had been awarded the Nobel Peace Prize. The Swedish peace activist who told me actually cried he was so upset by this incongruous honor. All the commentators were roundly denouncing the prize, although at that time, ObamaMania was generally high in Sweden.

Sunday, November 8, 2009
Aunt Cindy Wants You!
If Not Now, When?
If Not Me, Whom?

A great revolution is never the fault of the people, but of the government.
Johann Wolfgang von Goethe

Oh boy! Here comes Cindy Cynical again.

I know you want to hear that Obama is the Savior of the World—but the only thing Obama is saving is the Empire and the Corporatocracy. The new elitist health care bill is nothing but another handout to corporations and at the same time the Democrats limited a woman's right to reproductive choice over her own body. About 130 people will die today because they did not have access to health care, because they are uninsured or grossly under-insured—that's 47,000 a year. That's an Empire-imposed holocaust the size of a small city every year.

I know you want me to tell you that the economy is in recovery, but 17.5 percent unemployment and the fact that every 7.5 seconds someone's home will go into foreclosure and one million of our children here in the US will go to bed tonight and every night with hunger pangs gnawing at their bellies tell a different story than the Geithner-Summers-Bernanke fantasy "recovery."

I know you want to think that someone who was awarded the Nobel Peace Prize may actually be a person who works for peace, but in addition to the tens of thousands of troops Obama has already sent to the war torn zones, he will shortly announce an increase of at least 34,000 more for Afghanistan. This increase will incredibly happen even though members of the "antiwar" movement signed a petition asking him to "pretty please" not escalate the wars. How rude!

Soon pilots for drones (slaughter by robot) will be trained in Syracuse, NY and will also be controlled from there, too. How convenient: pilots can kiss their kids in the morning, go to work to remotely kill other people's kids, and then be home in time for dinner and the evening news.

I wish I could announce the cure for cancer and that cars can henceforth cleanly run on air and that the abuses of the Bush regime have been prosecuted and rectified, but I regrettably can't tell you any of these things either.

So, what are we going to do about it? Stay in sweet, yet disordered denial? Or get busy?

I choose to get busier.

This afternoon in DC, we had our first organizational meeting for Peace of the Action and here are some of the key things to which we came to a consensus.

CAMP

The "Camp Casey" aspect that was so crucial to the experience in confronting Bush in Crawford, TX will also be an integral part to Peace of the Action. Camp will be set up on March 13–14 on the Ellipse and will be the staging area and camping area for people coming to DC to take part in the Action.

There are many tent cities springing up around the country and we believe that our suffering should not be hidden from those that caused it, so we will set up right under their snooty noses.

Come to our Camp for food, basic shelter, and lots of warm community.

We are including social services, entertainment, and education pieces in our Camp life.

WHEN WILL WE BEGIN?

I had originally intended to begin Peace of the Action when we had 5000 people committed to joining us, but now we will begin on March 23rd no matter how many have signed up, to partner with the ANSWER Coalition's March 20th antiwar march (7th anniversary of the invasion of Iraq) and World Can't Wait's events on Friday, March 19th. We truly believe that this is going to be such an amazing and energizing action that "if we build it, you will come."

So, now everyone has target dates to plan to join us for the boldest antiwar action in recent history that will make all kinds of history! Make your plans! We will also have housing and ride-sharing boards on our website.

INVITATION

The committee and I would like to cordially and enthusiastically invite you to join us for Peace of the Action this spring until our demands are met (for all of the action, or any part you can make). We are all in it to win it, this time!

OUR DEMANDS

Troops out of Iraq and Afghanistan and close all bases.

No drone bombings.

Bring home contractors and paid mercenaries from those countries and Pakistan.

Reparations and political/diplomatic help for the people of those regions.

Fully fund VA programs to help reintegrate our troops healthfully back into society, physically, emotionally, and mentally.

ECONOMIC HEALTH

We in the coalition believe that we can't have economic health without the profound reduction of the US Military Empire and Peace of the Action will go very far in accomplishing this.

Troops and dollars home!

LOCAL ACTIONS

If you can't attend our actions in DC at any point (or even if you can), we will be encouraging and helping with local actions.

CINDY NOTE: Unveiling our developing plans for CampOutNow. There will be more posts about it between this one and March 2010.

Friday, November 27, 2009
You Get What You Vote For!

The so-called antiwar movement currently finds itself in somewhat of a quagmire: What to do when the man you raised money for, volunteered for, and yes, even voted for, actually fulfills one of his most repulsive campaign promises?

First of all, I never understood why, or how, peace people could support someone who voted to pay for the wars while he was a Senator and was quite clear on the fact that he would increase violence in Afghanistan and perform a slow, painful, and very incomplete withdrawal from Iraq. Principles that were proclaimed so loudly while Bush was president get shoved aside and buried now that a Democrat is president, and how do you get your principles back from the dung-pile of selling out?

Secondly, On January 23rd of a rapidly dissipating 2009, Barack Obama perpetrated his first war crime (as president) by authorizing a drone attack in Pakistan. In February of this same year, he ordered an increase of roughly 20,000 more troops to Afghanistan: more war crimes, no corresponding outcry. However, when I cried out, I was roundly attacked by the "left" for not giving Obama a "chance." Two thousand nine is going to be the most deadly year for our troops and Afghan and Pakistani civilians on record. I think George Bush is calling: he wants his Nobel Peace Prize back.

It is being widely reported (and it seems hotly anticipated by some)—even though the "antiwar" movement wrote a letter to Obama and asked him to "pretty please" not send any more troops to Afghanistan and had us calling the White House all day on Monday the 23rd when Obama was scheduled to hold his final "war summit"—that the US will commit 34,000 more troops to Afghanistan, which is a 50 percent increase in troop strength in the Land of Certain Empire Death.

What is the "antiwar" movement's response going to be? Candlelight vigils; "honk if you love peace" rallies; a hundred rounds of "We Shall Over Come" (someday, not today or tomorrow); or, is the "antiwar" movement going to say: "Phew, McChrystal asked for 80,000, but our letter worked—he's only sending 34,000?"

True story: In October of 2005, US troop deaths were going to reach 2000 within days and the "movement" was planning its response. I called for a die-in, with risk of arrest, in front of the White House and MoveOn.org called for a candlelight vigil in Lafayette Park. MoveOn.org moved their vigil to another location because they told me that their members weren't ready to do civil disobedience and some of them may be accidentally swept up in some kind of a "peace sweep." I said, "Fine, MoveOn.org, have a candlelight vigil for 2000 like you did for 1000 and next year you'll have one for 3000, then 4000, and then 5000." I think many of MoveOn.org's members were ready, I just don't think that MoveOn.org was then, or is now. They didn't do it when Bush was president, I can't imagine MoveOn.org standing up for peace when their man is the one doing the killing.

So, here we are four years, thousands of US troop deaths and hundreds of thousands of civilian deaths later, and the Pope of Hope, the Dalai O'Bama, the Nobel Laureate will soon be condemning thousands of more to the same fate, and his supporters have given him permission to do so, no matter how many letters they write, petitions they sign, or phone calls they make.

In the end, you always get what you vote for.

I knew that this surge was a done deal no matter how much political posturing and pandering occurred. I chained myself to the White House fence on October 5th and was arrested with 60 other people protesting the wars and demanding that peace be put on the proverbial table. But those were symbolic actions and the problems we are facing are deadly and in full Techno-Color, real. The time for symbolism and street-theater ended years ago, but moribund actions won't seem to just go away gracefully, so we will have to cut them off, cold turkey!

On Monday, November 30, the Peace of the Action Coalition will be sending out a press release condemning the escalation and announcing our Mother of all Protests (MOAP) that will begin in the spring.

If you're looking for some action, look no further than Peace of the Action and stayed fine-tuned for further details!

CINDY NOTE: Yes, Obama approved the "surge" in Afghanistan. Isn't "surge" such a lovely word? When I think of "surge" I think of a wave in the ocean: I love the ocean, I love waves. I hate the way warmongers "frame" their murderous ideas.

Saturday, December 5, 2009
Say What? Peace Prize for a War President?

I was in Stockholm, Sweden when it was announced that President Barack Obama had been awarded the Nobel Peace Prize and, even though the people of Sweden were still enamored of him, when they heard that, they (and I) were shocked.

We got over our shock a little while later when we snapped to our senses and realized what the NPP is all about—it's an establishment prize (usually) that rewards the status quo and Obama won't be the first warmonger to ever win it. Awarding the prize to

Obama, who has not done one concrete thing for peace, just confirmed that inconvenient truth.

A little known fact is that all of the other Nobels are awarded from Stockholm, but Alfred Nobel wanted the peace prize to be awarded from Oslo, because he didn't trust his own country-fellows to make such an important decision. Since it has been awarded to people like Woodrow Wilson, Menachem Begin, Yassir Arafat, Henry Kissinger, and Jimmy Carter, I wonder if Alfred could really trust Oslo, either!

A few weeks after I returned from Stockholm, I was invited to Oslo to be with that peace community when Obama received his medal and money in a ceremony on December 10th. The invitation was simple: "He's fighting three wars. This is an abomination. Please come!"

The undeserved nature of this "Peace Prize" was just brought into sharper clarity this past week when Obama announced that he would be sending tens of thousands of more troops to Afghanistan. There is no reason to send these troops and there is no reasonable expectation for "success," which is as ill-defined under this administration as it was during the last administration.

Nobel Laureate, my big toe!

CINDY NOTE: *Oh, looky, I will be off to Oslo soon!*

Thursday, December 10, 2009
How Dare They!

I have been in Oslo, Norway the past few days working with the Oslo peace community in their opposition to Barack Obama being awarded the Nobel Peace Prize.

I have been doing a lot of media in preparation for the rally that we had this evening that culminated in a march to the Grand Hotel, where the Laureate was to wave at us from a bulletproof glass-encased balcony.

My hosts here in Oslo are Afghan refugees who are working on an exciting movement to replace the US puppet leaders and the Taliban in Afghanistan and I am honored to be asked to be a part of it, and will have more details as the plan unfolds, but the organization is called: Peace and Democracy in Afghanistan. My hosts are understandably upset with Obama and upset with the Peace prize committee for this outlandish betrayal of peace!

I sat with my hosts and watched the speeches given by the Chairman of the Nobel committee (who seemed like he was going to bounce off the platform and float over to Obama and begin to French kiss him in ecstasy) and the Laureate and we were shocked and appalled at the way the speeches gave legitimacy and Robber Class honor to the "necessity" of war.

The protests today were large, energetic, youthful, and angry! It is nice to see some international rejection of the "hope-nosis" that has been infecting our world with rosey-colored violence and gold-plated oppression.

Below is the text of the speech that I gave at the "true peace" event this evening in the very cold, evening air of Oslo, Norway.

Hello friends! I have three words for the Nobel committee and for my president: "How dare you?"

How dare the committee give the Peace Prize (which will be known from here forward as the "Peace Prize") to Obama and how dare he accept it?

How dare the committee legitimize the war crimes and other crimes of the Bush regime by rewarding Obama for continuing them?

The committee said that Obama ordered the closure of Guantanamo prison, while it remains open and the torture policies have been broadened and expanded to Bagram in Afghanistan!

How dare they award the "Peace Prize" to a man who they say wants to reduce nuclear arms, but is waging a terrifying nuclear war in the Middle East by using weapons coated with depleted uranium that is causing a sharp rise in cancers and birth defects there?

How dare they award the prize to a man who they claim exemplifies American Values when those values are war, torture, environmental degradation, and drone bombing abroad and environmental and economic ruin at home?

This "Peace Prize" to Obama was nothing but a slap in the face to people in Iraq, Afghanistan, Pakistan, Palestine, Iran, North Korea, Colombia, Honduras, Venezuela and anywhere that Obama's boot of Empire is crushing or threatening to crush.

This "Peace Prize" is a slap in the face to parents like myself whose child has been killed in the Bush/Obama wars, now approved of by "Peace committees."

This award was a slap in the face to us—we who have been sacrificing and struggling for true peace for years.

If you listened really carefully to the speeches today—with ears not clogged by the hope-nosis of Empire—you heard Obama say, "War is Peace" and you heard the clarion call of the international Robber Class that the only way to peace is through war, war, and more war! The Robber Class has told us, once again, that there is no other way! War is the only way!

Well, I join with you in solidarity today to tell the Robber Class: Bullshit, we reject such stinking thinking and we reject the "honors" of the establishment as we say to them: "We refuse to play your violent games."

If they want awards, they can give them to each other. If they think that killing children is

"Peace," then they can send their own and leave ours the hell alone! If they want their wars then they can fight themselves!

The violent extremists of the world just rewarded themselves for their crimes in an orgy of self-congratulatory pageantry, but I want to say that I have not one enemy here or in Iraq, Afghanistan, or Pakistan.

My only enemy is yours too, the violent extremists of the world's Robber Class and we must join together to fight them, not fight in their wars, to bring true and lasting peace.

Thank you for inviting me here and giving me the honor of addressing true peace warriors!

CINDY NOTE: *I also have been over the idea that the warmongers should "go themselves" or "send their own children." I don't think anyone should be sent to kill innocents in other countries.*

Part Two
2010

CINDY NOTE: *Contrary to the claims of conservatives, I think the past evidence from 2009 shows that I am not in "Obama's pocket," or a hypocrite for not opposing Obama. Now, let's head to 2010!*

Peace of the Action

You've got to put your bodies upon the gears and upon the wheels, upon the levers, upon all the apparatus, and you've got to make it stop.

An eye for an eye would make the whole world blind.
Mahatma Gandhi

Three events over the holidays have caused me great consternation and they proved to me, if anything, that I am not so cynical and jaded that my government can't still shock me.

Of course, the first event has to be the "Crotch Bomber."

The Crotch Bomber story poses more questions than answers and, of course, Muttalabad has already been tried, convicted, and virtually executed by our media who have formulated an open and shut case against him without questioning any details except for "lax" security at airports and possible intelligence "failures." Credible eye-witnesses have said from the beginning that Abdulmutallab was ushered through the system at Schilpol airport in Amsterdam (an airport I have flown through twice in the last month) by a "sharp dressed man"—but the problem is apparently that we have not been subjected to perverted full-body scans every time we fly. So what is the US regime's answer to this incident? Give more military aid to the unstable regime of Yemen to fight "terrorism" in revenge for Abdulmutallabs's failed attempt (which was apparent revenge for US drones killing dozens of innocent Yemeni's just days before) *AND* subject air travelers to either the full body scan or full body search.

The next event that has me worried is the fact that eight CIA agents were just victims of a suicide attacker in Knost Province, Afghanistan. The attacker was also an agent and one of the eight dead. What motivated this attack? Did he attack the CIA because it's an agency that is the model of peace and democracy all over the world?

No, despite what the toady media and Obama say—the CIA is a hated agency involved in assassinations and coups all over the world (giving us the map and blowback we see today) for decades and the CIA has also been drone-bombing the crap out of Pakistan.

A recent report stated that those bombs have killed 700 civilians, and only "five" suspected Al-Qaeda—if we can even believe that figure—the liars are the ones telling us this. So what's the word about these killings coming from the Robber Class? The word is "revenge," even though the assassinations that the CIA is doing is also revenge for something extra-legal and morally reprehensible.

The third incident is the US military's execution of eight school children in Kunar, Afghanistan. According to reports, the US military flew in helicopters from Kabul to Kunar and entered a house, rousting out eight children (seven from the same family), handcuffing some, then dragging them out and summarily executing them. Have you heard of this "Haditha" or "My Lai" incident from your Robber Class "news" channels? I didn't think so.

As far as I am concerned, each one of the people involved in this horrific incident must be punished to the fullest extent of the law: from the soldiers who flew the helicopters, to the shooters, to the one (McChrystal?) who authorized this atrocity!

How do we stop this constant cycle of violence that is perpetrated, fomented, and encouraged by the US Empire? We have to realize that the people of Yemen have the same existential imperative, as do the 300 travelers aboard the flight from Amsterdam to Detroit!

We have to fully internalize that those 700 slaughtered people of Pakistan had as much right to life as the seven CIA operatives!

If we put ourselves in the home of the family where eight children were executed and try to visualize how we would feel if the occupying Empire broke into our home and killed every child that we had, and how terrorizing and devastating that would be, then maybe, just maybe, AND FINALLY, we would rise up against our own violent government?

I have dubbed 2010 the YEAR OF RESISTANCE and we must sacrifice some of our creature comforts for peace—not just peace here at home, but most of all, peace abroad!

Wednesday, January 27, 2010
Infomercial for the Empire

Twenty-Ten is a midterm election year, the Dems are hurting very badly—Obama needed to pull some propaganda out of his bag of tricks and he needed to be able to pronounce every word correctly so his base can say: "At least he's articulate."

I can just envision the weeks leading up to this non-event: "Joe, you wear the blue-striped tie—Barry, you wear the red-striped tie—and Nancy, you get a Botox shot, but make sure you can move your face a little before the speech."

Of course it was not a state of the union address. It was a giant infomercial for The Empire—at one point he even said: "I won't accept second place for the United States of America."

Well, the USA is number one in killing people—biggest terrorist state in decades—we have no peers in this aspect. We are even higher than number one here, if that's possible—we are the SUPER-COUNTRY and killing is our SUPER POWER!

The USA spends more on defense than the next ten lower countries combined. We're number one!

The USA incarcerates more people per capita than any other country. We're number one!

The USA is the number one polluter and user of natural resources than any other country. We're number one!

The USA has more bases on foreign soil than any other country. We're number one!

The USA IS NOT number one in quality, affordable, and easy accessible heath care. We're number 37!

The USA IS NOT number one in literacy. We're in a five-way tie for Number 11!

The USA IS NOT number one for life expectancy. We're number 37!

The USA IS NOT number one for infant mortality rates. We're number 33!

The USA IS NOT number one for quality of life. We're number 13!

The USA IS NOT number one for university graduates. China is number one and graduates TWICE as many than the USA.

Our homeless population is scandalous and the fact that one million children go to bed hungry every night in the USA is also a national shame.

Obama also said: "I will never quit." That doesn't fill me with hopium because the only thing he has done over the past years is make everything from foreign to domestic issues worse. Please "quit" Obama—for the sake of everyone—QUIT!

Peace of the Action won't quit and we are moving across the street from Obama's house to start shutting down the heart of the Empire until Peace is a reality—not just a slogan to mollify a base eager for crumbs from the Emperor's table.

Today was a bad day as we lost a truly wonderful human being who did more for us than Obama will ever do if he lives to be 87: Howard Zinn.

In Howard's memory, we must never give up.

CINDY NOTE: This piece was obviously written after Obama's State of the Union (SOTU) Speech.

February 1, 2010
The Goal of Modern Propaganda: Mythocracy

First Published in *Global Research*

> *The goal of modern propaganda is no longer to transform opinion*
> *but to arouse an active and mythical belief.*
> **Jacques Ellul**

On Super Bowl Sunday, the reason that I wrote my new book *Myth America: 20 Greatest Myths of the Robber Class and the Case for Revolution*, literally hit home.

Since it was the Holy Day of Obligation for our national religion of Football, I headed for my health club because I have always been a heretic. I arrived there a little before kick-off, so the club was still occupied, but after kick-off it was deserted.

After my solo water workout and swim in the pool I headed to the hot tub that was occupied by another spa patron—an older gentleman named Bill who seems to come to the club just to sit in the hot tub and chat. I get the feeling he is very lonely, and this following exchange may be why:

Bill: I think what you do disgraces your son, his memory, and what he died for.

Cindy: Oh really? Since he was killed in an illegal and immoral war, I think this nation disgraced him.

Bill: But they attacked us on 9-11.

Cindy: Who attacked us on 9-11?

Bill: Iraq and Saddam Hussein.

Cindy: Are you serious? If you believe the official story, 16 Saudi Arabians attacked us.

Bill: But Saddam killed his own people.

Cindy: We have killed over one million of Saddam's "own people," (at this point Cindy does air quotes).

Bill: But we didn't mean to.

Cindy: (Deep sigh), So, what team are you rooting for this afternoon?

At which point, Bill scrambled out of the hot tub and headed for the showers.

My "friend" Bill has been thoroughly propagandized from the right—there was no use sitting in the hot tub with the jets blasting and trying to reason with a man who thinks that over one million people can be killed "accidentally."

I didn't write *Myth America* for people like Bill who wouldn't recognize a fact if it flew out of his TV box and hit him on his bulbous nose. I wrote the book for our fellow citizens who have even a tiny inkling that what is our actual shared experience has very little to do with the Mythocracy that we live in.

I also wrote *Myth America* for people who knew that the wars of aggression were wrong when Bush was president, but magically transformed into born-again warniks when Obama took the oath of office. These newby warniks had begun to see through the propaganda over the last eight years, but allowed one of the more insidious myths to take over—the myth that there is a difference between an elected Democrat and an elected Republican. These are the same people who came to my talks after The Obama came to power to proclaim that the US needs to stay in Afghanistan to "protect the women."

During my campaign against House Speaker Nancy Pelosi in 2008, it became so clear to me that the only relevant division in this nation, indeed world, is a class division. I know I have been late to this game and analysis, but remember less than six years ago my entire world was my family and this suburban intellectually challenged sinkhole.

During my campaign I experienced the myths that "Elections Matter" and that the US has a "Free Press" as I struggled in a fierce campaign to even achieve ballot status as an independent and garner a few crumbs of media attention. Even the so-called "Liberal media" abandoned me, and when I did get media attention—even from the papers that endorsed me—the punch line always was, "but she has no chance."

I struggled with the working class to get labor to endorse me, but in each and every case members of my own class endorsed the Queen of the Robber Class, Nancy Pelosi. Nancy has done nothing for labor, except to operate her vineyards in wine country without unions, support most "free" trade agreements, and hire someone to iron her fabulously wealthy husband's shirts. So why did labor endorse Pelosi and not a hard working member of their own class with a labor platform that was hailed from all over this planet? Because she's a Democrat, that's why. Labor cares more about access to politicians than access to sane policies.

It was towards the end of my campaign when the infamous "bankster bailout" happened. After the bill failed in the House, Pelosi came out all haggard to whine about having to bail out the companies, but pushed the stuffing out of her caucus to ram it through the second time.

Democratic candidate and Senator from Illinois, Barack Obama, called members of the House to browbeat them to change their votes, and my neighboring Congresswoman, Barbara Lee of

Oakland, did a rare about-face and betrayed her principles and her poor constituents—that's when I finally woke up to what Robber Warren Buffet said: "It's class warfare all right, and its my class, the rich class that's making war, and we are winning." Well, in our Mythocracy, Buffet's class is really the only class that knows we are at war. Most of the rest of us believe that we live in a "democracy" where even the lowest of us can attain Robber Class status.

Well, in this Mythocracy, if there's a Robber Class, then what's the other class? The one that over 99 percent of us belong to? The Robbed Class—the class that must remain "Hope"notized by those myths and divided amongst ourselves so we don't even realize that just about everything we hold dear is being stolen from us, right out from under our own noses, with our apathetic acquiescence. It's the age-old Robber Class strategy of "divide and conquer."

What is the revolution that I write of?

First, it's the very revolutionary idea of recognizing that we do live in a Mythocracy, and the lower one is on the socio-economic ladder, the farther apart are the reality and myth of this country.

Secondly, the myths must be exposed and dispelled—my new PDF book is an addition to this conversation.

Thirdly, we must work together across racial, political, religious, gender, and sexual preference lines to build community and strength in our class to resist the larcenies of the Robber Class.

Finally, I foresee this top-heavy Empire of cards toppling in the foreseeable future. My revolution will create the necessary umbrella to be able to deflect some of the more damaging rubble that will come crashing down.

The Robber Class knows two things that we need to learn quickly:

They need us far more than we need them and there are far more of us then there are of them.

This is a revolution that we can win.

CINDY NOTE: The free PDF of this book is still available at Cindy Sheehan's Soapbox.

Sunday, February 14, 2010
Presidential Assassination Program
Cindy Sheehan's Soapbox

On today's Soapbox (2pm Pacific) CindySheehansSoapbox.com, Cindy chats with Constitutional authority and Civil Libertarian, Glenn Greenwald, about the US government's murder by presidential decree program as outlined in this op-ed that Greenwald wrote for Salon.com:

On the claimed "war exception" to the Constitution.

It seems as with the recent Supreme Court decision that gives corporations even more say in our government than they had before and with this new Presidential Assassination Program, that the US is even more of a rogue state under Obama's regime than we were under the Bush stain.

On May 31, 2007, Cindy wrote this:

"If we don't find alternatives to this corrupt 'two' party system our Representative Republic will die and be replaced with what we are rapidly descending into with nary a check or balance: a fascist corporate wasteland."

It seems like it is too late, we have come to this point.

Friday, February 19, 2010
Operation New Dawn

> *The very word "war," therefore, has become misleading.*
> *It would probably be accurate to say that by becoming continuous*
> *war has ceased to exist . . . War is Peace.*
> **George Orwell, 1984**

If I forget everything else in my life, I will never forget the night I walked in my front door with my dogs, Buster and Chewy, and saw the three military officers standing in my living room.

I knew the moment I saw them that Casey was dead. It doesn't take a genius to put that equation together. On one side of the equal sign is your recently deployed soldier-son, and on the other side are three Army officers standing in your house looking like they would rather be just about anywhere else.

I didn't go to sleep that night, or indeed for a few nights.

I didn't want to go to sleep and have to wake up after brief oblivion to the realization that my oldest son was dead: Killed in a war that, like most wars, never should have been fought in the first place. Casey's number came up and he became just one more in a long line of humans killed for profit. Casey certainly wasn't the first, and he certainly won't be the last, but my first-born preceded his parents and three of his grandparents in death.

It seemed like within minutes of the notification at 9pm on April 4, 2004, our house was filled with friends and the tears, screams, questions, and memories flowed freely. Around 6am, I went outside to sit on my porch swing. Through my tears, shock, and grief, I could see my neighborhood begin to awaken. People coming outside to pick up their papers or head for work. I wanted to scream at them: "Don't you know my son is dead? How can you pretend like the world is normal?" The world has never been "normal," but I have lived in an even more surreal version since Casey was killed.

Today, I found out that the "operation" that killed my son is over. "Operation Iraqi Freedom" got its name after the "great" Powers That Be figured out that "Operation Iraqi Liberation" stood for "OIL." Now, Obama's SecDef, Robert Gates, has changed that benign name to an even more New-Agey, Sweeter-than-Honey name: "Operation New Dawn." Doesn't that sound nice? Who doesn't like New Dawns? Except perhaps the people of Fallujah who were brutalized in a Marine siege back in 2004 that was inappropriately entitled, Operation New Dawn.

When Obama first took over the trappings of Empire he changed the name of the "Global War on Terror"—the GWOT— to OCO or Overseas Contingency Operation—doesn't that sound benevolent, too? Like the US Empire is involved in Overseas Aid. You have a need for "Aid?" We have a "contingency" for you!

Illegal invasions and occupations are now called "Interventions" as if the US and its allies are sweeping in and saving a country or society from a drug or alcohol problem, when clearly it is The Empire that is suffering from an addiction to mass murder and pillage.

It doesn't matter what the US decides to call its "Operations" part of us will reject the propaganda, and part of us will embrace it wanting very desperately to believe that our country is not a rogue state and/or that Obama is not as bad, or worse, than Bush.

No matter what label the war criminals in DC decide to put on their crimes, innocent people still die and our soldiers are still victims.

It doesn't matter for me either. One day, whether voluntarily or by force, these "Operations," "Contingencies," "Interventions," or "Crimes against humanity" will eventually end, but my oldest son will always be dead. There's absolutely no way in hell for The Empire to euphemize that reality to make it any less painful or easier for me to bear.

Accountability for Casey's death won't make the pain go away, either, but it may prevent other mothers and families from having to suffer from our nation's continuous wars.

Sunday, February 21, 2010
Don't Shoot the Messenger!

Back in the day, during time of war, a person to the opposing camp delivered messages. What a job to have, huh? Oftentimes, out of rage, revenge, or just because, the messenger was killed after the message was delivered.

Today, during times of war, the messages are delivered quite differently, but the business of delivering messages is still risky, especially if some people do not want to hear the truth.

Now "Attacking the Messenger" is a subdivision of the ad hominem logical fallacy, and boy, did I get attacked last week for having Glenn Greenwald on my show and exposing the Presidential Assassination Program. I haven't been so roundly, thoroughly, or more vilely attacked since I started to publicly say that the war in Iraq was based on lies—but this time from the other "side."

I got called "liar" and things that the rightwing reactionaries usually call me that can't be printed in polite company—for just pointing out the truth.

And like my guest said, "Where's the outcry" against this administration for ordering the assassinations of US citizens—and many times their families and neighbors? There was a huge outcry from the Democratic base when we found out the that the Bush Admin was spying on our phone calls, but not even a peep when we find out that the Obama regime is targeting US citizens in this extra-judicial crime spree. It's not a comfortable fact, but it's a fact, and anger should be directed properly. Your government is a rogue government—facts are facts and truth is the truth no matter who warms up the presidential chair in the Oval Office.

Anyway, I will keep telling the truth, and I don't "lie" about anything. If I ever get my facts wrong, I always correct that, but you can all be guaranteed that if I say something, it has been researched through credible sources! And, of course, you can always research whatever I say yourself.

CINDY NOTE: *This is what I was talking about when I said I was attacked for the Presidential Assassination Program show.*

Sunday, March 14, 2010
Beer with Obama

> *Change doesn't come from Washington. Change comes to Washington.*
> **Barack Obama**

Last summer we, here in the news-o-tainment capital of the world, were distracted with the shiny spectacle of the "Beer Affair."

You remember that one, right? In July, in Cambridge, Mass—police, in something that was a racially charged misunderstanding, confronted a college professor named Henry Louis Gates in his own home.

Then, our president—a legend in his own mind—said that the PD and police officer, Sgt. James Crowley, "acted stupidly." They did "act stupidly," but, of course, that's all beside the point.

There was a lot of unnecessary hoopla over the entire incident and after the dust settled, Obama invited both men to the White House to settle all differences and hurt feelings in the time-honored, manly way—over beer. I like to call this little incident: "Duff-Man Diplomacy."

We even found out which beer each man was drinking—I am not going to rehash this further, because it has already been done to death and it never should have reached such Paul Bunyanesque proportions anyway.

Tomorrow, March 15th, a few dozen intrepid souls will be setting up a Peace Camp (Camp OUT NOW) across the street from the White House because there appears that there was another misunderstanding, even more profoundly tragic than the Beer-scapades.

I think the misunderstanding of such catastrophic proportions is that Barack Obama is a "peace president." Many, many, many people voted for Obama thinking that he was going to take this nation in a direction diametrically opposed to the previous administration, but the reality has not matched the rhetoric in the least—unless you count the fact that he promised to send more troops to Afghanistan.

Well, we will have a big tent with red awnings that will have "WAR SUX" in big white lettering so the Obamas, tourists who are up in the Washington Monument, and travelers flying into National Airport, can't miss us.

It is really sad that as we near the seventh anniversary of the "dumb war," that the wars have all but fallen out of the consciousness of many Americans as we all struggle with keeping our noses above water. Our troops feel abandoned and the people of our occupied countries must be feeling that they have all but dropped off the proverbial radar screen.

During the month of March Camp OUT NOW will be asking for a meeting with Obama to set up a fully funded and grassroots Peace Council that will have a seat at the table when any matters of War are being discussed in the ubiquitous War Council.

Clearly, Obama WAS NOT the "change" that had been so eagerly anticipated. Obama and his team *ARE* the Washington insider elite—We the People are coming *TO* Washington to force the change we want to see.

And, we like beer, too—we will drink anything, Barack—and if you agree to meet with us, we'll even bring our own bottle openers.

CINDY NOTE: We didn't get invited for Beer with Obama.

Tuesday, March 23, 2010
Whose Streets? (Our Streets between 1pm and 4pm With a Permit)

On the 7th commemoration of the illegal and immoral invasion of Iraq, there was a rally and march in DC sponsored by the A.N.S.W.E.R. coalition that was attended by about eight thousand people.

For quite some time I have been having problems with marches on Saturday. It seems like we march past empty buildings and shake our fists at them and promise that if those empty buildings don't change their ways, we will be back next year to do the same thing. The arrests are symbolic and don't shut down anything, except in the case of large arrests, where the police stations are busy for a few hours.

As far as I know, there were no large civil disobediences scheduled for last Saturday's rally, but some coffins were built on the sidewalk in front of the White House and four protesters decided to lie down near them and not move. Two of these protesters were good friends of mine: Elaine Brower of Military Families Speak Out and Matthis Chiroux of Iraq Vets Against the War. When I went over to check out the action the four were begging the hundreds of others surrounding the protest to join them. The four were cordoned off with barriers and crime scene tape.

I began to plan a way to join Matthis and Elaine when I went to the front of the barrier and saw my dear friends, who have always been there for me, lying on the sidewalk by themselves. Just as I was figuring out how to get over the barriers, the section I was at collapsed onto the sidewalk and I took the opportunity to step over hoping that dozens, if not hundreds, would follow.

As soon as I crossed the barrier, I was slammed by a couple of cops, handcuffed, and then actually run around the front of the White House while the cops tried to find a paddy wagon to stick me in —about 50 people were running alongside of us yelling: "Let her go, let her go." When the officer and I finally got to the paddy wagon, I was surprised to find that only two others had followed me. One other crossed the line to bring our detained numbers up to eight.

During my speech at the rally, I iterated the importance of "throwing our bodies upon the gears" of the machine, as well as marching—I got a huge cheer and during the march the participants chanted: "Whose streets, our streets." Eight detainees? Apparently, the streets are only "ours" when we have a permit—god forbid we take them when the event is not permitted by the Police State!

Why, when the barrier was compromised, did more people not follow us to actually put their beliefs into higher relief than merely marching in a circle on Saturday? While we were being (tightly) handcuffed and loaded onto the hot paddy wagon, the crowd of on-lookers chanted, "This is what hypocrisy looks like."

I was, to say the least, very disheartened that hundreds of people didn't join us. Watching the video of my "crossing over," you can see a couple of people go over and then run back when the police come—but most of the people step back like the downed barrier is a livewire.

After a bumpy and sweaty ride, we eight arrive at the Park Police Station in Anacostia. As we were being processed, it started to become very clear that some of us were going to be detained until Monday. Ultimately, two of us were released and six of us were held. The two that were released were from DC and those of us held were out-of-towners. Immediately, we knew this explanation was total BS because I have been arrested in DC about 13 times now and I have always been from "out-of-town," and have never even been held overnight, let alone two nights.

Was it a coincidence that Camp OUT NOW had two major actions over the weekend to try and hold our campsite that I missed due to being jailed? I don't think so.

Well, those two days were some of the most miserable days of my life! We were taken to a lock-up and Elaine and I were put into a freezing room. Being unprepared for a two-day lock-up, I had only been wearing a t-shirt and flip-flops. For four women, our cell had one cement block bench that was about 7–8 feet long, so at least one of us always had to be on the stone-cold floor. Sleeping was fitful as it was very chilly all night—and very noisy!

Forty-six hours, and eight bologna-like and cheese-substitute sandwiches later, we were taken to the court for our arraignment and stayed in that cell for seven hours and were finally released at 5pm after we all pled "not-guilty" and were scheduled for a trial on June 9.

Basically, six of us stayed in jail for over 50 hours for an offense that ended up being the equivalent of a traffic ticket. We even had to go to traffic court to be arraigned. I am positive that everyone in DC who gets a traffic ticket and is from "out-of-town" does not have to stay over night. Then, I found out that the penalty for my charge "crossing a police line" doesn't even carry any jail time. I spent two nights in jail on an offense with no jail time! The maximum penalty is $300! Boy, I will be even more pissed if I go through a trial and have to pay $300 dollars after I have already spent two nights in jail.

To make matters even worse, I was the only one who was forced to come back for a trial even though Elaine has more DC arrests than I do. The other seven have chosen to go to trial with me, but they were given the option to "pay and forfeit" which means to pay the fine and forfeit your right to a trial.

The icing on the entire crappy cake came when the eight of us were given a "stay away order" from the White House—I asked the Judge how that could be legal since we weren't convicted of anything, but the Judge assured me that conditions could be placed on our release. I also think this is very suspicious considering our Camp OUT NOW actions were focusing on the White House.

Many times during the 53-hour ordeal, Elaine and I were asked if we thought it was "worth it," to go through so much hardship for so little gain.

My answer is, first of all, if more people crossed the line with me, we wouldn't have had to stay 50 hours in jail and I was very upset that we were left to hang out to dry like that. Secondly, the war didn't end while we were suffering—but knowing how awful it is to spend so much time in jail and be treated like one is a serial killer and not a protester—I would do it again and again, as I have.

There are literally billions of people suffering all over this planet due to my nation's militarism and greed, and I know many people would have traded places with me in a heartbeat and think the conditions were pretty damn good.

AND this never happened to me when Bush was president.

UPDATE: Three of us went to pick up our property this morning at the Park Police station and, as we were being jacked around, an officer named Thomas (Badge number 628) told me that if I "stopped getting arrested" I wouldn't have to go through all of this.

I said: "When the wars stop, I will stop." He actually then told me: "The wars will stop when we nuke them and take their oil."

Gee, I wonder why they are called "pigs."

CINDY NOTE: I was eventually found "not guilty" of the charges in July of that same year, although I had to observe that "stay away" order for four months.

Friday, March 26, 2010
Camp is Gone, but Not for Long!

Well, our great experiment didn't go as well as we planned here in DC. My vision was a Peace Camp that would serve the needs of the campers as far as housing and food were concerned (that part worked) and the campers would then commit aggressive acts of civil resistance (that part didn't) in the nation's capital to shut down the violent military-corporate empire that we live in. In the opinion of members of Peace of the Action, living here in the US gives us special responsibilities for stopping it.

Although we had hundreds of people come through camp, we were only allowed to keep it up for a week. Dozens were college students that worked very hard while they were here and we were sorry to see them go back to their schools after break. The thing that we were hoping would happen and never did was that hundreds of people would stay and help us claim the camp as a permanent presence on the mall.

It's true that the Park Police thwarted us and watched (and photographed) every move we made. However, if we had the numbers, we could have taken a more credible stand against the repression of our rights. When the Park Police came out and shut down camping on the first day, part of our name "Camp" was shut down, too.

We have wonderful organizers and I know I worked as much as is possible for one person, but we had to face facts that the will is just not in our fellow Americans to sacrifice a few creature comforts to create true and lasting change. It's so much easier to vote for a smooth-talking snake oil salesman than to roll up one's sleeves and do the dirty, hard, yet gratifying, work of empire change.

Even though we had some rough times in DC with the Police State and Camp OUT NOW is physically gone (for the time being), we are not giving up the spirit of shutting down this town for Peace.

Congress is once again taking up war supplemental funding. We can't just make phone calls and write petitions—we must organize and be in their faces here and in our home districts demanding that not one more penny be spent on killing and maiming people.

By the way, not only was our demand to meet with President Obama not granted—three of our Camp OUT NOW volunteers (including myself) have been given stay away orders from the White House.

We tried to get into the Senate Appropriations Committee meeting today at the Capitol and we were followed and harassed the entire time, and in the transparent age of Obama the hearing was closed to us citizens, anyway. I was able to watch the rerun on C-SPAN 3 and I can tell you all one thing, these wars are planned to continue indefinitely. I am not okay with that.

To take advantage of the energy and enthusiasm of our young people, we are planning on returning in June to set up Camp and start our actions again.

So we will be keeping the spirit of the Camp alive until the students get out of school and, hopefully, we can make a go of it in the summer.

It's really up to you—we have laid the foundation, now it's your turn to be the builders.

CINDY NOTE: *It's a pure wonder I have never given up!*

Thursday, April 1, 2010
SlayStation

First published in *Islam Times*

> *Unmanned aircraft systems (UAS) and the effects they provide have emerged as one of the most 'in demand' capabilities the USAF provides the Joint Force. The attributes of persistence, endurance, efficiency, and connectivity are proven force multipliers across the spectrum of global Joint military operations.*
> **USAF UAS Flight Plan 2009–2047**

Don't get me wrong, I am not in favor of "Manned Aircraft Systems" raining down bombs on civilians, but the idea of Murder by Joystick with the "Unmanned Aircraft Systems" (UAS) is especially sickening to me.

UAS, more commonly known as "drones," are controlled from thousands of miles away and are increasingly becoming the new wave of the Air Force. The Air Force was recently devastated by Congress cutting off funding for the obsolete F22 fighter jet and is very excited about its robotic killers.

Even the names of drones are monstrous, such as: Predator and Reaper—The Grim Reaper drone —choosing who lives or dies from an air-conditioned bunker at Creech Air Force base thousands of miles away from the bombing site:

Thousands of miles away from the carnage;

Thousands of miles away from the screaming and dying;

Light years away from morality and compassion.

With reports stating that, from the top down, the US military is filled with Christian zealots, I wonder who "authorizes" Murder by Joystick? Does the 6th Commandment say: "Thou shalt not murder; unless you can pretend you're playing a video game?" The mass murder of the 21st century couldn't have been even remotely conceived of a few millennia ago.

War has become more deadly to persons but increasingly more depersonalized. Today, needless civilian deaths outweigh unnecessary military deaths by a five to one ratio, but are still referred to as: "Collateral damage." Our military has become even further depersonalized by the utilization of paid mercenaries.

Not only is this kind of warfare taking a toll on civilians, but also military chaplains have reported that some of the "pilots" who control these weapons are having crises of conscience. Being me, I can't conceive of sitting in a comfy room and dropping bombs on children, then going home to eat dinner with my children, or attend their Scout meetings or sporting events. It is uplifting to know that some of our troops have consciences—I wish more would start to refuse these repugnant orders.

The Pentagon recently confirmed that even though US troops are moving out of Iraq, they would be replaced—sometimes by a two to one ratio—by mercenaries from such places as Uganda. This jaded nation of ours barely cares about the soldiers that are dying, how much less will we care about foreign paid mercenary killers and whether they have the right equipment or not?

The US Central Intelligence Agency collaborates with the Pakistani government to execute political enemies in the tribal regions of Pakistan, claiming that "al Qaeda" or "Taliban" leaders are being killed, when that is not the reality at all. While the government in Islamabad gives lip service to condemning CIA drone attacks, some of the drones are being launched from such airfields in Pakistan as Shamsi.

Currently the US is waging two undeclared wars with pre-emptive attacks in Yemen and promising tougher sanctions in Iran. US drones have been spotted over Venezuelan airspace. I predict that the escalating use of UAS's will just make it easier to wage not only illegal wars, but un-Constitutional wars as well.

In US culture today, it's just a short trip from the violent games on PlayStation and other video systems, to actually killing people with Slay-stations. We parents must be more proactive in banning violent games from our households.

SlayStation's game, Murder by Joystick, is just further moral bankruptcy from the Military Industrial Complex that, according to the UAF Flight Plan, is salivating and looking forward to the day when drones—using artificial intelligence—will carry nuclear weapons and won't need any direction from humans at all.

2047 is the target date for total Armageddon by UAS.

Note: When Bush was president there were 24 drone attacks in Pakistan from 2004–2008. In the 15 months that Obama has been president, there have been 72 attacks. Where's the change?

CINDY NOTE: I had been on this issue of UAVs since Obama's 3rd day in office. Others have jumped on it too late. Others wrote me and told me, "Cindy, you need to give Obama a chance."

Monday, April 26, 2010
Our Complex

Before the war is ended, the war party assumes the divine right to denounce and silence all opposition to war as unpatriotic and cowardly.
Robert "Fighting Bob" M. La Follette

Something "funny" happened on my way to Madison, WI yesterday.

I am in Madison to speak at an event against the "War Party" and its wars. I was to speak on how to do this outside of War Party Politics—based on my history of peace activism and my independent run against Nancy Pelosi in 2008. On the way here, I was informed that the room the event was to be held in at the University of Wisconsin (UW) was withdrawn due to "security concerns" because I am one of the speakers.

Getting down to the bottom of this is not easy. Steve, the student organizing this event here on the ground, was told on Friday that the organizers would have to put on security because I have made "controversial efforts" in the past. There is no basis for any security, because there have been no threats of violence against me. The sponsors could not afford the hefty cost of the security, so the indoor event was canceled.

So, the bottom line is, UW is not concerned FOR me, they are concerned ABOUT me.

Every so often, just for a reality check, I have to have my iPhone pinpoint my location—I am in Madison, Wisconsin—not Mobile, Alabama. Mobile was where the only actual physical attempt was made on my life (inside of the front tires slashed in a car I was riding in). I have spoken several times in Madison (and at the Fighting Bob Fest—where I also got an award) and have never felt anything other than support and love.

I have spoken in colleges and universities all over the world where I have actually received death threats and this is the first time, to my knowledge, that I have ever been shut out.

Hmm—just in the past month, I have been banned by the Catholic Church from any no-cost venue in Scranton, PA (including pressure on churches of other denominations) by the Catholic Bishop-elect AND I have a stay-away order from the White House—first ever as far as anyone can recall.

Why have I, an avowed Peace Monger, started to get so many bans? Is it because I have changed? Is it because I am saying anything different than I have been saying for the last six years? Is it because the wars are over and I still won't stop? No, it's because much of the country has gone insane while I remain the same.

People who should be opposing Obama, support him—people who should be supporting him, oppose him. The Tea Party is serving the purpose of putting a crazy and violent stamp on any kind of opposition at all, and any kind of opposition to Obama is being called "racist" or "seditious" by the very same people who called opposition "heroic" when Bush was president.

Recently, a 12-year-old girl was arrested in the office of a War Party Senator, and I wasn't the only one who got banned from the White House. Five others—including three men who have never been arrested in DC—also got banned from the perimeter of the White House. If one of us should dare disobey the stay-away order, it's a mandatory six months in jail.

How can I be a "security concern" when all my efforts have been peaceful for peace? If my efforts are ever successful, true security will reign over this planet.

Peace is a threat to only a few entities: the War Party and the War Profiteers.

Why would the University of Wisconsin do this?

Doing a cursory "google" search of the University of Wisconsin and its ties (like most universities) to the War Party and its profiteer-masters brings up some interesting facts.

UW gets a lot of "research" funding from defense industries and, as a state, Wisconsin is moving up the ladder of war profiteering graft.

It's not so easy to get current stats, but according to a report from 2004, these are some companies (weapons manufacturers) that UW is invested in:

Boeing	$1,015,535.00
Caterpillar Inc.	$74,813.00
General Dynamics	$153,150.00
General Electric	$1,309,462.00
Lockheed Martin	$548,553.00
Northrop Grumman	$762,619.00
Raytheon	$15,831.00
Total:	**$3,879,963.00**

So, just like everything and everywhere else, the Military industrial Complex has its evil tentacles here in a state that gave us the progressive gift of Robert La Follette.

The tiny, idyllic burg of Hood River, OR, fights for its death merchant, Insitu/Boeing and a University that was a hot bed of activism in the 1960s, UC Berkeley, has an active ROTC program and an evil war criminal teaching in its law school: John Yoo.

Since 9/11/2001, our rights have been steadily and increasingly eroded. I know mine have been suppressed even more under the current administration than the previous one.

We do have a Complex in this country—the Military Industrial one.

The MIC is obviously the boss.

Update: the University relented and is allowing us to use the room for the event.

CINDY NOTE: *Actually, the university gave us another, much smaller room and many people* *missed the talk because of the confusion. On, then off, then back on, then in a different room.*

Monday, May 3, 2010
"Teabaggish"

First appeared in *Islam Times*

I think, by now, that I have been called every nasty, dirty, demeaning, and just plain old, mean, name in the book.

I won't bore you with a list of names, but today I got called, "Teabaggish," by a "friend" who doesn't like that I occasionally point out truths. Truths that were truths on January 19, 2009 and are still true today.

Apparently, with this new epithet, I am being equated with the Glenn Beck following, slogan-slinging, knee-jerk reactionary, Sarah Palin lovers, who criticize Obama and the government. I hate to tell my "friend" but I have been doing this long before there was a Tea Party and Sarah Palin was still mayor of Wasilla. My "friend" knows this because he used to applaud me when I said exactly the same things when Bush was president.

I am still struggling with the Hope-nosis that has inflicted this country and the fact that it has infected the same people who were coming to the certainty that the US is an evil empire while Bush was president. Now that certainty is fading into the woodwork because there is a New Dawn (hey, isn't that the name of one of Obama's murderous operations in Afghanistan?)

In a recent speech the president gave at a commencement address in Michigan, he even said that if we call the government bad names, like "socialist" or "fascist," we are comparing the US to other "murderous regimes." Well, duh.

Either the killing of innocent and mostly brown people stopped on January 20, 2009, or I am "Teabaggish."

I can almost give a 100 percent guarantee that if George were still president, or if McCain had won, I wouldn't be called "Teabaggish" for speaking out against the escalation of the illegal occupation of Afghanistan and the continuation of the illegal occupation of Iraq. I bet if I pointed out the fact that UAV (Unmanned Aerial Vehicle) use has tripled in Pakistan since January 20, 2009, it wouldn't be met with hostility if it were McCain authorizing that usage.

And what about that Presidential Assassination Program whereupon the new president who is a "Constitutional Authority "can sign death warrants for any American and the "hit" will be carried out? To me this is one of the most egregious violations of civil and human rights that has ever been perpetrated in this country, and there is no bill in Congress to stop it, very little grassroots movement against it, and certainly no hue/outcry from the corporate media.

How can Obama just reserve this right to himself? Why is no one asking this question and demanding the answer? Then the next question that arises immediately following that one (if you're not Hope-notized) is—what will he come up with next? As my daughter recently said: "Why don't they just take away all of our rights and get it over with?"

Not only have I been called "Teabaggish" recently, but I have also been accused of constantly "whining" without offering solutions. Of course, I offer solutions all the time—but people like my nuevo-critics don't want to hear them.

As long as we here in our class continue to allow the elites to pull the proverbial wool over our eyes every four years to have us believe that WE have a choice for whom we vote for, or that there is any difference between Goldman Sachs Candidate A or Goldman Sachs Candidate B, these wars, economic degradation, and other oppressions will continue.

I don't offer get-free-quick schemes—I also don't propose false hope that perpetuates cults of personality or irrelevant and negative change. My solutions offer hard work and long hours, but the benefits are peace, justice, and economic equality. We can't count on our bought and paid politicians to make things right. It ain't going to happen no matter if even one of them talks pretty or is able to pronounce "noo-klee-er."

My solutions also require personal integrity and courage. And in this election year, we can exercise these two attributes and vow not to vote for another war-monger—if your Congress Rep votes for the 33 billion dollar war funding bill that is coming up, vote against them if there is a viable alternative. If not, have the courage NOT to vote.

I know that the corporate candidate from the War Party (One of the ones with the "D" or "R" behind their name) will probably still win, but at least your own conscience will be clear and your statement will be made.

Try it. You'll like it.

CINDY NOTE: *Some variations of "Teabaggish" that I have also been called over these past almost seven-years: "teatard," and "teajadist." Clever, huh? Because in the worldview of some, NOBODY could have principles and criticize the Dalai Bama from the left.*

___

Monday, May 3, 2010
The Drone Bomber

Jeez—hasn't the world suffered enough at the "antics" of the Robber Class at the annual White House Correspondents dinner?

I mean, crap, we have been "treated" to George Bush looking for the fabled WMD after so many people had been hilariously killed in Iraq (and that was just the beginning). And how will we ever get the picture of Karl Rove dancing and rapping out of our heads?

Over this past weekend, we were regaled with another lame performance by a president. Of course, with the audience laughing hysterically as if Obama were smashing watermelons, you wouldn't think the performance was lame—unless you can and still do think.

Obama joked about the new draconian and un-Constitutional law in Arizona—which isn't funny to millions of people. NAFTA and CAFTA and GMOs are deadly serious business and instead of joking about human rights violations, our government should be repealing these programs that force Latinos to risk their lives to come north to support their families.

Since the day the Nobel Laureate was sworn is as emperor, he has increased the use of CIA-controlled drone bombings in Pakistan. In fact, the raw numbers are triple those of the final five years of the Bush regime. Obama is the Drone Bomber for sure and thousands of civilians have been killed or chased from their homes into filthy refugee camps by Obama's war of terror.

To these people, joking about dropping Hellfire missiles on the Jonas Brothers is no laughing matter. Are presidents really that freaking insensitive, or do they just not care if their "jokes" are in the poorest of bad taste?

Yes, if you haven't heard, Obama did inform the Jonas Brothers who were in attendance at the dinner that if they had any romantic designs on his two young daughters that he would target them with "Predator drones."

The ironic thing about this threat is that this president has taken it upon himself to sign death warrants for Americans without due process. Again—not funny, dude.

In fact, you scare the hell out of me.

Thursday, May 6, 2010
Here Come Those Chickens Again

Chickens Coming Home to Roost
Proverb: When one has to face the consequences of mistakes or bad deeds.

As soon as I heard that Pakistani-American, Faisal Shahzad, was arrested for the so-called, "Times Square" attempted bombing (where an abandoned SUV filled with potential explosives was found in Times Square last weekend), my first thought was: "Those chickens are coming back to roost, again."

Then tonight, as I was driving, I heard on the radio news that Shahzad claimed that he did that because he was upset over the CIA drone-bombing program in Northern Pakistan. So, my initial suspicion was confirmed. Let's, for the time being, take Shahzad's "confessions" at face value. We really don't know what torture, lying, or other pressure was put on Shahzad, or why our government is so readily admitting that he was upset about drone bombings.

However, this incident also puts President Obama's recent remarks about threatening the Jonas Brothers with a Predator drone if they went near his two daughters in a different light, doesn't it? So many people on the "left" are defending Obama's joke—rationalizing it as vigorously as they condemned and attacked Bush over his WMD joke at a White House Correspondents dinner in 2004.

What if the bomb in Times Square went off and killed dozens of people, as happens frequently in Pakistan/Afghanistan/Iraq? Would Obama's joke still seem funny? I never thought joking about bombs that kill babies from the Joker that orders these bombings funny, anyway. But we all know that if Americans were killed, the shoe would be on an entirely different foot.

For example, this past May 4 was the 40th anniversary of the Kent State Massacre in Ohio. I spoke at SUNY Cortland at the event that the students put together there to commemorate that awful day.

I was pointing out to the crowd that four students being slaughtered by the US military was horrible 40 years ago, but millions of Vietnamese died at the hands of the same military, and since then millions more have been killed, displaced, or economically disadvantaged because of this wicked Empire.

Then, I guess I went too far in some of the young people's eyes, because I pointed out that on September 11, 2001—almost four thousands Americans tragically died—but on that same day (and every day since and every day after) tens of thousands of people died of starvation around the world. Then to make matters even worse, I compared the lives of the people who died of starvation favorably with the people who died on 9-11. I think I may have even said that they had the same exact existential right as those Americans! I heard from professors and the students that this caused a pretty big controversy on the campus.

Last December, the suicide bombing in Khost Province in Afghanistan at an American outpost that killed seven CIA agents was a revenge attack by a double agent in revenge for the drone killing of Hakimullah Mehsud and his family and neighbors—but didn't I just hear that he's still alive and just released a new video disputing his own recent death?

The one problem I have with 9/11 conspiracy theories is that sometimes the theories and the people who propose them discount one very important fact. Even though I never condone or support violence, Arab-Muslims had legitimate reasons to plan and carry out an attack—if they actually did is another question, though.

There will be a lot of unrighteous indignation over the Shahzad case and no one in power will even give a second thought to his legitimate frustration. The saddest and scariest thing about the entire episode to me is if the bombs did go off and kill innocent Americans, it would have been people who more than likely had no freaking idea that their government is slaughtering other innocent people with these weapons of terror.

Somewhere, sometime, the cycle of violence will have to stop—but who's going to stop it? We can't expect occupied peoples to stop resisting occupation. Self-defense and defending one's family and community is not only justified but a primal reaction.

Will the American people finally rise up against our government and demand an end to the US war of military and economic terror against the world, or will we keep electing Jokers thinking, yes even hoping, that anything will change?

CINDY NOTE: Five months after this, Shahzad was sentenced to life in prison.

Sunday, June 20, 2010
A Day in the Gulf

The man in charge of the government that both permitted and abetted the heinous corporate crime ("Drill, baby, drill!") should, by all rights, be in terminal disgrace. Instead, much of Obama's "base" behaves as if the First Black President is an innocent party—a victim of circumstances—rather than a facilitator of the corporate enterprise that has spawned the Mother of all Pollutions.
Glenn Ford of *Black Agenda Report*

I am in New Orleans at a People's Emergency Response to the cataclysm in the Gulf. It would be nice if the elitists in the world felt like this was an EMERGENCY, but it's obvious that the crisis plays into the hands of the globalists and the devastation does not bother them at all except for how this will affect them politically.

World Can't Wait organized the event in combo with activists in the New Orleans area. We have people from all over the country in attendance. Some people recognize that this is a global catastrophe—not a problem localized to a few shrimpers, fishers, and oil workers.

Today, I got an email from James Carville who is from this area and who has been a kind of critic of the Obama administration over the whole "Oil-Cano" incident in the Gulf, and it has a picture of Sarah Palin with "Drill, baby, drill" superimposed on it. This email is supposed to make us think that the fault of this cataclysm is totally confined to the Republican Party, and more specifically to the right-wing idiot faction of the RP.

What are we supposed to do with this information? Are we supposed to react to this email from the DCCC with horror and be profoundly grateful that McCain/Palin didn't win? If the Republican ticket got into the White House, there might have been an enormous explosion from a drilling in the Gulf of Mexico that is spewing tens of thousands of barrels of oil into the ocean, threatening life on this planet as we know it.

Oh, that did happen and the administration is Democratic.

We are supposed to forget that the Obama regime granted BP the license to drill where it was in

February of 2009.

We are supposed to forget that the Secretary of the Interior, Ben Salazar, is a great friend of the oil companies/offshore drilling.

We are supposed to forget that about three weeks before the spill, Obama and Salazar announced a comprehensive offshore drilling plan at Andrew's Air Force Base with much patriotic hullaballoo.

We are supposed to forget that Obama received more money from BP than any other candidate in the 2008 race.

We are supposed to forget that the US does not have a comprehensive energy program that does not include the use of fossil fuels (coal, oil, natural gas) or the promotion of clean, sustainable, and renewable sources of energy.

Like the unnecessary devastation after Katrina, this newest cataclysm began way before the well blew. The years of neglect of the levees and the poor communities surrounding them led to the biggest problems in New Orleans after the hurricane, and our decades of devotion to the oil companies that are raping and pillaging our planet led to the Deepwater Horizon catastrophe.

This is truly not a Democrat or Republican problem and conversely the solution won't come from there either.

I went down to Grand Isle with a contingent from the People's Gulf Emergency Response Conference and there's not a whole lot to report. The stench and the taste of the chemicals in the air was pretty bad—except that the locals say that the really bad smell and oil come in the morning and then it's cleaned up pretty quickly, because that's the "photo-op" locality. There were also orange booms along the shoreline about 20 feet from the ocean and we were told by security and sheriffs several times that if we crossed those barriers we would have to be "de-conned" and that it "wouldn't be pleasant." We heard that the media had moved on to Venice, LA where the slow creep of Armageddon was appearing next.

On the two and a half hour trip back and forth to Grand Isle from New Orleans, it was glaringly apparent that fishing and oil are the life of the Gulf—unfortunately, the most destructive one will probably survive without even a pause, and the one that has sustained the region and evolved from generations will die.

Along the main road in Grand Isle a resident constructed a "graveyard" in front of his home with crosses that had names of things that have been killed by the cronyism between the government and BP.

Some of the Gulf traditions that are dead or dying that were represented by the crosses were: Stargazing; Picnics; Frogs Croaking; Cajun Music; and Family Time.

If I had the opportunity to make a cross, I would have written: "My Grandchildren's Future."

We stopped at a Grand Isle diner for lunch and our server was very sweet. She told us that the "berms" that were constructed suit her just fine because she doesn't want to see the problem or think too hard about her very way of life being destroyed. She looked at us with very weary-teary eyes and simply said: "Thank you for caring."

CINDY NOTE: *According to the Harte Research Institute for Gulf of Mexico Studies at Texas A & M: But impacts from the 2010 BP Deepwater Horizon oil spill are still being felt and BP is preparing to re-enter Gulf with lease purchases recently approved, according to the summit advancer. Also, humans living in the area are very ill from the chemicals and no one will admit that the illnesses are chemically related.*

> *If Americans pulled back and started paying attention to this war,*
> *it would become even less popular.*
> **A senior adviser to head of NATO ops in Afghanistan,**
> **General Stanley McChrystal (via *Rolling Stone*)**

FUBAR: Military slang for: Fu#ked Up Beyond All/Any Repair/Recognition. FUBAR also has a close military acronym: SNAFU: Situation Normal All Fu#ked Up.

FUBAR and SNAFU can be traced back to WWII—you know that war. That's the war (the last constitutionally declared by Congress) that, along with the US Civil War, is the war that is held up as the shining example of the goodness, nay GREATNESS, of the United States of America. The war where we freed the entire planet of fascism, Nazi-ism, imperialism, and made the world safe for FREEDOM (and freedom's Siamese Twin: DEMOCRACY)!

So, if the people who were actually in the trenches were recognizing the war, even the GREAT ONE, was FUBAR, then we have only gone rapidly downhill from there. Even Marine Major General Smedley Butler (*War is a Racket*) pointed out that the "War to end all Wars" (WWI) just led to WWII and after he passed away in 1940: Korea, Vietnam, the Balkans, the First Gulf War, and now our stains in the Middle East. As a matter of fact, since WWII, we have NEVER been at peace.

The SNAFU over the *Rolling Stone* article where Stanley is openly and disrespectfully critical of Obama, Biden, Ambassador Eikenberry, and others is indicative of a few things to me:

First of all, there is a little known aspect of this developing story: McChrystal was given final approval over the version of the story that appeared in *Rolling Stone*—a person that achieves the elevated status in the elite world of McChrystal's rarely rises to the top without knowing the rules and without knowing how to play the game. And trust me, this is a "game." Does anyone believe that this story was a surprise to anyone in the Obama regime, or to McChrystal? No, obviously it wasn't—so why now?

Secondly—with a cataclysm off of our very shores that is further proof that our Military-Corporate Complex is not equipped to handle catastrophes—this SNAFU proves that the Military-Corporate Complex is not even equipped to handle wars. The Empire is crumbling, and it's crumbling even faster than I predicted—so I have to celebrate the news that just demonstrates how FUBAR things are in Afghanistan. Of course, the stats of civilian deaths (yeah, right—we are protecting civilians) and NATO and US troop deaths are there. There can be no disputing facts. No matter how much one wants to think that Obama is "better than Bush" or is "better than McCain" really has to look no further than these hard-core facts.

All of this posturing and speechifying is nothing but a distraction from the fact that our economy is FUBAR, the Gulf of Mexico is FUBAR, the wars are FUBAR—and Wikileaks is set to come out soon with another video of a bombing incident that killed over 100 civilians in Afghanistan and was covered up. When Obama appointed McChrystal to this job, he knew that he had already covered up the murder of Spc. Pat Tillman.

Also, on the heels of the Marjah Offensive ("bleeding ulcer" according to McChrystal), the Kandahar offensive is approaching and with June already being a deadly month, things will only get worse.

Thirdly, of course McChrystal is offering himself up as the sacrificial lamb of the FUBAR Empire.

Already, I am getting Democrats emailing me and telling me that it is "wonderful" that McChrystal is resigning because he "made Obama send more troops to Afghanistan." Again—are you serious? Obama gave top billing to the fact that he was going to send more troops to Afghanistan, as a campaign promise. When the "leak" came out that McChrystal wanted more troops near the end of 2009, all that did was give Obama the political space to do what he promised to do all along. "See, I didn't really want to send more troops to a mission that was FUBAR from the beginning, but my top-ranking General in the field made me!"

As the Iraq war winds down, Obama said, he wants to see troops redirected to Afghanistan. He said the fight against the Taliban and Al Qaeda was a war 'we have to win' and repeated his call for two more combat brigades in Afghanistan to counteract "deteriorating" conditions.

LA Times July 16, 2008

The problem is—and has been for decades—the Military-Corporate Complex. However, if we want valid change, we also have to look deeper.

Five months shy of two years ago, many of you went to the polls and voted for Obama because you were from mildly disappointed to wildly angry at the Bush administration. I get that emotion —I do. But even I realized that Bush was not THE problem, but only A problem. The real problem is the system that keeps killing our children and the children of other nations and cultures. It has been doing it from the beginning of our time and it will be doing it until our end if we don't recognize that an Empire exists to feed on others to enrich, empower, and give itself health. We cannot be a healthy society when we live in an Empire—no matter who sits on the throne.

The wars are FUBAR—the Empire is FUBAR. Even in the beginning it was a system for the elite. Now we are not only the down trodden, but the trodden on. Trampled on, but not defeated yet.

Peace of the Action is calling you to come to Washington, DC to confront the bleeding ulcers in the Gulf and in the Middle East and Asia. We also have to confront and come to terms with the fact that we are an Empire and it will be good in the long-term if it crumbles—and we are already feeling the gross-effects of the collapse in our homes and communities. Conditions in the economy and ecology will undoubtedly get far worse before they get better, but if we deal with these issues as a caring community—not as a class at war with itself—we can, and shall overcome.

Peace of the Action is also calling on all troops of good conscience to refuse to participate in these international war crimes against humanity—please don't allow yourself to be used as a token in this elitist game of destruction and death for profit! It's far better to pay consequences for being a conscientious objector, than to be dead at a very young age—or to kill innocent people.

Breaking news: As I was writing this, Obama announced that he accepted McChrystal's resignation and that General David Petraeus would be taking over. Swell—another insider of the Military-Corporate Complex. Of course, in Obama's speech, he never even hinted that the mission was FUBAR—or that it will be re-evaluated. The Empire rolls on, just rearranging the deck chairs on the Titanic. There is nothing "salvageable" about this disaster.

CINDY NOTE: *This according to Wikipedia, McChrystal hasn't been doing too badly for himself since he left the military:*

In 2010, after leaving the Army, McChrystal joined Yale University as a Jackson Institute for Global Affairs senior fellow. He teaches a course entitled "Leadership," a graduate-level seminar with some spots reserved for undergraduates. The course received 250 applications for 20 spots in 2011 and is being taught for a third time in 2013.

In November 2010, JetBlue Airways announced that McChrystal would join its board of directors. On February 16, 2011, Navistar International announced that McChrystal would join its board of directors.

McChrystal is Chairman of the Board of Siemens Government Systems, and is on the strategic advisory board of Knowledge International, a licensed arms dealer whose parent company is EAI, a business "very close" to the United Arab Emirates government. He co-founded and is a partner at the McChrystal Group LLC, an Alexandria, Virginia-based consulting firm.

Sunday, June 27, 2010
Where have all the Peaceniks Gone?

I believe it is human nature to want to be right (as in "correct" not "conservative.") I like to be right. I also like to research my facts because being wrong to me is embarrassing. The one time I would have loved to be in error, though, was in a conviction that began over two years ago. I was convinced that Barack Obama was not the progressive-peace-savior that many of my friends and colleagues were making him out to be.

But, I was right about that, and I think the facts have borne me out: the Overseas Contingency Operation (formerly known as George's War OF Terror) has become even more of a quagmire under the new regime; healthcare was not so much reformed or overhauled as it was a handout to the health insurance companies; the oppressive police state is increasing; no accountability for war criminals (few people will prosecute themselves); torture continues; financial industry reform looks like it is guaranteed for further rich v. poor conquest; and this administration has proven to be as good a friend to Big Oil as the last one.

To some of us, the problem is not so much that Obama has proven to be a dismal failure—because we know that he has been a huge success to the ruling class and corporations—but that partisan politics always overshadows common sense and true peace. We lost a lot of time giving Obama a "chance," and thousands have lost their lives and their ways of life.

I was outraged when, after three days in office, Obama authorized a drone strike into Northern Pakistan that killed dozens of civilians, but I was excoriated for being outraged. I was devastated when he announced an increase in troops (three times so far) to Afghanistan, and attacked for not caring about Afghan women (the ones our Empire are "protecting" by killing them and their children). I was laughed out of town when I was infuriated that Obama had declared himself "Judge, jury, and executioner" of American citizens. People who formerly supported me told me to "shut up and go away, you have had your 15 minutes of fame."

I was deeply hurt and lonely when everyone from celebrities to my friends in the peace-trenches abandoned me for someone who did not even have a principled campaign platform. However, I could not abandon my principles to support someone who did not conform to them.

Today, my friend, Rob Kall of Oped News wrote a scathing article about the financial aid "reform" bill after he spent significant time researching it. Rob is someone that I debated during the campaign and to see him write that he will do everything in his power to make sure that Obama is a "one-term president" was a very, dare I say, "hopeful" sign to me. I knew Rob would come around because he is insightful and compassionate.

It is very, very difficult to admit to making a mistake. I had to admit to making one of the most personally tragic errors possible—I failed my son and he is dead—killed by this Empire.

If you were an Obama supporter, I get that, but it's time to pull your head out of the clouds and realize that you got fooled again. It's hard to resist multi-million dollar marketing campaigns that give one the urge to rush out to buy the "new and improved, lemony-minty fresh" product, but it also usually doesn't take one long to figure out it was only the same old garbage in a new package.

The clock is ticking and until we all figure out that "It's The Empire, Stupid" (to borrow a ruling class phrase), nothing will change for the better.

We are trying to build a movement that is resistant to changing winds and that will stand strong on its principles to fight the tyrannical violence of this Empire with all of our strength, energy, and resources no matter who is in office.

I can also understand the urge to "have it both ways." However, you can't be intellectually honest with yourself, or your own heart, and support the Democratic Party. It is simply too incongruous. The only way to show that you are for peace and against racism, tyranny, and the destruction of the environment, is to not bend to, or bend over for, the War Party.

CINDY NOTE: True in 2010 and true today after Obama has expanded the wars dramatically, there are even fewer protests, now.

Friday, July 9, 2010
Requiem for the Antiwar Movement

When you vote for war, don't be surprised when you get it.
Cindy Sheehan

I will send at least two additional combat brigades to Afghanistan.
Presidential Candidate Barack Obama

This war (Iraq) prevents us from tackling every serious threat that we face, from a resurgent al-Qaeda in Afghanistan to a hostile Iranian regime intent on possessing nuclear weapons.
Presidential Candidate Barack Obama

And if we have actionable intelligence about high-level al-Qaeda targets (in Pakistan), we must act if Pakistan will or cannot.
Presidential Candidate Barack Obama

This article and these observations are going to piss some people off—but oh well. You will be angry with me, even though I am not the one who is ordering more war, paying for more war, torturing people and imprisoning them without due process, destroying the economy and the environment, blah, blah, blah. I have developed an incredibly thick skin and if I rankle, it's because I think time is running out to halt the disastrous trajectory this planet (via the US Military Corporate Complex) is on. I promise that I am not writing this because I am holding protests and no one is coming—these thoughts have been percolating in me for months now. (Note: Remember that old saying: "What if they gave a war and nobody came?" Well, here in DC I am living the opposite: "What if they gave an antiwar protest and nobody came?")

My grandbabies and other people's grandbabies WILL NOT live in a world where war-for-profit is so normal that state-sanctioned violence is rarely even questioned—and if it is, then the person questioning is the "loony tunes," the "mama moonbat," the "radical." That is one seriously messed-up world. You know it is and we are the only ones who have the key to unmessing it.

Last week, the Democratically controlled House of Representatives voted to give Barack Obama

33 billion more dollars to prosecute two idiotic and ill-advised wars. Of course they did—it wasn't the first time since 2007 that a Democratic Congress voted to fund wars, and it won't be the last—do you all know why? BECAUSE THE DEMOCRATS DON'T WANT PEACE—THEY ARE JUST ONE-HALF OF THE "WAR PARTY."

Why else did the Democrats vote for more war, more death, and more destruction? If you are a Democrat and voted for one of these scum—did you vote for them hoping that you would get more war? Did you vote for Obama hoping that he would dig this country into a deeper hole, and do you still believe that fucking things up even more is the way to solve problems?

Do you all know what else? The wars that were begun in the Bush presidency and fully funded and increased during the Obama regime belong to everyone who voted for Obama, too. If you listened to what Obama said, and not just how he said it, then you would have heard him promise you that he was going to SEND MORE TROOPS TO AFGHANISTAN. You would have heard him say that nothing was "off the table" for dealing with Iran.

During the campaign many colleagues and friends of mine assured me that Obama was just saying this hostile crap to "get elected" and once he was elected that he would "do the right thing." Well, first of all, why support such a pandering Jackwagon, and secondly, how has that ever worked? Three days after Obama swore to uphold and defend the Constitution, he drone-bombed a "target" in Pakistan killing 3 dozen civilians—and since that day he has elevated the art of drone bombings to new heights, while the so-called antiwar movement looks on in silent complacency and while Democratic operatives disguised as antiwar groups are hoping against hope that Obama comes out strong with a new antiwar marketing campaign to assure his "re-election." Even though not one progressive issue has been propagated during his term, these war supporters are looking forward to another four years of the dance of death. Right foot kill—left foot torture—spin around for environmental devastation—allemande left for health care fascism—and shimmy right for bankster bailouts. Wasn't eight years of this crap during the Bush stain enough for y'all?

Many antiwar groups and people who claim they are for peace lose their minds during election season thinking that the razor-thin difference between the Democrat and Republican is enough to go ape-shit crazy in working for the Democrat. Just take the last two Democratic candidates, for example. Kerry and Obama both supported more war. An "antiwar" movement de-legitimizes itself when it works hard for a candidate who does not promise total and rapid withdrawal of troops from wherever they happen to be at the time AND does not promise to end war as an imperial tool of corporate conquest.

The majority of the so-called antiwar movement, in fact, voted for a candidate that PROMISED to contract one war only to be able to profoundly EXPAND another. Obama all along said that he is not against all war, just "dumb wars." If there existed an antiwar movement that had integrity, it would have said that "all wars are dumb," and we withhold our support for just another dyed-in-the-wool warmonger.

What do we do now that we have another two and a half years of a hawk who thinks it is just hunky-dory that his supporters are under the delusion that he is a dove—he was awarded the war-establishment's highest prize wasn't he? He is, after all, a Nobel Laureate.

First of all, voting just doesn't cut it. Realistically, our choices are between War Party Candidate A and War Party Candidate B. A true peace candidate is marginalized, metaphorically spat upon, and reviled. This is not a nation that honors peace and non-violence. From the top down, we are a violent nation—so from the bottom up, we have to restructure society. Liberate yourself and remove your Obama bumper sticker that has a peace sign instead of the "O." If you are antiwar, you know in your heart that he is not a peace monger.

Secondly, our resources and energy are stretched thin. We live in a credit-based economy where good jobs are scarce. Many people, who have the same values, in this almost value-free society, constantly tell me that they would be with me if they could afford it.

Since my son was killed, which was as violent of a paradigm shift as anyone should have to endure, I have whittled my life down to a bare minimum. I have no car. I have no pets. I have no plants. I have no credit cards. My income is based on my donations from my itinerant peace travels and book sales. I have moved eight times since Casey died and now I can move with one small U-Haul. I have a cell phone and computer, a bed, clothes, a few dishes, a few valued books and peace paraphernalia and pictures of my children and grandbabies.

As HD Thoreau said: "You don't own your possessions, they own you." This consumer orgiastic society makes us literal slaves to a system that is detrimental to our health. Freeing oneself from those chains frees one to be a full-time, or near full-time activist. "Simplify, simplify, simplify."

Massive antiwar protest in this country is dead. We may as well acknowledge that and just bury the corpse, mourn, and then figure out a better way of doing things.

In the Christian tradition, death was only a prelude to a new and better life and farmers will tell you that a seed has to die before a health-nourishing plant can be born, and then there's the ever ubiquitous example of the ugly, hairy, and yucky caterpillar being reborn as a magnificent and beautiful butterfly. Have I hammered you with enough clichés yet?

The key to turning this caterpillar of a country into a beautiful butterfly is in Peace and recognizing that no matter if one is Bush, Obama, McCain, or Palin, these people don't want Peace, but we do.

I think we lose the raw humanity of war when we allow ourselves to wallow in War Party politics. When the Democratic Wing of the War Party took over the mis-management of the Empire, the antiwar movement was effectively neutralized even though the wars weren't.

So after we are done mourning, we get together as one human family to organize something that will bring positive change. We are not enemies with each other—we may be "enemies of the state," but the state is our enemy.

No more marching in circles, it makes us dizzy.

No more signing petitions, it gives us writer's cramp.

No more calling Congress-scum, the war machine is its master.

The establishment wants us to think that this busy-work has a chance to be effective—but when is the last time any of these tactics worked on a Federal level? Your president or your congress rep couldn't care less want you think or want. Your vote doesn't even count—in case you haven't heard, they steal votes and falsely manipulate you, anyway.

I am going to close with my organization's motivational quote. Peace of the ACTION takes our inspiration from a Mario Savio quote that he said on the steps of Sproul Hall at UC Berkeley, 46 years ago:

"There comes a time when the operation of the machine becomes so odious, makes you so sick at heart that you can't take part, you can't even passively take part. You have to put your bodies upon the gears and upon the levers, upon all the apparatus and you've got to make it stop. And you've got to indicate to the people who own it, to the people who run it, that unless you're free, the machine will be prevented from working at all."

CINDY NOTE: *This article has over 10,000 views—second place in my blog roll.*

Tuesday, July 13, 2010
Government Persecutors Read My Blog

On July 12, after one postponement, the POTA (Peace of the Action) 3, plus three, went to trial in DC Superior Court for our arrests after the ANSWER rally and march on March 20th (the 7th anniversary of the illegal and immoral invasion of Iraq).

On March 20, after the rally and march, Elaine Brower of MFSO (Military Families Speak Out) and Matthis Chiroux of IVAW (Iraq Vets Against the War) accompanied some mock coffins that were in the march to the sidewalk in front of the White House. Even though there were thousands of people in attendance, Matthis and Elaine (and two others that didn't end up going to trial) were the only ones that lay on the sidewalk.

I spoke at the rally, but did not go on the march. During the march, I went to lunch and back to Camp OUT NOW that Peace of the Action had erected on the lawn of the Washington Monument. Some of us agreed to meet at the West side of the White House fence at 4pm, because we had heard the Democrats were going to all go there to have a meeting with the president about the "health (corporate give-away) care" bill.

When I returned back to the White House, I saw some commotion that was happening near the centerline of the White House and went to check it out. That's when I saw Elaine and Matthis in the pen the Park Police had set up and planned to join them. Long story short: four of us were arrested for "crossing a police line." And four of us were arrested for "disorderly conduct." Six of us who were arrested (including myself) spent the next 52 hours in DC jail.

When we were arraigned (in waist and leg shackles) that Monday, we were given a stay-away order from the White House, and all the defendants, except me, were given the opportunity to pay the fine and forfeit the right to trial. They all rejected the offer and we were scheduled for trial on June 10.

On June 9, I was on my way to the airport in California at about 5:30am to go to DC for the trial when I got an email from one of our lawyers saying that the trial was postponed. We learned the next day that the trial was scheduled for July 12—when I happened to be in DC for Sizzlin' Summer Protests. The trial was yesterday.

A very creepy video that the DC National Park Service Police filmed during that day was the centerpiece of the persecutor's case. The video is creepy because of what the cameraperson focused on. He/she was at Camp OUT NOW earlier that day and then moved over to Lafayette Park and moved slowly from sign to sign—to faces (most familiar, long-time activists)—the cameraperson even focused on a *Worker's World* (socialist) newspaper on the sidewalk. It was just creepy—our government is constantly and voyeuristically surveilling us.

Persecutor for the government, Branch, brought only two officers, including Captain Beck, who was in charge that day, to testify. Captain Beck could only confirm that he witnessed four of the six of us committing our "crimes." In the video that Persecutor Branch showed you can see the "good" Captain Beck—who was only a Lieutenant that day—clearly shoving his bullhorn in my chest after my wrists were cuffed behind my back and the arresting officer is shown wrenching my arms up after two cops shoved me. The two others of the POTA 3, Jon Gold and Jim Veeder, aren't even shown in the police video crossing the line. The Government Persecutor brought only one very incoherent officer to testify to say that he had arrested Veeder (or the "white male with the aqua shirt.")

I took the stand at the end of the defense case and I testified that I came upon the scene when the resistance was already in progress and that when I saw Elaine and Matthis being penned in there that it was my intention to go and lie down next to them and the coffins in solidarity with the hundreds of thousands of people our nation has slaughtered in the name of profit.

Persecutor Branch thought she had damning "evidence" in two of my blogs where I wrote in one that I "crossed the police line." Well, I was arrested for "crossing a police line" and held in jail for 52 hours for "crossing a police line." Persecutor Branch said: "Then you agree with the charges?"

Wow, was that one of the dumbest questions ever? "If I agreed with the charges, I would have plead guilty and I wouldn't be here today," I answered her. "No further questions."

I, and my co-defendants, have spent a considerable amount of personal money, time, and energy to protest the Bush/Obama wars. Elaine Brower's convertible can probably drive down to DC from her NYC home by itself by now. Jon Gold has taken considerable time off of work to join Peace of the Action in DC last March and this July. Both Elaine and Jon had to take the 12th off to be here on trial. Matthis has to live with PTSD and part of his "therapy" is the antiwar sacrifices that he makes. If we "agreed" with being arrested for exercising our human freedoms and the freedoms guaranteed to us under the First Amendment, then we wouldn't have taken the time, expense, and energy to come to DC for trial after trial.

After the pitiful persecution presented by Persecutor Branch and after the spirited defense our lawyers presented (First Amendment, necessity of protesting an illegal and immoral war, the questionable legality of the police line), three of us (the POTA 3) were acquitted (the persecution didn't prove their case against us beyond a reasonable doubt) and Matthis, Leflora, and Elaine were convicted and given a $100.00 fine (suspended) and a mandatory $50.00 assessment to go to the Victims of Violent Crimes fund, which an amazing supporter, Larry Maxwell, paid after the verdict. Those convicted were convicted because the video clearly showed them and their infractions, and we other three were acquitted because the video did not clearly show our infractions. This seems to show some very lazy police-work to rely on videos that only they shoot. If the Persecutor had shown the Peace of the Action video, it would have been perfectly clear that I purposefully crossed that police line. Oh well—a win is a win!

This was actually the first time I was acquitted for charges stemming from protest and I wonder how Persecutor Branch feels about that one? I know our legal team was thrilled!

Elaine and I were in jail for the 52 hours—at least we got to stay together. When we weren't trying to sleep on the stone-cold cement floors, we talked about the pathetic antiwar movement and sort of felt sorry for ourselves being locked up for so long for such minor infractions that were still principled stands. However, we agreed then and we agreed yesterday after the trial was over, that we would do this again and keep doing it until the wars end and our troops quit killing innocent people for the Empire and come home to get the help they need to reintegrate healthfully and wholly back into society.

We can't help it—we are serial Peace Criminals.

I hope Persecutor Branch enjoys this blog.

Note—today we went to the White House to bid a not-so-fond farewell to Obama, and I got to go all the way up to the fence because our stay away orders were lifted!

Wednesday, July 28, 2010
I Have Become Uncomfortably Numb

I am numb, I think.

Since the US Corporate Military Industrial Complex forced me into the World of the Aware after my son's murder in Iraq, I feel that the news freshly assaults me on a daily basis.

I am numb, I think, from being abused by this Empire on a regular basis for years.

I am numb, I think, because it wears on one to care so deeply when so many citizens of my national community (reader excepted) barely even know we are at war, let alone that we live in a murderous Empire.

On Friday, July 23rd when we were awaiting the birth of my new grandson in California, 52 Afghan civilians were slaughtered by US/NATO (same thing) forces.

I am numb, I think, because 52 people who have the exactly equal (if not greater) existential imperative as my grandchildren and your grandchildren; my children and your children; and you and I—who live in a war zone imposed on them by the Empire—based on lies and solely for profit —were alive and now they are dead.

I am numb, I think, because their deaths don't make me feel safer—they make me feel like my existence is iffy and my numbness is a defense mechanism against what is only a news report to me, but life and death to millions of people who are in daily danger because The Empire that I live in sucks and most people who live here just don't care. They are already numb—but not from an overload of bad news, but from the constant SOMA of the TV, or consumerism, or by simply trying to survive in this "big dog-eat-little dog" Empire.

I am numb, I think, because Wikileaks released over 91,000 leaked documents dealing with the day-to-day operations in Afghanistan that detail obvious and hidden war crimes. Just like with the Collateral Damage video previously released—did anyone who has been paying attention learn something new and did anyone who isn't paying attention all of a sudden grow compassion skills? I doubt it—so I am numb, I think.

I am numb, I think, because many people elected a "Change" regime that has turned out to be a "Status Quo" regime and many of the people who voted for the Changer-in-Chief have become born-again Cheerleaders for War. The anti-Decider-in-Chief movement has all but fizzled out to nothing. That the "Changer" is no different or better than the "Decider" is not what has numbed me —it's the unreasonable support for the Changer that would cause me to stomp my feet in disgust, if it weren't for the numbness.

Deep down inside of me, there is the Cindy who is raging against the Democratic Congress' passage of the recent war-funding bill, but so I don't explode, I am outwardly calm. Pissed off Cindy has to be in here, or I wouldn't be writing this piece—but the rhetoric that I have written hundreds of times is now having the feeling of "been there, done that." Well, I am numb, I think, because I have visited this topic continually and words are just not cutting it. How many words are there for: murder, death, destruction, slaughter, starvation, predatory Capitalism, war profiteering, war, illegal, immoral, war crimes, callous, greedy, rape, pillage, plunder, blah, blah, blah!

We live in an Empire that on a daily basis murders dozens of people without blinking even before I drink my first cup of coffee and which always ignores the basic needs of its own citizens. But its citizens are quietly complacent and materially complicit in these crimes. Slaves of, and to, The Empire.

I am numb, I think.

The numbness in me is reinforced when I hear that the US is increasing hostilities against Venezuela, North Korea, and Iran. When will supporters of The Changer wake up?

Soon, I hope (at the risk of using The Changer's word) because this feeling of numbness is not healthy and just as twisted as the actual and hypocritical support for The Empire, depending on who inhabits the Oval Office.

I am numb, I think, but the Cindy who burns for justice and peace is still inside of me and I am sure she will be back out at some point.

Soon, I hope.

CINDY NOTE: *As of this writing, I think the numbness has been trying to settle back in: Ukraine, Iraq, Syria, on, and on. I wrote so many articles in the beginning, but you will soon see that they*

Thursday, August 5, 2010
My Reflections on the Fifth Anniversary of Camp Casey

Endless Wars for Endless Profits:

Before my son Casey was killed in Iraq on April 4, 2004, I was a mother of four, worried about all my children—but especially the one who was going to be deployed to Iraq—sometimes working as many as three jobs to survive, and only peripherally aware of the harsher realities of living in an Empire.

When Shocking and Awful rained down on Iraq, the military "operation" was then called: Operation Iraqi Liberation—but the geniuses in the War Selling Department figured out that the acronym was too obvious, so it was changed to Operation Iraqi Freedom, which is the name that was on all of my son's paperwork and medals after he was killed.

Back then "enhanced interrogation methods" were also known as "torture" while this nation was fighting a "War on Terror."

Since a Nobel Laureate has risen to the top of the Imperial Dung Heap (IDH), he has done good and well, as Nobel Laureates should: He has only changed the names of things at the directive of the War Selling Department. The "Global War on Terror" has been renamed to: "Overseas Contingency Operations"—whatever the hell that means, but the vagueness is intentional. The Empire is expert at ill-defining missions because if the missions were defined with precision, there would naturally have to be an end when the mission is really "accomplished."

Back sometime after the Nobel Laureate was installed on top of the IDH, the mission that killed my son was renamed: "Operation New Dawn." So every single one of our troops and Iraqis that have been killed since Obama's reign have been killed in something that resembles dish-washing detergent and most certainly the selling of it. "Operation New Dawn: New and Improved with more Lemony Freshness—and, boy, does it cut through grease!" Grease is the only thing that Operation New Dawn cuts through, though—since many of my fellow USAians want to believe that Obama is the "New and Improved" George Bush.

Obama has taken back a promise to have "Combat Troops" out of Iraq by September 1st of this year and now has pledged to have them out by the end of 2011—but of course, he has again redefined the mission and the troops are now on a "support and train" mission instead of a combat mission, so the Bots will believe that there is a new "Mission Accomplished." There will be some troops movement and more empty rhetoric about this as the next presidential season is rapidly coming to assault us with more Madison Avenue Trickery. And people on the so-called left and so-called antiwar movement were upset with John McCain when he said that troops would be in Iraq for "100 years?" Well, that is upsetting to me, also, but troops will be in Iraq for 100 years because WE only come out to fight when a Republican is in office and it is apparent that The Empire can tenaciously hang in there until the next cycle when a Democrat takes the "con" of The Empire and neutralizes the "Left" for another four to eight years.

Since I camped in Crawford, Texas beginning August 6, 2005, there has been little to celebrate and virtually no progress in a progressive direction regarding any policy.

Bush's troop "surge" in Iraq that was bought and paid for by Pelosi's Democratic Congress only "worked" because just about everybody that could be killed or displaced in or out of Iraq has been. In 2003, Iraq had a population of roughly 25 million and about 5 million of those have been killed or displaced—that's 1/5 of the population. Devastating figures—that would be comparable to 60 million USAians being killed or displaced! Significant and tragic figures that mean very little to most daily consumers of what passes for news here in the US.

In the Summer of 2005, BushCo and its wars were still maintaining slight popularity in polling (done by corporate sources), but there were millions of people in this nation and probably billions on the planet, that were against the wars and BushCo. Camp Casey captured the imagination and excitement of 15,000 who traveled to Crawford that August to be with us and tens of thousands throughout the world that held vigils in support of us and started their own Camp Caseys in solidarity with Camp Casey in Crawford.

Right after Camp Casey, we had many people travel to New Orleans to help with the hurricane relief and a Veterans for Peace bus took five tons of left over supplies after we closed Camp in August of 2005. We held a march and rally in DC on September 23rd that had over 500,000 participants. Still, everywhere I travel people tell me that, after my example, they became active in political, antiwar, or social justice movements.

So why are we still in too many wars?

Too often still, I receive emails from those on the so-called right that email me and call me a "hypocrite," "Democratic shill," "Obama tool," or other names indicating that they are under the false impression that I have retired since Obama became president, but nothing could be farther from the truth—I have NEVER stopped and I don't care who is the Corporatist in Chief—I never will until the wars are over and this nation has a saner foreign policy and a more humane domestic one.

The reason we still have wars is that, what I call the Robber Class, perpetuate Myths that keep us tied to them in very sick and harmful ways and the "antiwar" energy turned out to mostly be anti-Bush energy. Bush is gone, but his crimes remain.

Not only is August 6 the fifth anniversary of the beginning of Camp Casey, but it will also be the 65th anniversary of the first time the USA used an atomic weapon. I didn't plan on marching on Crawford the first time on Hiroshima Day, but I think it's fitting and a perfect example of the insanity of Empire.

To me, everyday is exactly like a nightmare from which I can't wake up. The Powers that Be lied to the world about Iraq having weapons of mass destruction and lied about some kind of connection between Osama bin Laden and Saddam Hussein and then admitted to lying—and the entire world yawned—and the killing continued and continues. The kicker in all this is that I have to live each and every day for the rest of my life knowing that my son died for these lies and that the people who have perpetrated these mass crimes against humanity walk among us freely and, as a matter of fact, are doing quite well for themselves. It's totally mind blowing to me and I get accused of being "angry." The thing about Casey dying in a war based on lies is because his recruiter lied to him. Our entire Imperial structure is constructed on lies and functions off of heartache.

The feistiness in me remains, but now I know that the enemies of peace are not just George Bush and the Republicans—the enemies of peace are widespread, diverse, in all segments of our society, and include the first female Speaker of the US House of Representatives, and Nobel Laureates.

Camp Casey was a miracle to me and I will never forget that summer and the high we were on thinking that we were going to finally make a difference, but the Empire knows how to neutralize those movements and we were distressed that the energy was inappropriately used to elect Democrats. But five years later, I am older and wiser and the proud grandmother of three grandbabies two years and under that have given me more love and joy than I thought was still possible in my life. The babies have also given me a renewed sense of urgency and commitment to making this planet a better place for all the babies.

Tuesday, August 10, 2010
Hopium and Hypocritium

The arrogance of the Bush administration could never be surpassed, right? Wrong!

Today, Whore House (again, with my apologies to my sex-worker friends) spokeswhore, Robert Gibbs, was quoted as saying this of the "professional left" who liken Obama to his predecessor:

"(They) need to be drug tested," and that these principled critics of the Empire are "crazy." This kind of hearkens back to earlier in the Changery when Rahm Emmanuel, Obama Chief of Staff and committed Zionist, called us: "F@#king Retards." Nice, huh?

Rahm Emmanuel is almost as sensitive as Dick Cheney and Robert Gibbs is almost as smart as Ari Fleischer—George's first Press Secretary.

These quotes of Gibbs' (who's not nearly as perky as Dana Perino) highlight two things for me: the slipperiness of the Obama regime and the stubborn hopenosis of its supporters.

First of all, we were force fed daily doses of mass-media propaganda during the presidential campaign telling us that Obama was a "community organizer," a "man of the people" and don't forget the famous, "If you want Obama to do the right thing, then you have to make him." Now the Changer in Chief's staff is telling us if we are critical of him from the "professional" left, we are drug-crazed lunatics—not principled opponents of the Empire.

I know I have been out in front of Chéz Obama (loudly) expressing my views on his foreign policy many times (so much so, I was banned from the Whore House for four months) and single-payer healthcare advocates were doing the same during the entire fascist healthcare give-away to the corporations. Our voices and vision for a more peaceful, sane, and healthier way of doing things have not even been given a seat at the proverbial table. So, what Gibbs is telling us is to: "Just shut the eff up—we don't care what you say or want."

During the same interview where Robert Gibbs called me (yes, I take it personally) a "drug-crazed lunatic," he also used the time-tested logical fallacy known as a non-sequitur (it does not follow) to say that we would only be happy if the president delivered "Canadian style healthcare," and "closed the Pentagon."

Of course, we advocated for single-payer healthcare and only a war-crazed maniacal empire needs a War Department the size of many small countries with budgets to match. But the "president" didn't even get in the same universe as "Canadian style healthcare" and has vastly increased funding to the Pentagon and Bush's wars of terror.

Also, the acceptance of this Imperial Faux Pas (IFP) illustrates how far this country is divided along faux political lines. The only change Obama has brought with him to the Whore House is negative, bad, bad, bad, change. We cannot, should not, must not, and better not criticize the Imperial First Family (IFF). However, we are supposed to take up pitchforks and torches when the barely functioning Sarah Palin says something stooopid and forget and forgive the Obamas for Imperial Excess (trips to Spain on our many dimes, $6000 handbags, etc.) and their stooopidity.

We also have to ask ourselves a very important question—why did Gibbs do this? Of course, these people don't make mistakes—even when they allow their true feelings to shine forth for the entire world to see, it is for very calculated reasons. Could it be because of the dismal jobless "recovery?" Could it be because of the obvious continuation and escalation of the wars? Could it be because the Obamas are finally being criticized for their "Let them eat cake" mentality? Could it be because

Gibbs wants to blame the "professional left" for Obama's failures and make it our fault when the Democrats get creamed in November?

So, I want to take Gibbs up on his offer—I will submit a vial of my urine to a location of his choosing—hell, I will even go and pee in the bathroom of the press corps room and hand him a warm sample, if that makes him happy—if he does the same. I seriously doubt that 535 members of Congress would pass the pee-test and I seriously doubt many denizens of the Whore House would, either.

I also wonder when Obama's supporters will quit smoking the Hopium or taking their daily dose of Hypocritium—those are the people who need to be drug tested, not the ones who have remained ideological pure. What is so "crazy" about wanting things like indiscriminate killing of civilians to end globally and social justice here locally?

I'll match my pee up against theirs any day!

CINDY NOTE: My offer to match my pee against theirs was never accepted.

Tuesday, August 17, 2010
Racketeers for Capitalism

I spent 33 years in the Marines. Most of my time being a high-class muscle man for Big Business, for Wall Street and the bankers. In short, I was a racketeer for capitalism.
Major General Smedley D. Butler, *War is a Racket* (1935)

I remember when the US war dead in Iraq reached 1000 sometime in the summer of 2005. My youngest child and her boyfriend accompanied me to a vigil in Davis, CA, where we held candles, pictures of Casey, each other, and sobbed—not just for Casey, but also for all the rest. And not just for the Americans, but for the Iraqis, too.

Then I remember when the needless toll reached 2000 in the fall of 2005—I got arrested with about 25 others in front of the White House—such organizations at MoveOn.org preferred candlelight vigils to direct action. I warned them if we didn't do something, then we would be mourning 3000—that total came in the early spring of 2007. Now the total for Iraq stands at 4415 and I was recently told by the founder of Veterans for Peace Arlington West Memorial on the beach in Santa Barbara (where I first visited five weeks after Casey was killed on Mother's Day) that they would no longer place a cross in the sand for my son, or the other 4414 dead in Iraq because Iraq is "old news."

Today, (August 17) we learn that in Afghanistan, three US troops, three NATO troops, and at least seven civilians were killed. This is another grim marker along the Imperial Road to Ruin as **Barack Obama's regime has managed to kill as many troops in Afghanistan in 19 months as the Bush stain did in seven years.**

I happen to believe that the wars and everything else became Obama's problems on January 20, 2009, but in reading comments about today's carnage on that bastion of centrism, the *Huffington Post*, many people either believe that the Afghanistan occupation just became Obama's War today, or that (in the case of at least one commenter), "Obama was forced to send more troops, and when one sends more troops, more of them will die." The matter-of-fact callousness of this remark stung like a hornet to me, and I bet the mothers of numbers 1227, 1228, and 1229 did not feel so cavalier when the Grim Reapers in dress khakis knocked on their doors today.

As little as we hear about US troops, as is our custom here in the Empire, the tragic slaughter of civilians in Iraq, Afghanistan, and Pakistan doesn't even deserve a blip on our radar screens. I watched three hours of MSDNC (MSNBC) tonight and the manipulative gyrations to find out how many ways they could talk about the "distraction" of the "mosque" at ground zero without talking about the one-million plus Arabs (Christians, Muslims, Jews, etc.) that the psychopathic US response to September 11, 2001 has killed, was pathetic and frustrating to watch.

There has been a bumper sticker saying for years that goes: "What if they gave a war and no one showed up?"

Well, "they," the ones that give the wars are not going to stop. "They" have too much at stake to give up the cash cow of wars for Imperial Profit, Power, and Expansion. "They" use the toady media to whip up nationalistic and patriotic fervor to get our kids to be thrown together with the victims in a meat grinder of destruction and we just sit here and allow them to do it.

The Empire preys on our kids using all the tools at its disposal: economic panic, high college tuition, high unemployment, and a mythology that the US has some existential right to steal the resources of other nations.

Not only do these occupations needlessly kill humans on both sides, but our troops are being dehumanized because of the institutional dehumanization of the so-called enemies, also. If you have not seen the Wikileaks Collateral Murder video, you have to watch it, but you also have to realize that these callous crimes are a daily occurrence in the "war" zones—not isolated incidents. We allow "Them" to turn our youth into animals for their sport so they can live opulent and obscene lifestyles while most of us struggle to even make ends meet.

To be proactive, we have to stop offering up our children to be sacrificed for the profit of the few.

Saturday, August 21, 2010
Deja Vu All Over Again

Dateline: September 27, 2017, Wasilla, AK.

Speaking from the Far-Western White House, President Sarah Palin today declared that combat operations "are over" in Iraq.

"I want to thank the American troops and their families for the heroic role they have played in freeing Iraq from a violent dictator and in protecting American interests in the Middle East," President Palin continued. "The troops that are not redeployed in Af/Pak, Korea, or Yemen, or Columbia, and remain in Iraq will now and forever be known as 'Enablers' and **Operation New Dawn** *will now be known as* **Operation High Noon**,*" the jubilant president, mother of eight, and grandmother of 12, finished.*

"The Palin administration feels confident that this will be one of the final times that 'end to combat operations' in Iraq will be declared, and this will be a robust withdrawal" a release from the White House press office stated.

Is the above scenario far-fetched? I don't think so—I have spent all week thinking that the rhetoric around the "end" to the combat mission in Iraq has to be satire from *The Onion*. I feel that nothing could be so bizarre.

Barack Obama called Iraq the "dumb war" in 2003—as is: "I am not against all wars, I am just against dumb wars," and from that tiny, lukewarm, and essentially hostile statement, he was called "anti-war." Indeed, when I found out that Obama had been awarded the Nobel Peace prize in 2009 —I accused the Swede (I was in Sweden at the time) who gave me the odd news, of lying, or reading another satire from *The Onion*.

My son Casey and at least 4000 more troops have been killed in Iraq since George Bush's famous

Captain Codpiece moment when he flew onto the deck of the Abraham Lincoln aircraft carrier near San Diego and declared an "end to major combat" in Iraq. At that point, my son's division, the First Cavalry's, imminent deployment to Iraq was canceled (but later rescheduled). I remember the day that happened. On May 1, 2003, Casey called me from Ft. Hood and we discussed the fact that the war was over.

Now, in a stultifying display of déjà vu, the Obama administration is declaring another end to combat in Iraq seven years, three months, and 18 days after BushCo's declaration. Not only is this an astounding display of re-framework, many people are going to believe it. I just saw a commentator on MSNBC(GE) telling everyone that President Barack Obama ended the war in Iraq ahead of schedule.

Dozens of Iraqis were killed this past week and I think they didn't get the memo about the war being over, either. People are still going to die—soldiers will still be killed because the Iraqis have always seen them as oppressors and occupiers, not saviors.

If the troops aren't combat troops any more, then let's take away their guns, tanks, drones, airplanes, helicopters, Humvees, bases, body armor, etc. and have them live in apartments in Baghdad—and speaking of that, why don't we de-fortify the Green Zone (that was also just rebranded to "International Zone) if everything is so hunky-dory. Also, the 3rd Armored Cav that is leaving for Iraq from Ft. Hood soon should refuse to go since the war is over!

The 4th Stryker Brigade from Ft. Lewis, Washington returned home a few days ago and they yelled: "We won," as they left the country. The US has won nothing in Iraq and what we have done to the Iraqi people (and are going to do to them) should be our infinite national shame.

Even when/if the US troop count ever truly equals zero in Iraq, the so-called war will never end for millions of people. Iraq is a hot zone of depleted uranium contamination as Vietnam is still a hot zone for Agent Orange. Empire is the curse that never stops defiling.

Even though this past week has been Bizzarro World, I know what I am going to do. I am going to pretend like the wars are still relevant and the people who are in danger have precious lives that are worth saving.

I only believed the "Mission Accomplished" BS on May 1, 2003, because I so desperately needed to.

Not this time.

Not ever again.

We'll leave Iraq when the last drop of oil and the last nickel is squeezed out of that most unfortunate of countries with some of the richest natural resources—not a second sooner.

CINDY NOTE: *As of this writing, the US under the Obama regime is committing more troops to fight the newest incarnation of enemy: "ISIS" or "ISIL" or "IS" or whatever.*

Friday, September 24, 2010
Did He Really Say That?

We can absorb a terrorist attack. We'll do everything we can to prevent it, but even a 9/11, even the biggest attack ever . . . we absorbed it and we are stronger.
Barack Obama in *Obama's Wars* by Bob Woodward

Again, the arrogance of US Robber Class politicians is astonishing!

71

I know I just have a modest internet talk show and a blog that only reaches thousands, but I am going to put in a request to interview Barack Obama, because I doubt, with the resignation of the only tough-ish person in the White House Press Corps, Helen Thomas, that any other so-called journalist has the guts to go against the Emperor and ask just one simple question—"Mr. President, who or what do you mean by 'us'?" Is it another case of: "It depends on what the meaning of the word 'is' is." (Bill Clinton).

Maybe Obama was suffering from the delusion of, "What doesn't kill us makes us stronger," but looking from the perspective of someone who was greatly weakened in so many ways by the attacks of 9/11, and from all of my other experiences since then, I can say what and who has not been made "stronger."

Many families here in the US have had members killed, maimed, or emotionally wounded starting on 9/11 and continuing every day since then. By this past week, 2010 was the deadliest year for our military in Afghanistan, already. It is just September, and 2010 has been only surpassed in carnage by the other year in the Obama regime—2009. And the other "crazy" thing is, troops keep dying in Iraq, even though that "war" is "over."

I can also say that the millions of people who have been killed, maimed, or displaced in Iraq, Afghanistan, and Pakistan (which Obama thinks is the "real threat") have not been strengthened in the short-term or long-term—but, hey—they don't really count, now, do they?

Since 9/11, I have been arrested many times for just exercising my civil rights to free speech and freedom of expression, and I am just one of thousands—I don't think our civil liberties are "stronger" since 9/11. In fact, just today, antiwar and social justice activists had their homes raided in all parts of this country by the FBI. I resent having to, for all intents and purposes, walk nude throughout airport security and I resent the entire police state mentality of airport personnel who, but for the "grace" of 9/11 could just as likely be saying: "Would you like that super-sized," as "I'm going to have to search you." Even their lives aren't better being wage slaves for the Police State.

Speaking of that, everyone I know in my wide circle of concern is either unemployed or underemployed. For example, my son, a new father, is working three jobs just to provide for his small family and hasn't worked in his trade as a land surveyor for a year and a half. Andy's story is not an unusual or special one. The job market has certainly not been made "stronger." The housing market has not been made "stronger" and OUR economy is as weak as my newborn grandson. It has no muscle tone or control and can only whine and scream because that's the only way it can express itself now. At least my grandbaby is adorable.

I can name a few institutions that have been made "stronger" since 9/11: The Police State and all its apparatus; the Military Industrial Complex and its tentacles—the Pentagon, the State Department, war profiteers, corporate media—Wall Street; the surviving banks; and especially the government. The rich are literally getting richer, and the poor are growing poorer. The income gap is wider than it ever has been since 1929!

Tragically—the numbers of people falling into poverty and into homelessness have been strengthened, as have the numbers of people who are losing their health insurance.

Whether Osama bin Laden perpetrated 9/11 from a cave in northern Afghanistan—or Dick Cheney planned it from his cave in Mordor—OBL's stated goal of total destruction of the US Empire is proceeding apace, and I can't fully comprehend what another "terrorist" attack would do to this nation. The institutions, people, and societal norms that were weakened by 9/11 will be further weakened and the ones that were made "stronger" will be further strengthened. I can foresee only a bleak future under Obama's Absorption Theory—complete tyranny in the U.S because of complete economic breakdown that will probably lead to isolated incidences of internal rebellion that will be violently suppressed in the name of "National Security and Stability."

I have read some Obamapologists saying that he was "correct;" that our nation was made "stronger." This line of thinking goes: *We were afraid at first, but eventually when WE were not attacked (by the terr'ists) again—we went about our daily lives as if nothing ever happened.* Well, I say: that's exactly what is wrong with this nation. Three-thousand Americans were killed that day, which wasn't bad enough—but almost 6000 (official count) Americans have been killed in the Middle East/Asia since then. And, as the mother of one of those, I can attest to the fact that not many people feel as connected to this tragic figure as they are to the ones murdered on 9/11. Our soldiers have been misused in this phony war of terror begun by Bush and perpetuated by Obama.

After 9/11, instead of becoming self-reflective, we mostly allowed our government to steal our flesh and blood, kill and torture millions of others, and descend into this Police State that is protected from accountability, because we the people are still afraid of our own shadows. We (as a whole) haven't "absorbed" crap—we have deflected it as far away from us as possible. Most of us are still afraid, but most of those that are still afraid are fearful of the wrong things. The real terrorists reside at 1600 Pennsylvania Avenue and other posh residences in the beltway.

We are speedily careening to November 2nd, when many of us will be going to the polls to vote for the "Party of No." Do you think I mean the Republicans? No, I mean the other "Party of No," the Democrats.

One thing the Obama regime has shown me is that the Democrats are also the Party of No: NO peace, NO justice, NO relevant healthcare reform, NO improvement in education, NO civil liberties, NO economic justice, NO environmental sustainability, NO jobs, NO anything that is positive for we that were made weaker after 9/11.

Yes, it's been a feast for the vampires of economic disaster and the pigs of war since 9/11 and I don't foresee any change coming at the ballot box. The ravenous feasters want your food, too—and they want you to believe that voting will hamper, or at least slow, their access to your measly crumbs. It obviously won't.

Go ahead and go vote for the Party of No (D or R) on November 2nd—but know that's what you are getting. Your vote for the Party of No (D or R) only strengthens the apparatus of control and oppression (I am going to go vote in California: Yes on 19!) and you get nothing in return.

CINDY NOTE: *My show, Cindy Sheehan's Soapbox, did reach out to the Obama press office for an interview and were rejected.*

Tuesday, October 5, 2010
Dissent in the Age of Obama

My first article for *Al Jazeera*

The welfare of the people in particular has always been the alibi of tyrants, and it provides the further advantage of giving the servants of tyranny a good conscience.
Albert Camus

Recently, the Federal Bureau of Investigations (FBI) raided the homes of at least eight antiwar/social justice activists here in the US

I happen to be a prominent antiwar activist myself, and have joked that I am a "little hurt" that I was not raided and perhaps I should try harder. Even though we have the urge to try and be lighthearted in this time of an increasing police state, with civil liberties on the retreat, it really isn't funny considering that the activists could face some serious charges stemming from these raids.

I have felt this harassment on a smaller scale myself and I know that defending oneself against a police state that has unlimited resources, time, and cruelty, can be quite expensive, time consuming, and annoying.

There is nothing noble about an agency that has reduced itself to being jackbooted enforcers of a neo-fascist police state, no matter how much the FBI has been romanticized in movies, television, and books.

For example, in one instance, early in the morning of September 24, at the home of Mick Kelly of Minneapolis, the door was battered in and flung across the room when his partner audaciously asked to see the FBI's warrant through the door's peephole. At Jessica Sundin's home, she walked downstairs to find seven agents ransacking her home while her partner and child looked on in shock.

These raids have terrifying implications for dissent here in the US.

First of all, these US citizens have been long-time and devoted antiwar activists who organized an antiwar rally that was violently suppressed by the US police state in Minneapolis-St. Paul, during the 2008 Republican National Convention. Because the Minneapolis activists have integrity, they had already announced that they would do the same if the Democrats hold their convention there in 2012.

I have observed that it was one thing to be anti-Bush, but to be anti-war in the age of Obama is not to be tolerated by many people. If you will also notice, the only people who seem to know about the raids are those of us already in the movement. There has been no huge outcry over this fresh outrage, either by the so-called movement or the corporate media.

I submit that if George Bush were still president, or if this happened under a McCain/Palin regime, there would be tens of thousands of people in the streets to protest. This is one of the reasons an escalation in police state oppression is so much more dangerous under Obama—even now, he gets a free pass from the very same people who should be adamantly opposed to such policies.

Secondly, I believe because the raids happened to basically 'unsung' and unknown, but very active workers in the movement, that the coordinated, early morning home invasions were designed to intimidate and frighten those of us who are still doing the work. The Obama regime would like nothing better than for us to shut up or go underground and to quit embarrassing it by pointing out its abject failures and highlighting its obvious crimes.

Just look at how the Democrats are demonizing activists who are trying to point out the inconvenient truth that the country (under a near Democratic tyranny) is sliding further into economic collapse, environmental decay, and perpetual war for enormous profit.

Barack and Joe, the *commandantes* of this police state, say that those who have the temerity to be critical are "asleep" and just need to "buck up." White House spokesperson, Robert Gibbs, recently stated that we on the "professional left" need to be "drug tested" if we are not addicted to the regimes' own drug: the Hopium of the Obama propaganda response team.

It seems like, even though some of those that have been nailed to the cross of national security do activism around South America, most of the activism is anti-war and pro-Palestinian rights. Being supportive of any Arab or Muslim, no matter how benign or courageous, is a very dangerous activity here in post-9/11 America.

The Supreme Court just decided (Wilner v. National Security Agency) that the National Security Agency (NSA) did not have to disclose if it was using warrantless wiretapping to spy on attorneys representing the extra-legal detention of prisoners in Guantanamo Bay, Cuba. Obtaining warrants, with cause, and attorney-client privilege were important principles of the US justice system, but even the neo-fascist Supreme Court is undermining the law—talk about "activist" judges!

Not only have activists been targeted here in the States, but also Obama has ominously declared himself judge, jury, and executioner of anyone that he deems a national security "threat." These are the actions of a tyrant and another assault against our rights and against the rule of law from a person who promised "complete transparency" from his administration.

We have learned that Obama's first victim under his presidential execution program is Anwar al-Awlaki, a US-born Muslim who is now in Yemen. Without showing proof of al-Awlaki's so-called executionable offenses and without a trial in a court of law, Obama has unloosed his hit squads on Awlaki. Is there anyone out there reading this who does not believe, or fear, that this program could quickly descend into summary executions within the borders of the US?

Al-Awlaki's father has filed a motion in federal court to stay the execution of his son until he gets his constitutionally guaranteed rights to due process, but Obama's justice department has refused to cooperate stating that to do so would 'undermine' that fabled, exploited, and ephemeral "national security."

When Obama behaves like Bush, only on steroids, he amply demonstrates why other people hate our country so much. Persons in other countries are not nearly as blind as Americans. They know that even though Obama went to Cairo to blather about building understanding between the US and the Muslim world, actions speak louder than words and Obama's actions drip with carnage and pain.

Obviously, the suppression of dissent here in the US, while outrageous and inexcusable, has not reached the level of the McCarthy witch-hunts of the 1950s—yet.

The longer we Americans remain silent in the face of these injustices, the more they will continue to occur and escalate.

Make your voice heard!

Saturday, October 16, 2010
Injustice in the Age of Obama: The Harrowing tale of Dr. Aafia Siddiqui

Since being the defendant in about six trials after I was arrested for protesting the Iraq and Afghanistan occupations, it's my experience that the police lie. Period.

However, the lies don't stop at street law enforcement level. From lies about WMD and connections to "al Qaeda," almost every institution of so-called authority—the Pentagon, State Department, CIA, FBI, all the way up to the Oval Office and back down—lie. Not white lies, but big, Mother of all BS (MOAB) lies that lead to the destruction of innocent lives. I.F Stone was most definitely on the ball when he proclaimed, "Governments lie."

Having clarified that, I would now like to examine a case that should be enshrined in the travesty of the US Justice Hall of Shame.

In February of this year, Aafia Siddiqui, a Pakistani mother of three, was convicted in US Federal (kangaroo) Court of seven counts, including two counts of "attempted murder of an American." On September 23, Judge Berman, who displayed an open bias against Dr. Siddiqui, sentenced her to 86 years in prison.

The tapestry of lies about Dr. Siddiqui—a cognitive neuroscientist, schooled at MIT and Brandeis —was woven during the Bush regime but fully maintained during her trial and sentencing this year by the Obama (in)Justice Department.

Before September 11, 2001, Aafia lived in Massachusetts with her husband, also a Pakistani citizen, and their two children. According to all reports, she was a quietly pious Muslim (which is still not a crime here in the States), who hosted play dates for her children. She was a good student who studied hard and maintained an exemplary record, causing little harm to anything, let alone anyone.

After 9/11, when she was pregnant with her third child, she encouraged her husband to move back to Pakistan to avoid the backlash against her Muslim children—which was a very prescient thing to do considering the Islamophobia that has only increased in this country since then.

Tortured "truth"

Following the move to Pakistan, Dr. Siddiqui and her husband divorced. Her life took a horrendous turn justly after. While Khalid Sheikh Mohammed (KSM)—supposed mastermind of the 9/11 plot —was being water-boarded by the CIA 183 times in one month, he gave Dr. Siddiqui up as a member of al-Qaeda. Was this a case of stolen identity, or was Mohammed just saying random words like you or I would to stop the torture?

There is some disputed "intelligence" that Aafia had married KSM's nephew, a tenuous allegation at best, and even so, guilt by association has no place in the hallowed US legal system.

Following KSM's torture-induced "insights," Dr. Siddiqui was listed by Bush's Justice Department as one of the seven most dangerous al-Qaeda operatives in the world. A mother of three equipped with a lethal ability to "thin-slice" your cognitive personality in seconds. If alleged association and a healthy interest in neuro-psychology are the definitive hallmarks of a "terrorist operative," then Malcolm Gladwell better start making some phone calls to Crane, Poole, and Schmidt.

A culture of falsehoods

Face it, we all know that since 9/11, there have been numerous false "terror" alerts and lies leading to the capture and torture of hundreds of innocent individuals—and the heinous treatment we have all witnessed from Abu Ghraib. Additionally, we are supposed to believe that multi-war criminal, Colin Powell, was "fooled" by faulty intelligence so much so that he paved the way for the invasion of Iraq by his false testimony at the UN, but we are also supposed to unquestioningly believe the US intelligence apparatus when they lie about others such as Dr. Siddiqui.

In any case, in a bizarre scenario—to make a very long story short—Dr. Siddiqui and her three children disappeared for five years from 2003 to 2008, resurfacing in Ghazni, Afghanistan with her oldest child, a son who was then eleven. She claimed that for the years she was missing, she was being held in various Pakistani and US prisons being tortured and repeatedly raped. Many prisoners, including Yvonne Ridley, maintain she was incarcerated in Bagram AFB and tortured for at least part of the five missing years.

After Dr. Siddiqui resurfaced, she was arrested and taken to an Afghan police station where four Americans—two military and two FBI agents—rushed to "question" her through interpreters. The FBI and military claim that they were taken to a room that had a curtain at one end and that they did not know that Dr. Siddiqui was lying asleep on a bed at the other side of the curtain. As you read below it will become blatantly obvious that personnel involved from both institutions totally fabricated their stories.

This is the Americans' version: They entered the room and one of the military dudes said he laid his weapon down (remember, they were there to interrogate one of the top most dangerous people in the world), and Siddiqui got up, grabbed the weapon, yelling obscenities and that she wanted to "kill Americans." All 5'3" of her raised the weapon to fire and she fired the rifle twice, missing everyone in the small room—in fact she even missed the walls, floor, and ceiling since no bullets from the rifle were ever recovered.

Then one of the Americans shot her twice in the stomach "in self-defence." It was shown at the trial that her fingerprints were not even on the weapon. The only bullets that were found that day were in Dr. Aafia's body. How many stories of military cover-ups have we heard about since 9/11? I can think of two right away without even trying hard: Pat Tillman and Jessica Lynch.

Hopeless injustice

Dr. Aafia's side is this: After she was arrested, she was again beaten and she fell asleep on a bed when she heard talking in the room she was in so she got out of the bed and someone shouted: "Oh no, she's loose!" Then she was shot—when she was wavering in and out of consciousness, she heard someone else say: "We could lose our jobs over this."

Even with no evidence that she fired any weapon, she was convicted (the jury found no pre-meditation) by a jury and sentenced to the aforementioned 86 years. It's interesting that the Feds did not pursue "terrorist" charges against Dr. Siddiqui because they were aware that the only evidence that existed was tortured out of KSM—so they literally ganged up on her to press the assault and attempted murder charges.

Even if Dr. Siddiqui did shoot at the Americans, reflect on this. Say this case was being tried in Pakistan under similar circumstances for an American woman named Dr. Betty Brown who was captured and repeatedly tortured and raped by the ISI—here in the states that woman would be a hero if she shot at her captors—not demonized and taken away from her life and her children.

I believe Dr. Aafia Siddiqui is a political prisoner and now the political bogey-woman for two US regimes.

In Pakistan, the response to her verdict and sentencing brought the predictable mass protests, burning of American flags and effigies of Obama, and calls for Pakistan to repatriate Dr. Siddiqui. They know who the real criminals are and who should be in prison for life! At present, Hilary's state department harps on about "soft power" and diplomacy, but what better way to quell US distrust in the Muslim world than to try such cases with due diligence and integrity.

In the US, not many people know about this case. Obviously many people were Hope-notized by the millions of dollars poured into the Obama PR machine—and believed when he said that his administration would be more transparent and lawful than the outlaws of the Bush era.

I guess they were mistaken.

Sunday, October 31, 2010
US: Myth of the Two Party System

Opinion—*Al Jazeera*

The two-party system has given this country the war of Lyndon Johnson, the Watergate of Nixon, and the incompetence of Carter. Saying we should keep the two-party system simply because it is working is like saying the Titanic voyage was a success because a few people survived on life rafts.
Eugene J. McCarthy, 1978

If John McCain were president, we can never be exactly sure what would be happening, but I think we can make some educated speculations.

First of all, the "banksters" would be receiving their carte blanche bailouts and Ben Bernanke would have been re-appointed as Chairman of the Federal Reserve.

Robert Gates would probably still be the secretary of defense and Sarah Palin would be offering late night comedians endless fodder for their monologues.

If John McCain happened to be the one infesting the Oval Office at this time, single-payer health care would surely be "off the table." I am confident that a health care "reform" bill probably would have contained massive giveaways to the insurance and big pharmaceutical industries, with no "robust" public option.

We citizens would, I'm sure, have been forced to purchase insurance from the very same insurance companies that spread out a largess of nearly $170m lobbying dollars to Congress in 2009. If we are one of the "lucky ones" that happen to already have coverage, we would have been taxed for the benefit.

McCain and "justice"

Without a doubt, McCain's Justice Department would be protecting war criminals—like John Yoo—of the preceding administration and the McCain Department of Justice (DOJ) would probably be vigorously defending the discriminatory practice of Don't Ask Don't Tell for the military.

More than likely, under this nightmarish scenario, McCain's Federal Bureau of Investigation would be committing home invasion break-ins (designated as "legal raids") to intimidate activists.

McCain probably would have given himself the power to be judge and jury over any American citizen that didn't approve of his foreign policy.

There is not even a shadow of doubt that McCain would be feigning strictness with Israel, while turning a blind eye to the continued expansions of Israeli settlements in the West Bank and the completely immoral and destructive blockade of Gaza.

If the unthinkable occurred and McCain beat Obama in 2008, official unemployment would be hovering around 10 percent (unofficial around 20 percent). And one in every five homes would be in danger of being foreclosed upon. We might even be experiencing the widest income disparity between the rich and poor that we have seen since before the stock market crash of 1929!

McCain, being the "brave" military man, may have tripled troop deployments to Afghanistan and the needless deaths of US troops and Afghan civilians would probably have increased dramatically. I am sure that McCain would have given huge contracts to the US war machine for drones, mercenaries, airplanes, and other military hardware.

Being a loyal Bushite, McCain would probably be conscientiously following the Status of Forces Agreement for the slow withdrawal from Iraq that was negotiated between the Bush government, and the puppet regime in Iraq.

At least we aren't bombing Iran!

I get informed all the time, that even though "Obama isn't so great," at least he hasn't invaded Iran yet, and McCain surely would have been bombing Iran by now.

Okay, so rhetoric towards Iran would be heightened, but whether McCain would have waged another military campaign during the current political climate would be an assumption too far.

Gosh, if McCain were president right now, the defense budget might be the largest—$741.2 billion—since World War II. He might have even asked for billions upon billions of supplemental funding for the wars in Iraq and Afghanistan. Horrors!

Of course, a McCain education budget would only be about 1/10th of the defense budget at $78 billion. And, a McCain education plan would probably contain lots of rigorous testing if the states were to want more desperately needed funds.

If McCain were president, there would be an active "antiwar" movement. However—as during the Bush years—the "movement" wouldn't be so much antiwar, but anti-war waged by the Republicans. The anti-Republican movement wants no systemic change, it just wants Democrats in office.

Blurring the political divide

However, in almost every case, Democrat equals the status quo.

Of course, in all of my above scenarios, Obama and his regime have done all of those things that people were afraid that McCain would do, but there's an extremely small outcry.

Here we are, once again, careening madly down the path to electoral ruin—where voting for the "lesser of two evils" has become a national pastime.

When the elite class gives the appearance of only two choices on the ballot, we end up voting "against" a candidate far more times than we vote "for" someone.

What's wrong with us? We are lazy, we are fearful, the establishment beats us down, we are ignorant, and we are defeated. Voting at least gives us the latent feeling that we are doing something, when we are really doing very little.

We righteously march down to our polling place, like good soldiers for the status quo. We vote. We get our little stickers with an American flag that proudly proclaims: I VOTED. But when we vote for a member of the political duopoly, we are only voting for "Dee or Dum."

The Democrats had their chance during the last four years, and instead of passing progressive legislation and ending the wars, they have pandered to the right, which has been emboldened by the power the Democrats gave it.

Now the Republicans are poised to take over at least the House of Representatives. And Democrats will begin to spew progressivism out of their lying mouths and abuse the energy of their newly-angry base to try to regain power—like the Republicans have done effectively for the past two years.

Will progressives ever learn that political pandering and fear-based voting never brings anything but defeat, or are we trapped in a vicious cycle of our own making?

Saturday, November 13, 2010
Savage Austerity

Yes, friends, governments in capitalist society are but committees of the rich to manage the affairs of the capitalist class.
James Connolly, Irish Freedom Fighter and founder of the Irish Labor Party

"We're all in this together," is the chorus the ruling class loves to sing while it simultaneously bestows "quantitative easing" upon banks after imposing "savage austerity" measures on the working class.

I have been worried about Obama's Bowles-Simpson "Cat Food Commission" (CFC) on reducing the deficit since it was announced, and it turns out my worries were well founded.

Besides suggesting raising the retirement age to an ungodly 69, savage cuts to Social Security and Medicare are proposed. Who needs Social Security and Medicare? Not the elite, but they are not forgotten in the CFC plan, the CFC also proposes to REDUCE taxes on the top earners from an already too low 35 percent, to an absolutely obscene 23 percent! Obama is following the international sport of the ruling class of forcing the least advantaged in society to pay for the crimes and excess of the One-Percent Club—those who sit at the top of the economic food chain controlling at least 50 percent of the nation's wealth.

One thing we must understand, especially in the US, is that Capitalism creates these crises to be able to "capitalize" on them. The bubbles of the past were generated for gross profit on the expansion, and economic vampirism on the contraction. We who are not in the One-Percent Club may feel some temporary prosperity on the expansion, but each contraction squeezes us tighter and tighter.

In the CFC, there are also modest cuts proposed to defense, but if any do go through (very doubtful), it will just be a symbolic gesture meant to prove to us that the parasites really are "in it" with us.

Why do we in the 99 Percent Guild just take it for granted that we will slave our lives away for the elite class? It not only will exploit our labor to make itself grow fatter, but it will also flood the banks with billions of counterfeit dollars to drive up prices of necessities and drive down the purchasing power of our hard-earned federal reserve notes. However, we are supposed to suffer through all this with the Protestant rectitude of our forbearers.

Instead of asking the working class to sacrifice even more "savagely," there are some obvious solutions to this threat of "savage austerity" and hyperinflation. One solution that would feed two birds with one worm would be to bring our troops out of Iraq and Afghanistan and then close at least 2/3rds of our bases around the world. The Pentagon budget is around $750 billion for 2011 and education gets a paltry one-tenth of that! The symbolic proposed cuts to defense are not satisfactory, nor will they stop the murder.

Alternative and renewable sources of energy must be enhanced and put into practice. When we bailed out the auto industries last year that would have been a perfect time to put people back to work to retool and move forward with more high-speed rail and public transportation. A massive public works program to move our nation from all fossil fuel to a completely renewable and sustainable future would put untold amounts of people to work doing meaningful labor at a living wage and it would make that future look brighter.

There must be an excess profit tax put on corporations and big oil's most favored status must change to pariah and the revenue we receive from the immoral profiteering can go to help pay for our new, clean energy and meaningful work policies. The One-Percent Club must pay "savage" tax on any income over a certain amount—the median household income in this country would be a good starting point. Conversely, Americans in the middle and lower income class should have their taxes dramatically cut to stimulate the economy. Tax cuts for the wealthy only stimulate the living standards of the wealthy. The CFC would end the only two meaningful deductions still left to the 99 Percent Club: health costs and mortgage interest.

Parasitism is a type of symbiotic relationship between organisms of different species where one organism, the parasite, benefits at the expense of the host. Well, the Capitalists are definitely a species of creature that benefits at the expense of its host—the workers and our prosperity. The intriguing thing about the parasitic behavior of the One Percent Club, though, is in its very name: One Percent. One percent of the economic parasites in the US are benefiting off of the rest of us.

Here though, it's almost as if we have invited our parasites to suck the life out of us, and we not only give them our comfy beds, we cook them a delicious breakfast, too, and compose a lovely Thank You note to them to add insult to injury.

I have spent the last 10 days in three European countries listening to how the people here are responding to the Savages and the cuts that are being proposed in their services, jobs, and ways of life. The experience has been educational and inspirational.

Recently, in England, students took to the streets in a massive display of protest against the huge increase in University tuition, and some of them occupied offices of Tory politicians. I met with leaders of unions that will not cooperate with the government or their union leaders who have been co-opted by the Labour Party that does not do anything to alleviate the suffering of labor.

In Dublin, tens of thousands have taken to the streets to protest perhaps the harshest austerity measures anywhere. The descendants of James Connolly will not take more oppression by the ruling class lying down.

Greece is a great example as reaction to the upcoming austerity in the US They have had five general strikes since May and, as I was leaving my hotel in Athens to go to a meeting, there were about 300 riot police beginning to cordon off the area around my hotel which was also close to an office of the Labor Ministry. Turning the corner, I ran into about 75 dock-workers who were carrying flags attached to three-inch dowels—instead of cowering under such an overwhelmingly potentially brutal reaction by the Police State, the dock workers were banging their flag poles on the ground. I wish I could have stayed around to watch as the workers were going to try to get into the ministry to protest their firings.

This global crisis of Capitalism gives us the golden opportunity to drive the final nail in the coffin of this oppressive and violent system. According to the UN Gini report, the US has the greatest income disparity of any so-called developed nation and implementing the recommendations of the CFC will make this fact even worse.

When Congress begins to debate the bill that will arise from the CFC report, we need to have a massive response: the Teamsters need to shut down ports and block roads; we need to boycott banking and credit; we need to boycott paying our federal income taxes; oil workers need to strike; we need to be in DC to occupy the offices of our Congressional Representatives (how about an across the board pay and benefit's cut for Congress and the president?) We just need to get out into the streets to do our part following in the footsteps of, not only our brothers and sisters in other countries, but giants in our own who sacrificed so much to win the hard earned concessions we have—or used to have.

An organized response that is committed, intelligent, militant, and courageous will take the US oligarchy by surprise and it's past time the USAians take part in the global struggle against savage austerity in a more meaningful way.

CINDY NOTE: *This article predated Occupy Wall Street by almost a year—I should have trademarked 1% and 99%.*

Thursday, December 23, 2010
Don't Go, Don't Kill (DGDK)

First published in *Al Jazeera* English

The recent repeal of the US military policy of "Don't ask, don't tell" (DADT) is far from being the human rights advancement some are touting it to be. I find it intellectually dishonest, in fact, illogical on any level to associate human rights with any military, let alone one that is currently dehumanizing two populations as well as numerous other victims of it's clandestine "security" policies.

Placing this major contention aside, the enactment of the bill might be an institutional step forward in the fight for "equality," however, institutions rarely reflect reality.

Do we really think that the US Congress vote to repeal the act and Obama signing the bill is going to stop the current systemic harassment of gays in the military?

While I am a staunch advocate for equality of marriage and same-sex partnership, I cannot—as a peace activist—rejoice in the fact that now homosexuals can openly serve next to heterosexuals in one of the least socially responsible organizations that currently exists on earth: The US military.

It is an organization tainted with a history of intolerance towards anyone who isn't a Caucasian male from the Mid-West. Even then I'm sure plenty fitting that description have faced the terror and torment enshrined into an institution that transforms the pride and enthusiasm of youth into a narrow zeal for dominating power relations.

Wrong battle for equality

It is hard to separate this issue from the activities of the military. War might be a "racket," but it is also the most devastating act one can be involved in. Whether you are the aggressor or a victimized civilian, no one can shake off the psychological scars of war. No one.

Its effects on the individual as well as collective human psyche are terminal. Championing equal rights is an issue of morality, war is immoral, and the US military is heading further and further down the path of immorality.

Even with the advent of WikiLeaks, transparency and accountability of US military activity has been sucked into a black hole of silence. Drone attacks, illegal cross-border interventions, extra-judicial assassinations all occur in the name of national interest. It is not in the interest of equal rights activists to support an institution that is intent on ignoring every protocol of human decency.

Face it, gays are now and have been in the military since before Valley Forge during the Revolutionary War.

The only difference being one can now admit their orientation without fear of official recrimination —a major boon for the equal rights movement! The capacity for increased carnage should not be celebrated as a victory!

I cannot help but think about those that are on the receiving end of US military aggression. So a minor change has occurred at the input juncture of the war machine, but the output remains the same: we dismantle systems of indigenous governance, support disingenuous often criminal overlords, commit endless acts of brutality, and worst of all leave entire nations rudderless, spiraling downwards into the same abyss that engulfs the US military's lack of accountability.

I wonder what the response towards DADT will be overseas? I wonder if mothers across the Swat Valley in Northern Pakistan are cheering the repeal of the act (most likely not), gathering in the streets to celebrate a victory in the global pursuit of human equality, only to be forced to take cover as yet another hellfire-laden drone appears on the horizon. Hell hath no fury, as a drone operated from somewhere south of the Mason-Dixon Line.

Don't equal human rights extend to those that the Empire has mislabeled as the "enemy?" Or do we now have to ignore the fact that innocent people are being slaughtered by the thousands?

Unjust binaries

We live in a world governed by binaries, straight or gay, them or us, freedom or tyranny. Until we break away from this norm, we shall forever be shackled to a narrow existence, manipulated by a political establishment that serves its own interests.

We should embrace complication, appreciate difference and most of all not be duped into accepting "victories" that clearly benefit an elite, that you and me (pardon the binary) will never be part of.

Some of us in the peace movement work really hard to keep our young people out of the hands of the war machine that preys on disadvantaged young people in inner cities and poor rural settings.

To see a demographic that is (without appearing to stereotypes) traditionally better educated, more politically progressive, and economically advantaged fight to join this killing machine is very disheartening.

I can see how one could view the repeal as a step forward, framed in the context dictated by the political elites of the Washington beltway. I can imagine much displeasure amongst the military brass—but I cannot reiterate enough how this is not a progressive moment in the social history of the United States.

The US military is not a human rights organization and nowhere near a healthy place to earn a living or raise a family. My email box is filled with stories of mostly straight soldiers and their families who were deeply harmed by life in the military.

Because of the callous and violent nature of the system, Post Traumatic Stress Disorder (PTSD) is on the rise and suicide rates among veterans and the spouses of active duty soldiers are skyrocketing.

Veterans still find it very difficult to access the services, benefits, and bonuses that were promised to them by their recruiters. I cannot imagine the repealing of DADT significantly improving the material conditions experienced by gays during military service.

While the children of war profiteers and politicians are protected from any kind of sacrifice, this Empire preys on the rest of our youth—gay/straight; male/female—and spits their mangled or dead bodies onto the dung heap of history, without a qualm or a twinge of conscience.

Joining the US military should never be an option for the socially conscious while our troops are being used as corporate tools for profit, or hired assassins for imperial expansion. Soldiers are called: "Bullet sponges," by their superiors and "dumb animals" by Henry Kissinger, the former secretary of state.

While soldiers are dehumanized and treated like dirt, they are taught to dehumanize "the other," and treat them as less than dirt. It is a vicious cycle, and the way to stop a vicious cycle is to denounce and reject it, not openly participate.

I want to bang my head against a wall when another young gay person commits suicide as a result of despicable bullying, yet people within the same community have fought hard for the right to openly join the biggest bully ever!

Don't go, don't kill!

CINDY NOTE: This is still ballyhooed as a great Obama accomplishment. Meh!

Wednesday, December 29, 2010
"Second Chances"

In case you don't know, Michael Vick is the current starting quarterback for the Philadelphia Eagles, but while he was QB of the Atlanta Falcons, he was arrested, tried, and convicted of running a dog-fighting ring that contained some of the most vile torture, cruelty, and death to man's "best-friend" that were tragically bred for Michael Vick's sick and twisted pleasures.

After spending 23 months, both in prison or under house arrest, Michael Vick was signed to play for the Philadelphia Eagles and he earned the position of starting QB with a seven million dollar, two-year contract.

I believe prisons should be rehabilitative and not punitive, but was justice served and did Michael Vick pay his debt to society for his horrendous crimes? Is he redeemed? Of course, what he did was heinous and inhumane and thinking about it fills me with disgust, but our president is not similarly conflicted. On Sunday, from Hawaii, Obama reportedly called Jeffrey Lurie, owner of the Eagles and huge donor to Barack Obama and other Democrats to "thank" him for giving Vick a "second chance."

Hmmm—"Second chances" are almost miraculous for some people and impossible for others. One similar call could take Mumia off of death row, or pardon railroaded defense attorney, Lynne Stewart, or get Pvt. Bradley Manning out of his inhumane imprisonment (this list could fill a book, I am afraid, so I'll stop now).

Also, a study by the Independent Committee on Reentry and Employment, for example, found that up to 60 percent of ex-cons in New York were still unemployed one year after release. Stats on this are difficult to find, like most statistics on unemployment (which only count those that are receiving unemployment checks, or applying for them), but I am almost 100 percent sure that 100 percent of the 60 percent are not Michael Vicks or fictional, Gordon Gekkos, looking for multi-million dollar salary scores after incarceration. Most certainly, many of these "ex-cons" looking for work didn't commit as heinous of a crime as Vick did, either, but that's something we can only speculate on.

Many humans (including myself) have a soft spot in their hearts for animals. In America, we seem very fond of our dogs. In fact, I remember back in March of 2008, a video emerged on the Interwebs showing a US Marine named Lance Corporal Motari throwing a puppy off of a cliff while on duty in Iraq. The outrage was enormous and, according to Snopes.Com, the Marine Corps eventually discharged the Marine and one of his buddies. My thought at the time was: "Of course, Marines can throw puppies off of cliffs, they kick Iraqi doors in, kill innocent people, and spray population centers with white phosphorous, among other war crimes. What's a puppy?"

So, in my mind, the "second chance" for Michael Vick evolves to the video of Marines throwing a puppy from a cliff which itself evolves to the Wikileaks Collateral Murder Video that was released last March. This video clearly shows an Army unit in the air and on the ground attacking journalists and children and laughing about it on tape. The Collateral Murder video has 302 thousand hits on Google, yet when one Googles Michael Vick and Barack Obama, we get 10.7 MILLION hits! What's wrong with this picture?

Almost three thousand of our fellow humans were killed on 9/11, and their murderers still haven't been brought to justice, whether you think Osama bin Laden or Dick Cheney was the "master-mind." One is either dead, or in hiding, and the other hiding out in the open with his phalanx of Secret Service and evil sneer to protect him. Both of them are extremely wealthy, in any case, and are protected from accountability by the institutions that gave birth to their evil and help sustain them with phony investigations predicated on institutional, not justice. There are no "second chances" for those killed on 9/11 or their families who miss them and long for their presence.

After 9/11, whether Dick Cheney planned the crime, or not, he and the cabal of evil that surrounded him invaded two countries in search of massive profits, but talked a gullible public into believing that these high crimes and crimes against humanity (wars of aggression, according to the Nuremburg Tribunals, are the highest form of war crime) were for "justice." I think, unless one is the most recalcitrant neocon or Fox Noised American, most of us realize by now that the wars that still rage on after a decade were bogus and based on fairy tales supported by centuries of a mythic America that, if she doesn't "do the right thing," at least she always has "good intentions."

The few that still support the wars, often use "3000 Americans were killed on 9/11" as their excuse for revenge, but even if we only count US troop deaths, over twice that number have died now from the war and hundreds from suicide or other illnesses caused by deployment. Aren't these "Americans," too? They have no "second chance" to make better choices. I can't help it, but sometimes I go over the dozens of different choices Casey could have made differently to be alive today—even if the bullet that made mincemeat out of his beautiful brain was a few inches to the right or left. Sometimes, I can't bear the fact that I didn't carry through with my threat to hit him with my car the last time he was home. Sigh, "second chances" don't usually appear to us down here in the working-class.

Then the biggest class of humans who don't get much of a "second chance" are the millions killed or displaced by the "hot wars" of Iraq/Af/Pak and the other almost 1000 places the US military is currently deployed around the world like a thinly-sliced Christmas ham. Also, we never hear about the millions of people "living" off of less than $3 a day, while Vick, Osama, Obama, George, and Dick get their millions and the banksters get their billions.

Reading the stories of how Vick's associates tortured the dogs broke my heart, but former Justice Department employee, John Yoo, wrote the justification for HUMAN torture methods that included water-boarding (Vicks' scum actually hung dogs in the pool to drown them for not performing well), yet Yoo has a cushy professorship at UC Berkeley teaching Constitutional Law of all things. George Bush reports yelling: "Hell, yeah" when asked about the use of waterboarding and he got millions of dollars for a book he didn't write and gets thousands of dollars reading speeches to people that have been prepared for him. The scum of the Bush regime don't even need "second chances," because Obama protects them with that institutional immunity guaranteed to the worst of the worst.

The 22,000 children per day who die quietly from illness, dehydration and/or starvation due to poverty are the silent scream that is never heard and most of them were born with very slim chances to survive past age five. The explosions on 9/11 drowned out the fact that for every one American killed that day, three children died—the apathy of our materialistic lives hasn't allowed that stunningly sad fact to penetrate our "rat race" existence every day before 9/11/2001 and every day since.

This isn't about whether Michael Vick has been rehabilitated or not, or whether he deserves a second chance—I am about as much the "second chance monitor" as the POTUS is—it's about perspective. The one person with so much power and so little compassionate perspective is Barack Obama. With his blood-drenched hands, Obama theoretically has the power to stop allowing imperial torture and death and to order a halt to economic tsunamis. Then literally billions of good people could get that magical "second chance."

I guess a phone call to a large campaign contributor is far easier than actually doing the right thing!

CINDY NOTE: And that is the final entry for 2010! Phew—quite a busy year protesting war and oppression for someone who "disappeared."

Part Three
2011

> *My Administration is committed to creating an unprecedented level of openness in Government. We will work together to ensure the public trust and establish a system of transparency, public participation, and collaboration. Openness will strengthen our democracy and promote efficiency and effectiveness in Government. Government should be transparent. Transparency promotes accountability and provides information for citizens about what their Government is doing.*
>
> **A message from President Obama to his staff**
> **Taken from the White House Website**

From the outset of Barack Obama's political career, up until his presidential election victory, a large part of his political platform was the concept of transparency in government. As a legal scholar of Constitutional Law, having taught the subject at the prestigious University of Chicago Law School, his promotion of political decision-making transparency, at the time, seemed to be more substance than rhetoric.

The political chattering classes were championing his credentials; many talking heads on the "liberal left" were predicting the closure of Guantanamo, amendments to the Military Commissions Act of 2006 removing the suspension of habeas corpus, thorough Congressional investigations into warrantless wiretapping, etc., etc.—the "wish list" was endless. The previous president had spent the majority of his time in office eroding our Constitutional rights and civil liberties at home and tarnishing our image abroad—all sandwiched between his primary pursuit in office: family holidays at Kennebunkport.

Obama was going to be different, he planned to send Mr. Lobbyist out of Washington; government was going to be clean, efficient and focused on the public good—he knew exactly the dirty secrets of government. An Obama 2008 document entitled "Restoring Trust and improving Transparency" states:

"Oil and gas executives met with Vice President Cheney to write our energy laws, with the goal of increasing their profits and saddling the public with their environmental and public health costs; Cheney went to the Supreme Court to keep the names of these lobbyists secret."

The jig was up for backdoor deals and the time of what Harvard Law Professor Lawrence Lessig calls "institutionalized corruption" was over. A new sheriff was coming to town.

Health Care: A New Hope
So in January 2009, the nation turned to "the great hope," Barack Obama, a man so familiar with the US Constitution one could imagine him being able to recite it backwards. As it turns out, it seems he interprets it backwards as well.

The first major event on the political calendar was health-care reform. Democrats (and the tens of millions without health-care insurance) were hoping to succeed where the Clintons had previously failed. Progressives were optimistically exuding large swathes of hope, dreaming of a public option. The Beltway political landscape was about to undergo a facelift, with the health-care insurance lobby—one of the biggest "cartels" in town—about to receive a swift boot to the unmentionables. Better yet we were all going to see it live on national TV—Obama promised at least eight times that a debate on the health-care issue would be televised.

We got screwed. We did get a televised debate—several Democrats went up against several Republicans spewing their respective talking points, no doubt written by political consultants and not by people in the medical/public health field—an event watched by the eight or nine people constantly tuned into C-Span and the three others streaming it from the White House website.

Don't worry, if you missed the health-care discussion, you're in the company of the elected officials who allegedly took part in it.

The real debate took place behind the closed doors of the Oval Office, with a strict guest list including insurance executives and none other than the lobbyists who were supposedly being ushered out of town and back to Dodge.

Worst still, health-care reform had miraculously overnight transformed into health-care insurance reform. Somehow the health-care insurance industry had snagged the deal of the century—Obama had agreed to a policy that included a provision that every American had to buy health-care insurance!

Talk of a public option had been locked in a box, left in Dennis Kucinich's office on Capitol Hill, with the keys somewhere at the bottom of the Potomac—placed there to taunt him for the rest of his political life. I don't remember having the opportunity to tune into my local affiliate of the "I'm liberal, really I am" channel to watch that discussion. Were those meetings available for view in your market?

Shining a light on the dark side

Okay, so Obama dropped the ball on health care. Lobbyists are extremely well entrenched in Washington DC. Maybe he was softening them up for the knockout punch some time down the line —or not. So turning once again to Obama's transparency platform, from the aforementioned campaign document, a rich source of political perfidy: "*It is no coincidence that the disastrous policies of the Bush-Cheney years have been accompanied by unprecedented secrecy . . . .*"

In his literary "masterpiece" *Decision Points*, George Bush, no doubt through the auspices of a ghostwriter, transparently admits (enthusiastically to the point of being overzealous) that he ordered the use of waterboarding, an act that clearly falls under the traditional definition of torture. We, the US, openly admit to torturing individuals. What little moral capital the US once held has disintegrated faster than that of Tiger Woods.

Many of us knew years ago that waterboarding (along with other inhumane practices) was being used on (mostly) illegally detained individuals in prisons that remain open and active under the Obama regime. Is the Obama regime prosecuting or even investigating these crimes that have been openly admitted to by the instigators like Berkeley Law professor John Yoo and the torturers? Heck no! Obama has famously said that we need to "look forward, not backward."

Next time I get pulled over for speeding I hope the police officer has the moral vision of our president and accepts my pleas of "I won't do that again, I promise." I mean if it works for mass torture, surely—humor aside, the entire corruption of the interpretation of Constitutional Law in regards to Gitmo/ "terror" detainees has not only led to a substantial reduction in the civil rights of most Americans; but also made it legally impossible to lawfully prosecute those who were genuinely out to cause harm. The case is building against teachers of Constitutional Law. It seems such a career is the best preparation for a life of subverting the Constitution.

Robot Santa

Not only is Obama against rescinding the scope of presidential executive orders—extended via the various post 9/11 security Act amendments collectively referred to as the Patriot Act—he has added a few extras, one being what I like to refer to as his "Presidential Execution Program (PEP)." PEP talks in the Oval Office have a distinctly different outcome to pep talks in the locker room.

Obama has bestowed upon himself the decision of which "suspected" "evil doer" (we might as well use Bush rhetoric, since we are still very much beholden to his policies) gets to live or die. Very much reminiscent of the demented Robot Santa from Futurama, Obama maintains a list of "naughty" individuals whose fate will undoubtedly involve a drone, some hellfires and, ironically, little hope.

According to attorney, Maria LaHood, of the Centre for Constitutional Rights, who represents the father of the only person we know for sure that is on the list, Anwar al Awlaki, the list is not only secretive, but a Federal Court recently barred any discussion of releasing even the standards for what puts one on Obama's hit list. Who knows, Anwar al Awlaki may be guilty of some treasonable offense, but where in the name of our legal system does a mere president of the USA get to decide without due process in a court of law who must die?

I can't even begin to fathom the lack of moral outrage in this country against the PEP—no matter where any of us are on the political spectrum. Such an affront to morality and legal procedure should be met with the most extreme rejection and hostility. Yet, I doubt if a majority of Americans even know that such a program exists.

Corporate welfare, public despair
Another flagrant violation of transparency began last April when the biggest environmental disaster in US history occurred in the Gulf of Mexico after an oil rig leased by BP blew up due to lax maintenance and weak governmental regulations favoring oil companies. A recent report from a study done on this catastrophe boldly states that the Obama administration engaged in a concerted cover up to underestimate the amount of oil released and the impact it had on the environment, humans, and animal life.

The lingering affects of the oil mixed in with the dispersant, Corexit, are combining to give the residents of that region horrible health complications. Also, according to the above-mentioned report, the oil was only dispersed, not disappeared, and could be in the fragile ecosystem for decades before it fully goes away! The cover up of a disaster of this magnitude should be fodder for prosecution and removal from office of everyone involved—but while Ken Feinberg's Law firm pockets $850,000 per MONTH to administer the 20 billion BP victims' fund, the people suffer economically and physically with very limited accountability, if any.

On his first day in office Obama did restore the Freedom of Information Act, but, according to the *Los Angeles Times*, 14 months after the beginning of this era of "transparency," the Obama regime had denied more FOIA requests than that of Bush! Of course, the recent War on Transparency waged by the Obama administration has to be the current persecution of the WikiLeaks organization and one of its founders, Julian Assange. Even vice president of the USA, Joe Biden, recently said that the disclosures provided no "substantive damage," even though there was some embarrassment to the "Empire."

If, as Biden says, the WikiLeaks disclosures don't do substantive damage to the Empire (if they did, there's always the thousands of nukes we have to back us up), then why the persecution of Assange and the threat of severely limiting everyone's free and unfettered access to the internet? In the same week the latest document dump happened. The US government closed down 70 websites, just to show us that it could, and now the United Nations is discussing a global governmental committee to regulate the world-wide-web!

The hidden truth
Transparency should, but doesn't, begin at the top of the power pyramid. The increasing surveillance and persecution of peace and social justice activists coupled with the escalating use of full-body scanners in US airports tells me that the only "transparency" Obama wanted was for our clothes and our lives, not his administration.

What is the moral of the series of articles on Barack Obama? Do I believe that Obama is "evil incarnate?" No, but I believe the system that he is at the same time an advocate for, and tool of, is becoming increasingly evil, misguided, and out of control with its wars abroad and oppressions at home.

Whether Obama came into office with a naive agenda of liberating the US Public from the hold of the Lobbying Industry, or if he played the Left like Yo-Yo Ma plays the Cello, doesn't really matter. What matters is we are essentially experiencing the third term of G W Bush minus a few wins on the domestic front for the center left—albeit wins by the two branches of government Obama doesn't reside in. The status quo has had us gripped for over a decade now: It's time for a change.

Sunday, January 9, 2011
Violence: From Tucson to Datta Khel

Violence is a part of America.
I don't want to single out rap music. Let's be honest. America's the most violent country in the history of the world, that's just the way it is.
We're all affected by it.
Spike Lee

I do not know a method of drawing up an indictment against a whole people.
Edmund Burke

January 8, 2011 was a tough day—six people were killed and many more wounded in a cowardly act of unspeakable violence.

These people awakened on that day, ate their breakfasts, played with their children/grandchildren/parents/friends, made love, brushed their teeth, used the toilet, and any number of other "normal" activities we do every day, and they probably didn't even imagine that it would be their last day on earth—beating hearts silenced by hatred, ignorance, and bigotry. Lives cut short and futures canceled by a murderous and unconscionable massacre.

I hope for the sake of the victims' families and for international justice that those responsible for this massacre will be held accountable, but unfortunately, they are not even in custody—or even "persons of interest" in this despicable crime.

Oh, did you think I was talking about the "massacre in Tucson" that has been in all the news? Although, that was also a horrible, unspeakable act of violence, I am actually talking about the fact that at least six people were killed in North Waziristan by a Hellfire missile dropped from one of Obama's drones.

Since Obama is Commander in Chief, I want him arrested for these, and other murders. Not only has Obama tripled troop strength to Afghanistan, he has quadrupled bombings in Pakistan by un-manned aerial vehicles since he ordered his first drone strike on January 23, 2009. Being an over-achiever and Nobel Peace Laureate, I guess he didn't want to be outdone by his predecessor in the senseless carnage department.

Obama is targeting whomever he wants to target with his Presidential Execution Program and has been indiscriminately using drones in Yemen. The serial-imperial killer Barack Obama had this to say about the tragedy in Tucson on January 8:

"Such a senseless and terrible act of violence has no place in a free society."

First of all, I wonder what country Obama lives in and, secondly, he presides as president of the Empire over much of these "terrible acts of violence."

While we're at it, throw Secretary of Defense Robert Gates into the brig at Quantico with no possibility of bail and treat him the same way PFC Bradley Manning has been treated—23 hours per day of solitary confinement with no books, no TV, no exercise, no variation of lighting, no communication with fellow prisoners, etc.

Since the CIA is the institution that facilitates the drone-bombing crimes in Pakistan, I want Leon Panetta arrested. Since the CIA is also responsible for torture and false imprisonment in many "black sites" around the world, I want him incarcerated in Guantanamo or Bagram and detained indefinitely until or if his military commission is ready.

Not forgetting the Bush administration that set these programs in motion, I would like Bush, Cheney, Rumsfeld, Rice, Yoo, etc., arrested and incarcerated until their kangaroo courts are convened—the same kind of ridiculous trial that was afforded to Dr. Aafia Siddiqui. Being "kangaroo courts," when they are found inevitably guilty, I hope they are each given 86 years, plus life, in prison, like Dr. Siddiqui was.

The drones that carry out these despicable attacks on "suspected terrorists" and their neighborhoods and families are piloted from Air Force bases in the US—the pilot who followed an illegal order (condemned by the UN, among others) should be court-martialed and tried for his part in the war crime that occurred on January 8. In our top-down, violent society, though, people that kill civilians in Iraq, Pakistan, and Afghanistan are usually given commendations; but people that shoot "raunchy videos" are relieved of duty.

Vietnam war criminal, John McCain, who dropped bombs on innocent civilians during his stint and was responsible for "wet-starting" his jet while "hot dogging" on his aircraft carrier, the USS Forrestal, and incinerating 134 of his fellow crewman, called the Tucson shooter "a disgrace." How ironic that such a criminal (who also crashed five jets and graduated very near the bottom of his class at Annapolis) would call anyone else a "disgrace."

We live in a society where we are taught that violence solves everything, indeed, scoundrels like McCain rise to the very top. Those of us who strive and advocate for non-violent, creative solutions to problems are perceived as being "crazy, weak and traitorous," while history bears out that those using guns, tanks, planes, and drones are the weak ones.

Although top-down violence is oftentimes rewarded, bottom-up violence is usually vigorously prosecuted, even though, it's possible, that if the same amount of resources and commitment were devoted to education, mental health care, and our communities, many of these bottom-up crimes could be prevented. You know the old saying: Prevention is the best medicine.

Whether it was the tragic massacre in North Waziristan, or the tragic massacre in Arizona, the same rotten imperial system is to blame—but only those of us on the bottom of the so-called food chain are required to pay for our crimes.

Bombs are dropped on real people by real people who basically want the same things out of life: love, happiness, security and prosperity. Violence is also perpetrated by individuals—like some sort of Palinesque sicko that snuffs out the life of a nine-year-old (and others) because of some manufactured psychosis perpetuated by the collaborators in the US media.

What did young Christina Greene ever do to the demented shooter in Arizona that deserved her unnecessary death at the too young age of nine? Christina was tragically collateral damage and my heart breaks for her family. Similarly, what did the hundreds of thousands of the nameless and uncounted youngsters in our war-torn countries ever do to us? They are tragically just collateral damage, too, and my heart is torn apart for their families. Twenty-two-year-old white men and

91

women kill nine-year-old people in our war torn countries every single day and I hear few politicians or news commentators crying over their mangled bodies. The disproportionate outcry over the attempted murder of a US Congressperson over the murders of innocent people by our wars is the elitist way of saying: "Our lives count more than theirs or yours."

The only people that are our enemies and the enemies of universal love, happiness, security, and prosperity are sitting happily in their comfy and opulent homes (in Wasilla or DC) while at least one-dozen families are in profound mourning right now.

There is only one solution to this acute problem—whether the pilot who killed six in North Waziristan, or the shooter that killed six in Tucson—we have to stop killing each other to satisfy the blood lust and greed of the Robber Class.

We lose, they win.

My heart goes out to the people in Tucson, Datta Khel, and everywhere who are the victims or survivors of violence.

As an American, the shame I feel for my country is profound.

Sunday, January 23, 2011
Afghani-Scammed

Statesmen will invent cheap lies, putting blame upon the nation that is attacked, and every man will be glad of those conscience-soothing falsities, and will diligently study them, and refuse to examine any refutations of them; and thus he will by and by convince himself that the war is just, and will thank God for the better sleep he enjoys after this process of grotesque self-deception.
Mark Twain—*Chronicle of Young Satan*

The current president of the USA is no less skilled at being the Liar-in-Chief than the last one—after all, to be fair, that is the job description of the CEO of the Empire. Near the end of 2010, the president (whom, in instances pertaining to the eternal war in Afghanistan, I call: "Barackistan O'Bomber"), had this to say:

"Today, al-Qaeda's senior leadership in the border region is under more pressure than at any point since they fled Afghanistan nine years ago. Senior leaders have been killed. It's harder for them to recruit . . . . It's harder for them to plot and launch attacks. In short, al-Qaeda is hunkered down."

So, "in short" the US occupying forces are making progress, but the progress is slow, and more troops and hardware will be needed to ferret out this very few people that are "hunkered down," plotting more attacks on defenseless Americans. At a cost of one million dollars per year, per soldier, someone is benefiting from this violent occupation, but it's not the people of Afghanistan, as the people of that war-torn country (that "coincidentally is rich in minerals, oil, and natural gas) struggle to survive.

Another "ace in the hole" of supporting violent Imperial aims is the USA's top "diplomat" Hillary Clinton who, being skilled at fear-based rhetoric, warned us that if we "abandon" Afghanistan now, like we did after the USSR failed to subdue the country (being closer and using all of its advanced weaponry), it would be a "grave mistake." The graves that the US/NATO forces are digging with their Hellfire missiles in the border regions of Af/Pak mean little to the hellions of the Empire, as human life means so little compared to the rich natural resources of that region.

There is very little left to be said if you buy into the scam that the invasion and subsequent occupation of Afghanistan was justified because the US was "attacked" on 9/11—however, here is a brief review of facts, not scam.

Afghanistan didn't attack us on 9/11. Even if one believes the lies of the Empire about the "official story," the nationality of the hijackers were overwhelmingly Saudi Arabians—and the US didn't go half-cocked into Saudi Arabia to invade its buddies there. No, in fact, in 2010, the US sold 60 billion dollars worth of arms to Saudi Arabia, making it the largest such sale in history—which makes the next fact a little more interesting.

Al Qaeda was a construct of the CIA and the CIA-armed Osama bin Laden and Saudi Arabia funded him to wage jihad against the Soviet Union. Al Qaeda was originally a CIA database of thousands of Mujahadeen who were recruited and trained by the CIA. Our troops are being killed by first and second generation CIA operatives in Afghanistan and Pakistan and, knowing what I know now, I have very little illusion that the CIA didn't know what it was doing or that the Mujahadeen would eventually use those weapons against the US. Being the biggest dope dealer in the world, the CIA had big stakes in Afghanistan's poppy fields.

Two of the biggest lies the Empire tells about US crimes in Afghanistan are that we are there to: A) Redevelop the country (like Haiti); and B) Protect the women. "Protecting the women" of Afghanistan is one thing the liberals here in the US and Laura Bush have in common as a justification for the occupation.

On Sunday, January 23, 2011, my guest on Cindy Sheehan's Soapbox was Spogmai (Spaj-My) Akseer, who is a bright young woman on the steering committee of the international organization Afghans for Peace (AFP). Spogmai was born in Afghanistan and now lives in Canada. She travels to Afghanistan frequently and she clearly dispelled the above two myths.

Spogmai and AFP believe that the occupation of Afghanistan is for the financial benefit of global war profiteers, some NGO's, and the elite of Afghanistan. Spogmai has seen very little progress in the way of development for the average citizen of Afghanistan. If I believed in Hell, it would be a comfort to know that there was a special level for War Profiteers who must spend eternity paying for their inhumanity by living in a constant state of deprivation and war. But as Spogmai has personally witnessed in her many trips to Afghanistan, unusable schools have been built, roads to nowhere have been constructed, and there is zero accountability for the contractor who builds useless infrastructure then leaves the country with a tidy bundle of US taxpayer dollars in his bank account. In a country rife with corruption and scandal there is enough blame and fraud to go around.

I told Spogmai a story about a time, last July, when I was vigiling in front of the White House (in Lafayette Park, because I had a "stay-away" order from the White House at that time) and a phalanx of very elegantly and expensively dressed Afghans emerged from a meeting. The women of the party, who knew who I was, came up to me and through a translator explained to me how they had been in the White House to meet with the president (something which I have always been denied) so they could tell him how desperate the situation is in Afghanistan and how our troops needed to stay there, even though they "regret" the deaths of our young people. Occupations always benefit the elitists of every country through similar carpet bagging corruption as the Karzais and their cronies—it even happened in our own South during the Reconstruction period. There is nothing new here—and what else is an age-old story is how the non-elites of the world lap this crap up believing in the myth of the "accidental war/tragedy profiteer." Isn't this part of the "American Dream" to be in the "right place" at the "right time?" How fortuitous! There is no way to "get rich quicker" than through the war and its profitable aftermath.

Afghanistan is just one tragedy in the long list of scams every Empire has perpetrated in the name of profit and population control.

The destruction of the way of life of we non-elites will only stop when we stop participating in our own demise.

Spogmai and Afghans for Peace work for peace, development, and Afghan sovereignty. It's very dangerous for the people in Afghanistan to speak out against the occupiers and the elite in their own country, so we must, whether Afghan or not, struggle in solidarity FOR these noble goals against the violence and with the people who are paying the most for the disease of Empire.

Sunday, February 13, 2011
Once Upon a Time in the Evil Empire

America is a Nation with a mission—and that mission comes from our most basic beliefs. We have no desire to dominate, no ambitions of empire.

Our aim is a democratic peace—a peace founded upon the dignity and rights of every man and woman.

Emperor George the III

Once upon a time in the Evil Empire there arose to the Most Powerful Office in the Land a very stupidly evil man named George Walker Bush (the III George of the Empire).

George the III had been a less than mediocre student in school; he failed in every business that he tried to operate, and as governor of one of the far-flung provinces of the Evil Empire called Texas, he was an unmitigated disaster. The axe of his executioner swung wildly and he dismantled the education system while ruining the environment.

George Walker Bush was not much different than any other Ruler of the Evil Empire in his Evilness, but the arrogant stupidity of his Evilness began to turn off many of the Subjects of the Evil Empire. What was also so different about George the III was that he stole the office in not a subtle coup, as in previous times, but in an obvious coup that ripped any semblance of democracy to shreds.

In the first year of the Reign of George the III, the Evil Empire was attacked around the globe because of its Evil Ways and George the III and his Consort, Richard the Sick-Hearted, sent the Armies of the Evil Empire to various regions of the planet to murder, rape, and pillage, thus causing more hatred and resentment towards the Evil Empire, and anon, the Subjects of the Evil Empire also became very restless.

The Subjects of the Evil Empire rose up in great numbers to oust George and Richard, but the Royal Ass-wipes in the Parliament refused to depose the dictators until the appointed time that they were to leave the Highest Office in the Land.

George and Richard returned to the comfortable lives of the Evil Empire's Nobility, but when they left, they left two wars raging and an economic crisis that was the worst the Subjects had experienced in generations.

Lo, and in the Year of the Lord 2008, an Angel appeared unto the Evil Empire (on CNN) and said: "Rejoice, you highly favored Ones! The Lord is with you. Blessed are you among Nations!" And unto the Evil Empire was given a savior: Barack Obama.

The Subjects in the Kingdom of Democrats responded with great rejoicing and the memory of the trials and tribulations of the last eight years receded from Memory—although the trials and tribulations remained.

In the Kingdom of the Republicans, though, the same trials and tribulations that Blinded them during the reign of George the III and Richard the Sick-Hearted miraculously appeared to them and they became most distressed and formed their rage into Tea Parties where no actual tea was served along with the stupidity and racism.

What is the point of the above Fairy Tale? The US is a Mythocracy where the puppets in apparent leadership roles dance to the whims of the real rulers of this country: the Corporatocracy.

Basically, what Economic Hit Men are trained to do is to build up the American empire. To create situations where as many resources as possible flow into this country, to our corporations, and our government, and in fact we've been very successful.
John Perkins (Confessions of an Economic Hitman)

This fact is not a crazy conspiracy theory and the US isn't the only country run by the super-wealthy—Anti-globalization movements like the ones against the economic oligarchies of the G8, G20, WTO, and World Bank understand this simple fact.

Look at the recent democratic uprising in Egypt. The puppet of this global oligarchy, Mubarak, hung onto to power for 18 days, even sending in thugs to kill hundreds of anti-Mubarak protesters, stalling the inevitability of his departure.

Why did Mubarak stay for so long? He told CNN's, Christiane Amanpour, that he didn't even want to be "president" anymore, after 30 years of rape and pillage. He stayed, according to a recent article in the *UK Telegraph*, to make sure his wealth, estimated upwards of 70 billion dollars was secure. Mubarak was not about to beat a hasty retreat without making sure every last penny was securely away from being frozen by Swiss authorities or re-appropriated back to the people he stole it from.

Mubarak was never a public servant of the people of Egypt—public servants don't amass Pharaoh-sized fortunes. He was given billions of pieces of silver to betray his people and the people of Palestine with this blood money.

The oligarchy's hand-picked, hand-puppet in Afghanistan, Hamid Karzai, and his family sit on a goldmine for them and their masters: vast mineral deposits and the CIA-opium trade. According to Wikileaks documents released late last year, the US is "distressed" at the corruption in Afghanistan and millions (if not billions) of dollars that flow into Afghanistan from US taxpayers, flow right back out of the country to such places as Dubai, where Karzai and his cronies can be assured that if they are chased out of Afghanistan by a popular uprising, their wealth is secured. If the US is so "distressed" by all the corruption and graft in Afghanistan, why is Karzai allowed to remain? It's not because he has been "democratically" elected in a process that is blatantly fraudulent—no, it's because he's a willing dancer with the hand of the puppeteer firmly ensconced in his nether-regions.

There are some nations that are able to remain relatively independent of the global oligarchy, and one such nation sits just 90 miles off the tip of Florida: Cuba.

Although Cuba was used as a wedge between the US and the USSR during the Cold War, it has never been a military or economic threat to us—what it is down there is a constant reminder to the Global Imperialists that, no matter how tiny, there are still places that can remain free and survive.

The propaganda about Cuba is stunningly wrong and pathetically obvious, and one doesn't have to dig too deeply in the mire to find out the truth; but ask yourself this: Why is the US obsessed with Cuba and the Castros when it has supported too many dictatorships in Latin America to count? Why was Allende overthrown in favor of the appalling murderer and oppressor Pinochet in Chile?

Why is the Empire obsessed with democratically elected and supported Hugo Chavez in Venezuela, yet props up a violent Narco-State like Colombia?

The still recent CIA-backed coup (they're all CIA backed) in Honduras deposed Zelaya to install a more oligarchy friendly regime, is another example of blatant hypocrisy.

The reason the Karzais and Mubaraks of the world are so beloved by the globalists and hated by the people is the same reason that the Chavezes and Castros of the world are hated by the globalists and loved by their people (and others who have been inspired by their stands)—leaders like Chavez and Castro have insulted this Corporatocracy by insisting that the wealth and resources of their respective countries belong to the people of that nation.

Let's hope that the uprisings against the elites of this world that didn't start in Egypt, but was so obvious there, continue.

Our brothers and sisters in Latin America have been doing an admirable, if unsung job, rising up against the puppet-masters from the bottom to the top in some cases.

Here we sit in the seat of the globalist's wet dream—the United States of America. Ah, America, where the people on the bottom of the economic ladder still think it's possible to claw, fight, kick, and scratch our way to the top and we won't allow any pesky facts to get in the way of our quest for this impossible Madison Avenue induced nightmare.

If most of us can't even discern that it doesn't matter who dances for the elite in the Oval Office, then all is lost before we even begin.

Emperor Obama, and Emperor Bush before him, were installed in their positions by the same institutions that installed Mubarak and Karzai. The difference is, with our complicit media, many of us still firmly believe in the illusion of political "choice."

The elites of the world never call these people dictators, but their people do.

Will this Once Upon a Time have a happy ending for the heroes? Only the people themselves can decide that.

Wednesday, March 9, 2011
Empire Means Never Having to Mean It's Sorry

The US is deeply sorry . . . these deaths shouldn't have happened.
General David Petraeus
After nine Afghan children gathering wood were slaughtered by the US

On March 3, occupying forces in Afghanistan killed nine children gathering wood in Kunar Province. This time, instead of despicably accusing Afghan parents of killing their own children to laughably cast the US in a bad light (we don't need any help), according to the *L.A. Times,* Petraeus "swiftly" apologized.

Well, as someone who has had a child killed in this Imperial insanity, I know that apologies and blood money are just not enough to assuage the overwhelming grief one feels when a child precedes a parent to the stone-cold permanence of death. If there is any worse thing than burying a child, burying one so that others can realize vastly improved bottom-lines has to be way up there.

Having a child killed in needless and senseless wars is as needless and senseless as having one killed by a drunk driver. Even though there are strict laws in my state to punish people who drive while they are under the influence, apparently there are no strict laws against committing war crimes and crimes against humanity. There is not even a "War Criminal's Anonymous," where arbiters of peace and justice can send these brazen and unrepentant criminals to, after nine youngsters are murdered in calculated cold-blood.

Tragedy can be described as a very sad or disastrous event. Tragic things happen to people every day at the hands of the Empire, and since the USA is the world's top-evil Empire, the people that are on the receiving end are the ones that should have the most claims on our sympathy. However, we also know it is a fact that many US troops come home with what used to be called "shell shock," but is now called Post Traumatic Stress Disorder. I would hope the ground-level soldier who made the "mistake" (but make no mistake about it—there are no "mistakes" in illegal wars of aggression—every activity is criminal) that killed these children in Afghanistan has the conscience of a human being and is at the very least troubled by what he or she did.

We call things that kill people without remorse: Monsters.

Well, the Monster Petraeus claims that the US is "deeply sorry" for the deaths of the Afghan boys, but we know that few people at the helm of this demented ship of state are truly "sorry" that anyone is getting killed, let alone nine desperately poor children in Afghanistan—over a million people have been killed since 9/11/2001 and if any tears have been shed by the warmongers, they are of the crocodile variety, to be sure.

How about the rest of the people who reside and pay taxes in this Empire—do they even know about this incident? In the Charlie Sheen/Newt Gingrich soaked news-o-tainment industry, these deaths haven't even been mentioned. When that tax check to Uncle Sam is written every year, or when he takes his pound of flesh every payday, does the average American even stop to think what their money pays for?

Our tax dollars don't just go to pay for wanton murder, they also go to keep the Guantanamo Bay torture facility open.

During the marathon-infomercial some people like to call a "presidential campaign," then candidate Obama was very clear that he would close Guantanamo Torture Facility and "restore habeas corpus" to those detained. Candidate Obama correctly identified the existence of such a place as a detriment to America's "image;" yet, as president, Obama recently signed an executive order to restore Military tribunals and has not kept his promise, nor carried out his other executive order to close the prison.

According to British journalist, Andy Worthington, dozens of teens, sometimes 12–13 years old, have been incarcerated in Guantanamo. Who's going to say "sorry" to them for having their lives stolen along with the unspeakable torture and inhumane treatment they received at the hands of the Beacon of Democracy?

One member of this Gitmo Youth Group, Mohammed Jawad of Afghanistan, was tortured in Gitmo, confessed to the crime he was accused of, and held in detention for seven years based on a confession gleaned from torture! Imagine being 12 years old, arrested by foreign occupiers, and then tortured. What would you say? Would you "sing like a bird," as US officials derisively said about this child? Now imagine your own child or another relative being treated worse than an animal and imprisoned for one-third of their young life for nothing. No "swift" apology came for Jawad, and nothing, especially an empty apology, could give him back his life, anyway.

Speaking of torture, PFC Bradley Manning has been tortured at Quantico for over a year now for allegedly "leaking" information to the whistleblower site Wikileaks. Bradley has been held in solitary confinement for 23 hours a day for nearly a year now. He has been charged with 22 counts, including "aiding and abetting the enemy" and faces execution if convicted. The civilian and military leaders of this Empire "aid and abet the enemy" everyday by their actions, orders, greed, and insanity. In fact, they are the ones that are the enemy, and if he did leak the material, Manning exposed them he did not "aid" them.

In fact, one of the things Manning allegedly leaked is the "Collateral Murder" video, which is an egregious example of military mayhem that shows an Apache helicopter crew in Baghdad strafing some journalists and a van with two children inside that rushes to the aid of the journalists. When the crew discovers that children were in the van, you hear a soldier with a deficient soul say, "Oh well, that's what you get when you bring children to a war zone." Actually, quite the opposite, the

US illegally and immorally brought the "war zone" to the children and is sending the children of our nation to slaughter the children of others.

The Empire reminds me of my nearly three-year-old grandson Jonah—whenever he knows he has done something he shouldn't, he says "I sowwy, I sowwy," right away thinking his "swift" apology will expunge his guilt and avoid punishment.

Jonah doesn't really mean it either, but he's too young to know the difference.

Monster Petraeus was correct about one thing—these deaths should never have happened, but the nine youngsters in Afghanistan weren't the first ones killed and they won't, unfortunately, be the last.

War is so ridiculous with grown men behaving like out-of-control toddlers with live ammo, planes, helicopters, and bombs—time for this Empire to crumble as all Empires have in the past.

Just leave our children out of it.

Thursday, March 17, 2011
Barack-a-lujah! I Have Seen the Light!

Thanks to the helpful feedback I have received over these past few years, I have seen the enormous error of my ways.

I used to be against ALL wars and the use of violence, but (and I must admit a little confusion on this one, at first) now it seems that I am against wars, acts of war, and violence ONLY if a Republican is president. Now I understand with perfect clarity that it was good to protest Bush—and if the US-UN resolution against Libya was done when Bush was president, it would have been wrong—but now it's "compassionate." I must admit, I was a little shocked to find out that the US actually commits compassionate acts and, again, silly me—I thought most acts of war and war were for profit. I realize that only a jerk (or racist) would think that now. I have repented.

I cringe with embarrassment when I think of the wasted years imagining that there could be any other way to solve problems without killing more innocent people! It's okay to bomb Libyans to save Libyans (or Iraqis to save Iraqis; or Afghans to save Afghans; or Yemenis to save Yemenis, etc.) because a Democratic president who has been given the cover of the UN Security Council may bomb them. Yep, it's all starting to make sense. With all the continuing conflicts, imagining a world without war was starting to seem useless—and now I know it was! Phew!

This is another kooky idea I had—that the Security Council of the UN oftentimes, if not always, bowed to the will of the global oligarchy—or should we say, OILigarchy. I chuckle, because apparently that notion was either dead wrong, or was just a fact of life up until January 20, 2009.

Here's another mistaken notion that I labored under all these years: Torture is inhumane and a war crime. Up until just last week, I thought the US torture camp at Guantanamo Bay, Cuba should be closed and that military tribunals should not resume—but President Obama signed an executive order to keep Gitmo open and resume military tribunals. Wow, it's like from almost one day to the next, torture and illegal, indefinite detention became acceptable practices.

Pssst—since I am in confession mode, I want to, with a red face, confess something else. Please, I hope you laugh with me and not at me, but this is so hard to admit. I thought I learned that US citizens were to be arrested only with reasonable cause, given their due process, and THEN punished if found guilty. I must admit I still thought that was wrong earlier today, but when I was (not so) gently and repeatedly reminded that we have a change agent as president, the scales fell from my eyes and now I get it! If Barack Obama (D) thinks that a US citizen needs to be executed without a trial or even a handshake, then by golly that person must need to be killed. Barack

Obama (D) is a Constitutional scholar after all and I am sure his interpretation of the Bill of Rights is the correct one. Who am I to argue? What a relief—*thinking* is so unnecessary and hard!

Now the skeptical, old, and ignorant Cindy Sheehan would have thought that the US was only concerned with the regime in Libya "killing its own citizens" because Libya has large crude oil reserves, but that was before I reflected on the fact that Barack Obama (D) has told us that offshore drilling and nuclear power is safe! Like my new hero Barack Obama (D) keeps saying, we do need to "reduce" US dependence on "foreign oil," but not before we kill as many people as we must to get all of that oil. The old me also would have thought that we needed to entirely eliminate our dependence on petroleum and petroleum products all together, but if Barack Obama (D) says it's safe, that's good enough for me!

I just hope the people of Libya realize that it's way more of an honor to be killed by a US bomb than by a Libyan bomb, and what an honor it is that the US is paying attention to their internal strife, because we don't always do that—we like to pick and choose—and Libya, it's probably just a coincidence that we choose YOU because you have oil. My country would never do anything wrong when a Democrat is president and I will forget history, too, because I don't need it anymore.

I also must admit that I used to spend a lot of time worrying about Pfc. Bradley Manning being incarcerated and tortured at Quantico for allegedly dumping info about US policy to Wikileaks. Now I believe that if he did that to my wonderful president, he must deserve the treatment he is getting. Manning, that traitor, is lucky President Obama (D) hasn't just decided to drop a Hellfire missile on him from one of those righteous drones he loves to use! Additionally, if Obama (D) says that Manning's treatment is "appropriate," I believe him now. Worrying about Bradley was keeping me up at night and now I wish I had the money back that I incorrectly donated to his legal defense fund so I can send it to the Committee to Re-Elect the President.

The old axiom is true! Confession is good for the soul!

I hope with this confession and subsequent penance (10 Our Fathers, 20 Hail Mary's and a pledge to vote Democrat for the rest of my life) that I am accepted back into the fold of the Democratic Party. I will also voluntarily swear to uphold health-care- for-profit and to love Wall Street, the war machine, and the bankers with all my heart while detesting working people and those people who want to "kill Americans" for absolutely no reason.

In Obama I trust. What a relief! Having a conscience is very isolating.

Let's Party with a capital D because if I can CHANGE, then there is HOPE for everyone, and anyone else who is still lost wandering nearly alone in that wilderness of integrity.

Come home!

War is Peace!

Freedom is Slavery!

Ignorance is Strength.

$2 + 2 = 5$

Monday, March 21, 2011
An Open Letter to War Loving (Democratic/Republican) Frauds

Dear War Loving (Democratic or Republican) Fraud,

I know many of you don't really care, but in exactly 15 days, it will be seven years since my oldest son Casey (whom I never "abandoned" and raised with his father and three siblings until he went into the Army when he was 21) was killed in this Empire's insane War OF Terror. Was Casey the first, or the last? No, but he was my first and the shock knocked me out of my quiet complacency —which was just as wrong as the Empire's unending wars.

When I began protesting Bush was president and my protest and the energy that grew around it was used by you Democrats to regain political power in the federal government. Four years later, and a change of Executive, this nation is still mired in Arab countries waging a war against Arabs of all, or no, faith. Now brought to us by the Blue Team.

Three days after the current evil Emperor was installed by the oligarchy, he ordered a drone bombing in Northern Pakistan (a country that we are supposedly not at war with) that killed 36 civilians, and since then he has been absolutely mad about drone bombings, increasing Bush's total over 300 percent in far fewer years. Even though I never supported Obama who funded wars as a Senator and who is NOT a peace president, I said at the time: "Three days in and already a war criminal." I was thoroughly attacked by Democrats who once affiliated as "peace" activists for not giving Obama "time."

Well, Gitmo is still open, military tribunals will resume for men who have been illegally detained for up to a decade now, US Tomahawk missiles are raining down on innocents in Libya (killing people to save them is the NEW PEACE), dictators are still supported, Israel is still occupying and oppressing Palestine, activists are being targeted by Obama's DOJ while BushCo are being protected, the USA PATRIOT ACT was renewed, the Gulf is dying—and where is the outrage?

This is where I think the outrage is—the oligarchy of this country is clever; they knew that it would take a person of color with an Islamic name who sold his soul many years ago to fulfill the neocon agenda of planetary dominance (see: Project for a New American Century). So if one criticizes Obama, then we are attacked by War Loving Democrats for being "divisive fanatics," "racist," "Tea Baggers," "crazy," etcetera. Could McCain be getting away with bombing North Africa? Or does that take an African-American to give political cover to the war jackals?

The last four paragraphs were for War Loving Democrats, Greens, and Socialists—yes, I have heard from all three groups denouncing me for being against bombing Libyans to save them (same thing BushCo said about Iraqis, by the way—and the very same rhetoric used for Vietnam, etc.)

This next part is for War Loving Republicans and "Independents."

What? Are you people morons? First of all, you should be dancing in the streets praising the name of Obama like your comrades in the Democratic Party who hypocritically support his murders. Face it, YOU OVERTLY LOVE WAR when a Republican is doing it. Admit it, you salivate over killing innocents so those "jihadist" babies won't crawl over here to cut your throats and make your women wear burkas! How dare you attack me and complain that I don't protest Obama's wars when you should be out supporting him with all of your violent hearts and souls.

Before you write to attack ME for being a hypocrite, I suggest a five-minute exercise in "googling."

If you do that, then you'll see that since before he was even elected I opposed Obama, while I was running for election in San Francisco AGAINST a Democrat, Nancy (War Lover and Torture Supporter) Pelosi.

You'll also see that I wrote a book in January of 2009 detailing everything I discovered that was wrong with this Empire and the myths that bind both sides to the establishment. Then you'll find that I traveled to Martha's Vineyard in 2009 when the Obamas took a $50,000 per week vacation there to demand a meeting with him to ask him "What Noble Cause?"

But that's not all, my War Loving Republican "friends."

In March of 2010, I set up a Peace Camp called Camp Out Now on the lawn of the Washington Monument for two weeks protesting Obama and his wars. Near the end of that Camp I was arrested in front of the White House and jailed for 52 hours, then given a four month "stay away" order from the White House—does this sound like someone who supports, or is supported by the Obama regime?

Not being one to abandon my principles so quickly, I went back in July for two weeks to try and do the same thing.

I have protested the regime's drone bombing campaign in front of CIA HQ in Langley, VA AND at the Smithsonian Institute where the harbingers of massacre are proudly displayed. I even traveled to Oslo, Norway to protest his awardence of the Nobel Peace Prize.

So, War Lovers on the "right"—hate me if you will—but hate me because I am diametrically opposed to everything you stand for, not because I am a "hypocrite." Look inside yourselves and realize that Obama is ONE OF YOU—scary isn't it?

And War Lovers from the "left"—hate me if you will, too, but not because I am a "fanatic" (how can one be a fanatic about non-violence?), hate me because the light I shine back at you exposes your own lack of integrity around these issues—be honest and look deeply inside yourself and see that if it were McCain/Palin or Bush/Cheney bombing the crap out of Libya, you would be furious with me, not at me.

Peace Before Partisan Politics,

Cindy Sheehan

PS: Being against the US and its toadies bombing Libyans DOES NOT mean I am for Qaddafi killing Libyans either (or anyone killing Libyans, or others, for that matter.)

PPS: In his own words: *"The President does not have power under the Constitution to unilaterally authorize a military attack in a situation that does not involve stopping an actual or imminent threat to the nation."* – Barack Obama, *Boston Globe*, December 20, 2007

Monday, April 25, 2011
One Wedding and Unlimited Funerals

I guess I must be a glutton for punishment because I just snapped off CiaNN in frustration and anger for about the 5000th time.

Yesterday, I was treated to Candy ("I never met a warmonger I didn't love") Crowley fairly gushing with bloodlust—kill Qaddafi, bomb-the-shit-out-of-the-Libyan-people—over her three warmonger guests: Republican Senators Lindsey Graham (R-Closet); John McCain (R-Mordor); and Joseph Lieberman (R-Tel Aviv)—okay, I know that Lieberman is technically an "I," but he out Republicans Ronald Reagan in every instance.

If one has an insatiable thirst for institutional violence on a massive and very extravagant scale—like Miss Crowley—then who else would you have on your program to talk about the US/British/NATO war crimes in Libya? Certainly not Cindy Sheehan, Cynthia McKinney, or Dennis Kucinich? Heck no! If one of us were interviewed on CiaNN, we may actually tell the truth about what's really happening in Libya and the tiny cat's paw of doubt may begin to creep into the minds of the average consumer of CiaNN's "All war, All the time," news-o-tainment.

Today the airwaves are all atwitter about the impending ROYAL WEDDING! The CiaNN mouthpiece for everything establishment—(sorry it wasn't Candy, but I don't know what her name is, but does it really matter, anyway?)—was interviewing some British talking-twit who could hardly contain his spittle of excitement as he fairly swooned over the impending nuptials of William and Kate (plus 8?) and opined to the CiaNNer that, even though the "subjects" are facing "harsh austerity measures," EVERYONE in Great Britain is salivating over the prospect of a ROYAL SPECTACLE.

Really? I remember a few months ago, Will's dad, the sad-sack Charles, and his wife, the inconceivable, Camilla, left a Robber Class to-do on Regent (irony?) Street in London, and their limo was pounced upon, rocked, and stoned by a group of students protesting the steep increase in school fees after they recognized the Royal Scandals. The film of this incident shows, not a frightened Chucky and Cammie, but a highly insulted and shocked ("We are not amused") royal couple!

England, along with Greece and France, has been ground-zero for the increasingly militant protests against the savage global austerity measures being put in place to protect the vast fortunes of people like Great Britain's Royal Family—(give me a break—appropriate their assets and put them in public housing in Liverpool—the only thing giving them "special" status is the accident of their inbred births) while putting the rest of us into increasing income insecurity.

I am sure there are some people in Great Britain who want to see a Royal Spectacle—even those in the class that suffers directly because of the Royal Scandals. I know this because a large percentage of the population here in the US think that the Robber Class deserves their own special obscene perks. Weddings, like Princess Chelsea's, which cost in the millions instead of the hundreds like ours, are celebrated, not raided. Princess Chelsea held a $1500 a plate reception and people who could pay three months rent with one plate of Clinton swill defended this Robber Class excess!

Then there are the King and Queen of America who don't find anything amiss with taking expensive vacations with their Subjects footing huge portions of the bill, while unemployment is still at Depression-era levels, and when the Subjects, who are lucky enough to have jobs, can't afford even a "staycation." When the Obamas took their first $50,000/week vacation in 2009 on Martha's Vineyard I was incensed and expressed it (as is my custom). One male Imperial Subject asked me, "Cindy, where do you expect him to stay? A Motel 6 in Orlando, Florida?" My answer was, "Hell yeah! If it's good enough for us, it's good enough for them."

Besides the fact that I will get sick to the point of vomiting over the Royal Scandals' new Royal Spectacle this week, Great Britain and the USA are involved in three major shooting wars which are killing many people (and, ironically, being famous for dropping Hellfire missiles on Arab wedding parties) in parts of the world that are resisting being made Subjects to the collaboration of the Robber Class of these two countries.

The only coverage we will see on US Lamestream Media about Robber Class violence is existentially supportive—and I do mean "existentially," because the Robber Class Media has every intention of lining its own pockets with the booty that war brings!

The only solution to the ills that plague us from this global bourgeoisie is a peasant's (working-class) revolution—and the only way we will ever see one of those is if we stop being co-dependent with the very people who welcome our extinction after our usefulness to them is used up.

If you don't believe me, all you have to do is a little research into worldwide attacks against education AND the elderly.

Closer to home, King Bush "misunderestimated" his "mandate" to privatize Social Security, so the US Branch of the Global Robber Class had to install a more sympathetic puppet who has a "free pass" from "liberals" who think any criticism of the new King is "racist." This meme comes mostly because of the fraudulent, yet convenient, Tea Party Society.

King Obama is getting away with far more than John McCain (R-Mordor) ever could have.

Here in my state, California, a group of us are planning to March On and Occupy Sacramento protesting the savage austerity measures being placed on our state's most "vulnerable" beginning on Worker's Day, May 1.

More information can be found at Strike California.

The goal of modern propaganda is no longer to transform opinion
but to arouse an active and mythical belief.
Jacques Ellul, philosopher

Class, let's review what Barack (Nobel Peace Laureate) has done since achieving the office of POTUS:

On day three, he ordered his first drone bombing strike in the tribal regions of North Pakistan thus murdering a reported 36 civilians. Since that day, the US has used this tactic of abject terror 192 more times resulting in hundreds of civilian deaths. In the four years the Bush Stain used this tactic of terror it was used 43 times. In this area, Obama is definitely an overachiever.

Let's stay with Afghanistan—Obama has tripled troop strength there and, according to justforeignpolicy.org, since Obama has taken office, 910 US troops have been killed in Afghanistan, compared to 575 in seven years that Bush was president. Now, don't get me wrong, I am not defending the Bush Stain, I am just pointing out that in some aspects that of Obama is far worse.

He promised during his campaign that if he were elected POTUS, he would "end the war in Iraq." He even said, "You can take that to the bank." What we don't know is if that was one of the banks that failed since the bailouts began in 2008, with Obama's avid support.

Well, troop strength in Iraq is down, while almost 6000 Americans are working at the embassy in Baghdad that is 104 acres huge. Does it seem like we are leaving Iraq any time soon, and what do we need an embassy the size of Vatican City in a country that we supposedly are in the process of leaving?

Besides Iraq, Afghanistan, and Pakistan, the Nobel Laureate has started a new bombing war in Libya where the use of Unmanned Aerial Vehicles (drones) is also happening. The day before Osama bin Laden was allegedly killed by US Navy SEALS, the UN/NATO/US violated the "no fly zone" by going out of it to Tripoli and killing one of Qaddafi's sons and three of his grandchildren. Is that the plan, there? *Bloomberg News* (not exactly a leftwing source) says that "thousands" have been killed since the bombing campaign two months ago and hundreds of thousands have fled the country. Obama, like Bush before him, is a disgusting "Deather," but if one doesn't believe someone who has already lied about so many things, that makes one a "Deather?"

The Bush/Obama freak show didn't invent using "convenient" enemies, nor did it invent killing hundreds of thousands of innocent people exploiting these enemies. It's not that I don't believe Obama about Osama because he's Obama, I don't believe him because he is just one in a long line of butt-naked Emperors.

It was widely reported and ridiculed today that I don't believe that Osama bin Laden is dead and that makes me a "Deather." I guess this slur is a riff on the "Birther" movement that claims that the current POTUS was not born in the US and therefore is not qualified to be in office—I think the Birther movement is a ruse and distraction from the real issues, as is OBL's latest death.

First of all, I find it cute that the Lamestream media is reading my Facebook wall and reporting it as "news." That's almost as ridiculous as reporting what Obama said on Sunday evening as "news." The only proof of Osama being dead again that we were offered was Obama telling us that there was a DNA match between the man killed by the Navy SEALS and OBL. Even if it is possible to get DNA done so quickly, and the regime did have bin Laden DNA lying around a lab somewhere, where is the empirical proof? I read one analysis where a wagging tongue said we know because "people who know" have told us. Now we don't actually have to see proof? So we just accept the words as proof? Here's some more food for thought—one doesn't have to be dead to have a DNA test done. They don't kill deadbeat dads to prove paternity, do they?

Another thing we were told without any proof, other than Obama saying so, is that Osama bin Laden was hastily buried at sea to conform to Islam. A) Islam does not encourage burial at sea. B) Where is the video? In this day and age, one would think the Empire would want to be very careful about proving its case. C) The nearest Sea is hundreds of miles away from Islamabad where OBL was allegedly killed again. D) Islam DOES NOT say "within 24 hours." It just says, as soon as possible. E) When did this Empire ever care about Islam? Look up Dr. Aafia Siddiqui and how her religious sensibilities were/are assaulted—then look at the photos from Abu Ghraib, or recall the Koran being flushed down the toilet.

Then, after the US put out a photo-shopped picture of the "dead" OBL, it was quickly proven and reported to be a fraud. The White House responded to this exposure claiming that it didn't release the "real photo" because it was too "grisly." The Empire thinks you and I are stupid—and it is sad that many of us are.

Secondly (from my "first of all" above), I never said anywhere, not even on my Facebook wall, that I don't think Osama bin Laden is dead—this is just another smokescreen. I said that I don't believe the story that protruded from the evil collusion of the Empire and its toady Lamestream media like a cancerous mole that has metastasized to the size of a grapefruit. Like I told Anderson Cooper in August of 2005, "reporting" is not regurgitating the spiel of the Emperor or his spokesliar.

I have written over and over on my Facebook wall since this whole farce began that, even though I don't believe one word of the story yesterday, there are many things that OBL could be, but being killed yesterday by Navy SEALS was not one of them.

FACT: Osama bin Laden and al Qaida were constructs of the CIA.

FACT: The US armed the Mujahadeen and the CIA trained it during its resistance against the occupation and violence of the USSR.

FACT: OBL NEVER claimed responsibility for 9/11.

FACT: The Taliban were willing to extradite him to a neutral third country after 9/11, if the US showed proof that he was guilty of "masterminding" 9/11. The US refused and commenced bombing.

FACT: Any of the wealthy, Saudi, bin Laden family that was in the US on 9/12/2001, were flown out of the country, although all other flights were grounded.

FACT: Benazir Bhutto, Pakistani politician and hardly a wild-eyed radical, told David Frost in an interview dated November 2, 2007, that Osama had already been murdered.

FACT: Up until May 2, 2011, the supposed new death day of OBL, the FBI didn't even list him as one of the Ten Most Wanted for 9/11—hmmm, interesting?

FACT: The US admits to presenting a fake photograph of the dead again OBL to the world.

FACT: Millions of people are dead, displaced, wounded, tortured, imprisoned, or heartbroken since 9/11/2001, and the perpetrators of these crimes, the Bush Stain, are running around freely, arrogantly, and wrongly.

Why would the president, who can pronounce "nuclear," boldly lie to the world (again) about the US's convenient enemy? Because the distraction of the Royal Wedding is over and Obama's policies were beginning to reek? Even people who chastised me for being against the humanitarian bombing of civilians in Libya were starting to come around.

The economy is in the toilet and partially due to the new US misadventure in the oil producing world, we are paying four-dollars plus per gallon for fuel. The ongoing Fukushima disaster is too scary for us to think about so we needed something to be jingoistic over and to buy Chinese-made American flags so we could wave them wildly while dancing in the streets?

Many wagging tongues have exulted over the fact that this "triumph" assures Obama's re-election in 2012—I guess that means that A) He won't need to raise the one billion dollars his campaign is seeking; and B) The new re-killing of OBL was Obama's campaign kick-off.

I am disgusted beyond belief that the persons responsible for my son's death are being protected by Obama's DOJ, but I am freaking amazed that everyone doesn't automatically sprinkle a healthy dose of skepticism on any pronouncement of The Empire by now.

Why didn't Osama get re-executed during Bush's regime? Because after 2005, Bush had negative credibility—and the same people who are celebrating OBL's newest murder would have recognized the lies for what they are.

Well, the only thing some of us can be grateful for is the fact that this has to be the final time that Osama meets his maker—the Empire shot its wad on this one—but does this mean that I don't have to take my shoes off and be physically molested every time I fly, now? Is the US war of terror against the Arab world now over? (Not according to the Secretary of War—oops, State—Hillary Clinton).

All I do know for sure is that this Empire is the Empire of Death—and to call someone who questions the fables a "Deather" is just blatant demonization and a reactionary response to fortify the fraud.

CINDY NOTE: In this first CINDY NOTE of 2011, I want to iterate that there is still no proof that Obama killed Osama despite Hollywood's fake-making movies about it.

Thursday, June 9, 2011
Police State Much?

Totalitarianism is patriotism institutionalized.
Steve Allen

"Patriotic" Americans are still berating me for "demeaning" my son's "sacrifice." A typical message goes something like this:

"Your son died to give you the right to spew your filth against this country. If it wasn't for the military and people like your son, you wouldn't have the freedom to protest."

Oh, really? If I have the "freedom to protest" then why have I been arrested so many times and why did I have a four-month restraining order from protesting near the White House last year that would have landed my buns in jail for six-months if I violated it? Why are activists still being arrested for solely exercising what used to be our fundamental rights?

In fact, Louisiana attorney, Bill Quigley, has documented that more than 2600 activists have been arrested since Obama was sworn in as president in 2009.

The Constitutional-Lawyer-turned-POTUS is committing atrocities against peace, justice, and human rights at a pace that Bush and Cheney only dreamed possible. If Obama can't have one of us arrested or executed on his orders, then he will gladly diagnose our principled questioning as a mental disorder. Obama even told Steve Pelley of *60 Minutes* that if any American dare question his obvious lies around the re-death of Osama bin Laden, then they should have "their heads examined."

I find it extremely interesting that the fundamental values of peace, truth, and justice have been turned into a mental disorder by the POTUS who, as I have pointed out before, has committed innumerable atrocities against these values. However, what I am finding increasingly alarming is the USA's rapid descent into a police state.

On June 7, my sister and I were driving from Sacramento to Los Angeles on I-5—this is a trip that both she and I have made dozens of times since my family moved near Sacramento in 1993. We almost immediately noticed the elevated presence of cop 'copters hovering over the interstate and over nearby communities. Neither of us had ever witnessed so many military convoys nor such a police presence in any of the previous times we made the trip. While we speculated about it I had to come to a complete stop on I-105 when it looked like a Los Angeles Sheriff's 'copter was about to land on the roof of my rented car. Hmm, there is definitely a shift happening, but it's often hard to pin things down.

Well, the very next day, I learned about two events that shocked even me—I thought the Empire couldn't shock me, but I was wrong.

The very day that my sister and I were traveling the length of our gorgeous state, a Stockton, California man was having his door broken down by what he thought was a S.W.A.T. Goon Squad.

According to Kenneth Wright—a single father of three young children ages 3, 7 and 11—he heard some commotion outside his Stockton home, so he looked out his upstairs window and saw 15 cops that looked like members of S.W.A.T. Before he could get downstairs to the door, they had battered it down and entered his home. Wright spent the next six hours handcuffed in the back of a cop car with his three frightened children.

Is Kenneth Wright the alleged murderer of thousands of brown people in the Middle East and North Africa? Has this scoundrel cheated millions of people out of their retirement/life savings? Did Mr. Wright authorize the use of torture, or even invade one country illegally?

No, of course not. It turns out that the cops who broke down Mr. Wright's door brutalizing him and traumatizing his children weren't local or state law enforcement, but an Education Goon Squad that had been granted some kind of vicious police state authority because Mr. Wright's ex-wife allegedly committed "fraud" on her student loans.

How many of us have student loans that are in danger of being defaulted on because we can't find a job? The primary question is, though, why do most of us have to commit ourselves to years of debt to get a University education which should be free in the most wealthiest country in the world?

The scandal of the rising cost and increasing inaccessibility of higher education can be directly related to the oppression and exploitation of the people that handle Obama like the Marionette that he is.

If the above story doesn't terrify you, then what about this one:

In the wee hours of Memorial Day, cops in Miami were involved in a high-speed chase that ended with the injuries of four innocent bystanders and the shooting execution of the SUSPECT. Witnesses to the crimes of the P.D. videotaped the entire incident and were, themselves, subjected to police brutality as the Miami cops held guns to their heads and smashed their cell phones. Luckily, one of the victims had the presence of mind to secure the SIM card of his phone in his mouth.

Ask yourself: "How terrified would I be if I just witnessed cops brutally shooting a man to death, then holding a gun to my head?"

The Robber Class obviously doesn't want hungry people fed, sick people healed, uneducated people schooled, homeless people housed, or poor people prosperous. Their agenda is total domination of the world's resources and complete income inequality in our own country.

The next time you fly and either have to subject your body to unacceptable levels of radiation in one of the Pervo-Scanners or get molested by TSA, think to yourself: "This is how it starts—my nation is being turned into a police state with nary a whimper."

At least I loudly protest these violations when I fly and I educate everyone within earshot (including the TSA) that Michael Chertoff (former director of the NSA under Bush) profits from the full-body X-ray machines in airports. The last time a TSA agent was illegally molesting me because I refused to go through one of the Pervo-Scanners, she said: "Am I hurting you?" And I answered: "Yes, you are beating the crap out of my Fourth Amendment."

The above stories illustrate that we no longer even have the pretense to the rights to privacy or against illegal search and seizure. Even if the state grants warrants, or passes laws that our privates are now fair game for government perversity, oftentimes these laws directly contravene the Constitution.

However, with the recent reauthorization of the USA PATRIOT ACT, the Constitution has again been rendered "null and void."

The obvious solution to what ails our nation is to end the wars and invest part of the money in education—forgive student loans and provide free/low-cost university education to everyone in this country. Ending the wars will not only have a positive effect on our economy, but we won't be creating enemies faster than we can kill them, so all of this jack-booted police state thuggery would not be necessary.

With the profit motive being so tempting to the Robber Class, it seems like one of the only recourses left to us now is to film everything that happens around us and hide the SIM cards from our phones in one of our body's crevices—we can at least be witnesses to and document Obama's rush to total totalitarianism.

CINDY NOTE: As of this writing, the descent into a police state has quickened.

Sunday, June 12, 2011
Children and War

Recently, I was listening to KGO radio, and in case you don't know, KGO is the ABC affiliate super-station here in San Francisco that can be heard by millions of people with it's mega-wattage transmitter.

Gene Burns happened to be the host at that time. The night that I was listening, Mr. Burns was wondering why the US is bombing Libya, but not Syria, because Syria is "torturing and killing children," and Mr. Burns didn't know how the people of the world could stand by and watch this happen.

I wish I could have gotten through on the call-in line because I would have asked Mr. Burns how he feels about the USA torturing and killing children in places like Libya, Iraq, Afghanistan, Pakistan, and Yemen? These are the active places the US is bombing, but what about the children that were held or are being held in places like Guantanamo Bay, Cuba; Abu Ghraib in Iraq, or Bagram AFB in Afghanistan? Why are the "people of the world" standing by and watching the US destroy civilization as it murders and tortures children?

It is my suspicion that even the most hardcore war supporter knows that women and children are the ones that suffer the most from war—but as War Madam, Madeline Albright, notoriously said in an interview with Lesley Stahl of CBS: the slaughter of over 500,000 Iraqi children during the sanctions period during the Clinton regime was "worth it." Monsters don't always have to have long claws, bloody fangs, or inhabit our nightmares—they can look like somebody's Grammy—and that's what I call a waking terror.

As a mother of a victim of US Imperialism, my well of empathy is bottomless, but I am not like Gene Burns. I don't think we should just be upset when "rogue" regimes kill or torture children—because the US is the largest rogue regime in recorded history. The rogue Empire counts on people like Gene Burns to provide cover for its crimes, in part, by over-sensationalizing the crimes of others.

Because of the definition of "collateral damage" ("We don't do body counts," General Tommy Franks), it is hard to pin down the exact number of children that have been killed by the US's War OF Terror since 2001—in fact, it's almost impossible, but a safe guesstimate is hundreds of thousands. However, one is exactly one too many.

What I can do for you is tell you some statistics on how children are treated here in the US:

HOMELESS CHILDREN: *1.5 million*
http://www.time.com/time/nation/article/0,8599,1883966,00.html

HUNGRY CHILDREN: *16.7 million*
http://www.bread.org/hunger/us/

CHILDREN LIVING IN POVERTY: *13 million*
http://www.nccp.org/publications/pub_684.html

CHILDREN LIVING WITHOUT HEALTH INSURANCE: *10.6 million*
http://en.wikipedia.org/wiki/Health_insurance_coverage_in_the_United_States

PERCENTAGE OF STUDENTS WHO DON'T GRADUATE FROM HIGH SCHOOL: *30*
http://www.bgca.org/whywecare/Pages/EducationCrisis.aspx

JUVENILES INCARCERATED IN THE US: *92,854 (2006)*
http://en.wikipedia.org/wiki/Youth_incarceration_in_the_United_States

CHILDREN DETAINED BY US IN GITMO? *22*
http://dandelionsalad.wordpress.com/2011/06/11/wikileaks-and-the-22-children-of-guantanamo-by-andy-worthington/

CHILDREN SYRIAN FORCES ARE ACCUSED OF KILLING: *30*
http://www.yalibnan.com/2011/06/01/unicef-says-30-children-killed-in-syrian-protests/

Children should be the ultimate expression of love, joy, and hope in all societies—and I am not trying to excuse Syrian forces for what has happened. Killing/torturing a child (adult) is an abomination, but what I am trying to do is put things in perspective.

Why would the dark forces that run the US care about murdering brown children with odd sounding names in far away places when it doesn't even care about the children here within our own borders?

Today (Sunday, June 12), on CBS's *Meet the Press,* war monster, Senator Lindsey Graham of SC, said that the time was "very close" to attacking Syria, and it's time to let President Assad know that "all options are on the table."

If we do attack Syria, then the Nobel Laureate POTUS would be at war with at least six countries. I hope that Graham is just having a wet dream about Syria, but I fear he is correct because the US can't allow anybody else to kill people—our War Machine already has a near monopoly on murder.

CINDY NOTE: *And "voila" as of this writing, with very little antiwar opposition, the US is bombing Syria.*

Saturday, July 2, 2011
The Sign-On Letter to Barack We'd Like to See

Dear Barry,

We have signed numerous letters to you calling for you to do numerous things that many of us would like to see you do—including, but not limited to:

- Institute a National Single-Payer Health Care system
- Bring US troops home from Iraq and Afghanistan
- Quit bombing Pakistan with Unmanned Aerial Vehicles (Drones)
- Not bomb Libya
- Free Bradley Manning
- End the use of nuclear technology for energy
- Investigate the Bush crime cabal
- Investigate and punish those responsible for contaminating the Gulf of Mexico
- Denounce US sanctions against Venezuela
- Do not reauthorize the illegal and immoral USA PATRIOT ACT
- Do not resume military tribunals in Guantanamo
- Close Guantanamo
- Rapidly develop a zero carbon economy
- End unconditional US support of Israel in its immoral occupation of Palestine (including withholding over 3 billion dollars/year in foreign aid).

You've made it pretty clear in the last two and a half years, however, that you don't have to listen to principled criticism of your actions from the "left." You and members of your administration have very blatantly accused those who dare to challenge you from the left side of the political spectrum as either "crazy" or "on drugs."

It's funny (sad) that you continually pander to, and simultaneously blame, the political fascist, racist right when its policies are violent and economically oppressive to the working-class. On any (every) given day that means your political decisions are, yes, violent and economically oppressive, ecologically destructive, and socially irresponsible.

Barry—we aren't begging you to do anything, and our letter carries no clout because we never supported you and we never intend to support you; rather, we just wanted to write this to let you know that we aren't buying the Imperial BS for which you are currently Head Salesman.

We want to let you know that there are a few people out here in the realm who see you for the fraud that you are.

Oh, the Emperor does have clothes, all right, but they are the lederhosen of a marionette cheerfully and willfully dancing for his corporate puppeteers.

Cheers!

Cindy Sheehan, Grieving mother and admitted idealist
Gregory Vickrey, Board Member, Peace of the Action
Dorothy Reilly
David Baldinger
Pegg Rapp
Nancy Jakubiak, Clarksville, In
Matthew Koob
Jerry ClapSo Avissato
Anna Marie Stenberg, Grandmother who is ashamed to be an American
Missy Beattie, Board member of Peace of the Action
Elizabeth F. Kaplan, Mother/Matriot
Don DeBar, Ossining, NY
Jon Gold, Advocate for 9/11 Justice
Heather Harman, Mother and Human Being
Malcolm Chaddock, Member, Veterans For Peace Ch. 72 Portland, OR
Cory Morningstar, Climate Justice Advocate
Larry Maxwell
David Swanson, author of War is a Lie

Thursday, July 28, 2011
Memo to the Evil Actors in DC

Even though some people have said: "Cindy Speaks for Me," I have never claimed that I am a spokesperson for anybody but myself—but I do know a lot of people agree with me. So, this is a memo from us.

You evil actors are all putting on another show over there in DC, and we are supposed to believe that any of you are serious, or seriously care about the people of this nation, or your make-believe "oath of office." You all put your hand on a bible, or other religious tome of your choosing, and swore to protect the rule of law, but you may as well have put your hand on a copy of "Death of a Salesman," or "Romeo and Juliet" for all your "swearing" means to any of you.

Barack Obama was allegedly chosen as lead character in this farce to change the script of Empire and economic exploitation. Then, in a very unbelievable plot twist, he was also chosen as Nobel Peace Laureate because there was hope that the script would change. However, Obama has proven to be an excellent reader of tele-prompters, but lousy at improv. The script reads "perpetual war for perpetual profit" (stage north, south, east, and west) and Obama is currently bombing at least five countries (Afghanistan, Pakistan, Libya, Somalia, Yemen) and is maintaining a profound (and profoundly expensive) occupational presence in Iraq (boo, hiss).

The US Empire currently maintains approximately 1000 military outposts in over 150 countries all over the world. The US military/ "Pentagram" consumes the largest amount of our tax and borrowed dollars. However, the script reads: never cut "defense."

I would like all of you mountebanks in Washington DCeit to know that there are many of us out here who don't buy the political circle-jerk that you are subjecting us to around this whole debt ceiling distraction. When Obama gets his shorts in a bunch and storms out of a meeting, or Eric Cantor (R) does similar, we know that you all go offstage, smoke a ciggy, laugh at we "easy marks" in the audience who stupidly shell out most of our livelihood to you charlatans onstage so you can high-five each other and go back out for Act Number Infinity.

Some of us *are* smarter than fifth graders, and we know this is all an act written by your masters with the money—and, in the end, it will be a tragedy for 99 percent of us who fall into the bottom five percent of the economic food chain.

Even though you treat all of us USAians like we are a nation of morons—clearly, some of us are not and we have seen this production ad infinitum—the reruns are even worse than the original. So why don't you all just skip the boring parts and pass a bill that won't make even a scratch in the wallets of the wealthy, but cuts more services and benefits to the rest of us.

Then the Democrats can say: "Wah, wah, the wicked Republicans made us cut a bunch of stuff." And the Republicans can say: "Wah, wah, we wanted to cut even more stuff, but the dastardly Democrats wouldn't let us." Then we can all get back to *Dancing with the Greatest American Idol* and FOR GOD'S SAKE, football season is almost starting—give us a frickin' break here!

Also (as an incentive to you murderers), if you can all just wrap up this charade ASAP, maybe you can add another country or two to your bombing list? Just kidding, of course, because if I were in charge of things, the crapload of wars and the 1K of military bases would be the first things to be cut—not just cut, but slashed, dashed, sliced, diced, and demolished—but that would mess up the script you scoundrels follow so sacra-religiously, wouldn't it?

I also would like to inform you that I do quite a bit of traveling outside of Circus, USA and the rest of the world pretty much thinks you are a bunch of clowns—evil for sure, but ridiculous all the same.

So, Obama, say: "Blah, blah, blah." Boehner say: "Blah, blah, blah." Wolf Blitzer say: "Blah, blah, blah." Mr. and Mrs. Odd Couple Skeletor say: "Blah, blah, blah." Geithner say, "Blah, blah, blah." The rest of you say, "Aye" or "Nay," or don't show up that day, or whatever your part is in this script of dangerous buffoonery and let's just get it the hell over with.

We get it and we want you to know that you can't fool some of us any of the time.

Saturday, August 13, 2011
The People vs. The Machine

Since the summer of 2005, when I began a camp in front of the vacation "ranch" of George Bush, I have traveled to many countries and all over the US meeting with people who have been in long struggles against neoliberalism. Most of us in the US are familiar with the term "neoconservative," but "neoliberal" is also a well-understood and often used term in other areas.

Wikipedia has a very good explanation of neoliberalism:

The term "neoliberalism" has also come into wide use in cultural studies to describe an internationally prevailing ideological paradigm that leads to social, cultural, and political practices and policies that use the language of markets, efficiency, consumer choice, transactional thinking, and individual autonomy to shift risk from governments and corporations onto individuals and to extend this kind of market logic into the realm of social and affective relationships.

Opponents of neoliberalism would identify several enemy organizations that foster global neoliberalism: the World Bank, the World Trade Organization (WTO), the International Monetary Fund (IMF), and the US Military—not to mention the collusion of most governments with private corporations in this headlong rush to economic disaster.

What I observe in the US is the financial chickens coming home to roost after decades-long foreign expansion and wars. I firmly believe that Barack Obama was (s)elected to put a minority face on this expansion to help quell rising protests against the aggressive wars abroad and the war against the poor here at home. Everything he has done during his disastrous first term in office has been

111

done to shore up the economic defenses of the economic elite: expand wars, TARP, health care "reform" bill, bankster bailouts, and the recent debt ceiling debacle.

I was recently in Hana-shi, Okinawa Prefecture in Southern Japan. While there, I visited a protest camp in Henoko, where activists have been protesting against the expansion of a US Marine Corps base called Camp Schwab.

Fifteen years ago when this protest started the "profound wisdom" of the mighty Empire was to build an island offshore with landfill, which would spoil the natural beauty of the ocean, and further harm species of endangered manatee and sea tortoise.

Through guerilla protests with boats and the taking over of platforms, the activists stopped the offshore base from being built, and so, the Empire decided to move the expansion onshore and build landing strips next to the already existing base, which would basically do the same thing as the offshore addition.

I was assured by the activists at the protest site that has been there for a decade and a half that, while Okinawa is home to 80 percent of the US's military presence in Japan, a vast majority of the residents do not want the US occupying their island any longer. I was asked the same question I have often wrestled with myself: If Japan is a "democracy" then why isn't the government responding to the wishes of the people of Okinawa? Same, same in the US—most of us want the wars to end and the tax loopholes for the wealthy and corporations to be slammed shut, but we are not listened to in either country.

Henoko is not the only place I have been where the people struggle against US bases and militarism—it is quite common, actually. If only more world leaders were like Ecuadorean President Rafael Correa who refused to renew the lease of Manta Air Base in Ecuador when he became president. He said: "We'll renew the base on one condition: that they let us put a base in Miami—an Ecuadorean base."

Most of the time it is peace activists fighting against US military bases—in Italy, in Japan, in South Korea, in Germany—but, as at Henoko, the environmental devastation the US brings with its occupations is also a component of any struggle.

The answer to these global problems is one that centers on peace and opposition to neoliberal policies.

Our indigenous brothers and sisters won a major victory against development on their sacred lands in Vallejo, CA. After an encampment that lasted over 100 days, the park's commission finally granted a cultural easement that would avoid the areas that are sacred to most tribes in California and farther north.

In Val di Susa, Italy—where I was recently—activists have been fighting for 20 years against the construction of a high-speed rail line that would slash their valley like a scar. It looks like this long fight will end in their victory, soon (we hope).

Along with Henoko, these are small, or regional victories, but every struggle honors and inspires the next one. The only way we can win the ultimate overthrow of a system that cares about everything for profit and nothing for the lives of people is to support each other, learn from each other, mourn with each other, and celebrate with each other.

The only way we can ever lose is to stop fighting.

We can never give up the fight!

Thursday, September 29, 2011
Show a Little Mercy; Free the Cuban Five!

Nothing can make injustice just but mercy.
Robert Frost

For quite some time I have been involved in the call to free the "Hikers," Shane Bauer and Josh Fattal, from Iranian prison. I put "Hikers" in quotation marks, because this is the term they have become known by in the media—not because I believe there was anything more nefarious in their actions. I was first contacted by Josh's brother, and subsequently have gotten to know Shane's mother, Cindy Hickey, better—I even once had her on my radio show, Cindy Sheehan's Soapbox.

I was delighted on September 21st, the day Shane and Josh, convicted of spying and given an eight-year sentence, were shown the highest mercy by the country of Iran and released. I had been invited to meet with President Mahmoud Ahmadinejad in NYC that day, but financial circumstances prevented me from making a last minute trip from California. I wish I had been able to go to thank him personally, but while I was not in NYC, I was at my home in California basically doing a deathwatch for Troy Anthony Davis who was ultimately "lynched" by the State of Georgia for the 1989 murder of a cop that he most likely did not commit. However, I have noticed a pattern, if a cop is killed, someone must die—it doesn't really matter if that person is actually the one that committed the murder.

On the 5th of July, two Fullerton, California cops beat Kelly Thomas, a homeless and mentally ill man who was begging for his life and for his dad to help him. Kelly died five days later on the 10th —a crime that was videotaped by passersby with cell phone cameras AND a transit camera because the incident occurred at a bus station. The charges against these murderers for a heinous crime were essentially slaps on the wrist, á la Johannes Meserle, the assassin of unarmed, Oscar Grant.

What is the common thread in the above cases? The state kills "Cop Killers" and Killer Cops literally get away with their murders. Manuel Ramos and Jay Cicinelli, the murderers of Kelly Thomas, are on paid administrative leave—the taxpayers are funding their little paid vacation (with full benefits intact).

Besides the cruelty of the police state killings of Kelly Thomas and Oscar Grant and more recently a young black man, Kenneth Harding, who didn't have evidence of paying his MUNI fare in San Francisco, the cops surely must know that their crimes will be videotaped in this age of almost universal citizen access to this technology—yet the police state still commits its crimes supremely confident in the knowledge that they will assuredly "get away" with them. That's a bone-chilling thought!

To me, the guilt or innocence of a person is not what's important in the issue of capital punishment —what's important is that the use of this state murder is barbaric and needs to end. Troy Anthony Davis was not shown mercy by the State of Georgia, or by the Barbaric State of America. Kelly Thomas and Kenneth Harding were tragically not shown mercy by members of the police state, but the cops will be shown plenty of that elusive virtue because it's usually only reserved for the wealthy or members of this police state.

The day that the Hikers were released, the Pérez of this country said, "I am thrilled. They never should have been in prison in the first place." Well, I would like to tell you about FIVE men currently languishing in US Federal Prison who never should be there "in the first place" either. It's the little known case of the Cuban Five, or the "Five Heroes" as they are referred to in Cuba.

Many acts of terrorism against Cuba have been planned from the right-wing Cuban exile community in Miami. These terrorists have killed thousands of Cubans and so the Cuban Five, as they would come to be known, were sent to the US to infiltrate this terrorist cell based in South Florida so as to be able to transmit messages back to Cuba to save lives in their homeland.

René González, Ramón Labaniño, Fernando González, Antonío Guerrero, and Gerardo Hernández left their families to go to the US.

To make a long story short, in an act of good will, Cuban authorities decided to share information gathered by the Five with the FBI, and instead of rounding up the real terrorists, the Five were rounded up, put on trial in a kangaroo court in Miami where a fair trial was just not possible, and sentenced to 15 years to life in prison.

The Five Heroes did nothing against the US and never gathered any intelligence against our government—yet they have been in prison since 1998.

I have met their mothers, wives, and children all over the world and I have also been in solidarity with the movement to free the Five for several years.

I know that President Hugo Chávez of Venezuela used his good influence with President Ahmadinejad of Iran (in fact, as I am told, worked harder than the US did for the Hikers' freedom) and I am wondering after so many have called for the release of the Five if there's any humanitarian that the leaders of this nation would listen to? Of course, the "Communist Dictator," Hugo Chávez, has no influence here in the US—he himself is on the same path of demonization that Castro, Ahmadinejad, Qaddafy, et al, are on.

The Cuban Five never should have been in prison, and 13 years is a long time for innocent men to be incarcerated.

It's time for Obama to show the same mercy as was just shown two of our innocent citizens by Iran and send the Five Heroes home to their families.

It's not only the humane thing to do; it's the just thing to do.

CINDY NOTE: Two of the five, Rene Gonzalez and Antonio Guerrero are back in Cuba after serving their sentences; three of the five still languish in federal prison.

Saturday, October 8, 2011
Transcript for Cynthia McKinney (10/2) Show

CS: Cindy Sheehan

CM: Cynthia McKinney

CS: Welcome back to Cindy Sheehan's Soapbox. I am your host, Cindy Sheehan, and you are listening at CindySheehansSoapbox.com.

I am recording this from a faculty member's office at Dominican University in a suburb of Chicago, Illinois. I'm going to be speaking there as soon as I finish recording our conversation and interview at Cindy Sheehan's Soapbox.

I am speaking to the students and the subject is called Women in the Peace Movement. I'm also supposed to talk about the case of the Cuban Five and I'm writing an article about that, which I am going to post at Cindy Sheehan's Soapbox blogspot. I am also going to talk about Cuban American relations. I just found out something very exciting. I probably will be going back to Cuba next month to do a colloquium around the Cuban Five in Holguin, Cuba. Cuba is a country and a subject that is very near and dear to my heart.

Today we are going to be speaking to somebody who is also near and dear to my heart and a very good friend of mine. A very courageous woman. A friend of Cindy Sheehan's Soapbox and probably somebody you consider a friend whether you've met her or not and somebody who is, to me, always on the side of peace and justice.

Our guest today is ex-congresswoman from the state of Georgia Cynthia McKinney.

Cynthia McKinney, welcome back to Cindy Sheehan's Soapbox.

CM: I know it's been too long Cindy. I have been missing you.

CS: Well, you've been extremely busy; well we've both been busy, but you've been extraordinarily busy in the past few months haven't you? Tell my listeners, I think most of my listeners know what you've been up to, but tell them about your grueling schedule since you returned from Libya.

CM: Well, oh my goodness. I went on a tour and it just kept expanding, so I think the final count was 29 cities in about 40 days.

CS: Wow.

CM: It was literally amazing. The reason—it was like in 30 days—I had to take a week out because I started a PHD program and I actually had to do some work.

The reason that I have been sort of low key is, of course, that I got very behind in my work; and I have been putting my nose literally to the grindstone to make sure that I get all of my work done, so that eventually, maybe, I can get back out on the road. But you caught me at a very interesting time because all of the—this is the first day actually that I have had to unpack and wash my clothes and repack. Then go through the mountain of materials that people gave me along the tour. So the message is, if you haven't heard from me, it is coming. Those of you who were there with me on the tour and gave me a packet of information or gave me your card and told me to get back to you that is what I am in the process of doing, literally, right now.

When you called me, Cindy, that's what I was doing, going through everything so I can make the contact and reconnect with the people. Literally, thousands of people in the 29 cities that included three cities in Canada. Every venue was a standing-room-only crowd and the reason, I believe, is because by now the people have clearly understood that they cannot rely on what they see on the television, what they hear over the airwaves. They can't rely on that and they have to search for other opportunities to hear what's going on. And then, hopefully, what they will do is weigh the two and then make their own minds up.

CS: I saw you when you were out on your tour at a really overflow crowd in San Francisco. Part of the people that were there were criticizing you and were saying that your report was false. And I am here in Chicago, like I said, and the person who is driving me around saw you when you were in this area and said the same thing happened. What do you think was behind those people? Who do you think were behind those people? Who do you think was behind their coming out and basically saying what you were saying was false: that the rebels are heroic revolutionaries and Gadhaffi is public enemy number one around the world. What do you think was behind that?

CM: Well it's very interesting. There are some people that have legitimate grievances with government. It would have legitimate grievances with the Jamahiriya. And I would caution you, Cindy, that Libya is 6.5 million people, it's not one person. So when we talk about Gadhaffi let's also recognize that there is a system of government there that is larger than one person. So now, if there are legitimate grievances, I think the way to deal with those legitimate grievances is in the international arena, the international court system. But I have grievances. Look, I am from the State of Georgia and we just murdered an innocent boy. I would never call France and Britain to come and bomb my country and use depleted uranium in my country if I had legitimate grievances. I believe that my grievances against the United States are legitimate. But we use a different way to exercise our right and attempt to get heard.

So these people, first of all, they called in depleted uranium, helicopter gun ships, no telling what other kinds of weapons caused the wounds that I saw when I was at the hospital. It looked like the weapons that were used against the people of Gaza that are called dime weapons, which is a new kind of weaponry. So that is what was going on when I was there.

Now, of course, the situation is far worse and Libya has been completely destroyed. Completely destroyed in the way that Iraq was completely destroyed, Afghanistan completely destroyed. Pakistan, well on its way to being destroyed as a political entity unless the people of Pakistan stand up and say no to NATO led by the United States, which has a plan to engulf Pakistan in confusion, chaos and, ultimately, a loss of control from the people.

Unfortunately, now what I have been told by the people I have been in contact with, who I was there with, they told me that Tripoli—you would not recognize Tripoli and that saddens me because, if you can imagine, Tripoli has a million and a half people and they're dropping bombs as people are driving to work or whatever, they're dropping bombs.

The partners they were called, the African migrants who had come to Libya because Libya gave them the opportunity to work in dignity and to raise their families, and to send their remittances back home so that their families back home could live in a modicum of dignity. Those people were and still are the ones that were there are no longer there at least in the way were, at least the group that I am about to mention. They gathered at [inaudible] and there was one Libyan who was in, he was abroad. He was a dentist and he decided when all this happened he would come back and he served as my translator, my interpreter when I would go into [inaudible] to see what was going on. They would have a party every night and when NATO sent those bombs into [inaudible] they were bombing innocent people. Some of those people, the crowds began to grow because as more and more people became homeless due to the bombing they would set up their tents and they would also join what started out as the Partners who had come and these are largely Africans from other parts of the continent who were so loyal to the opportunity that they had been given to live with a modicum of dignity that they said they would stay there instead of going back home. So they stayed at [inaudible] and they would have the drummers come out and they would dance and chant and do whatever. And this went on every night and every night NATO would bomb. Then NATO bombed them. NATO didn't bomb beside them. NATO bombed them! Just about a week and a half ago two weeks ago I got a message that the dentist who used to perform my translations for me is no longer answering his cell phone he's probably dead.

CS: Oh, that's terrible.

CM: I am just beside myself with outrage at people who want to reduce criminal behavior to opposition to a political figure. There are people who dislike me intensely.

CS: Un Huh. I know the feeling.

CM: And there one of them was a journalist. I have to tell this story. This journalist who said on his show that I should be lynched. This was when I was in congress. I had become accustomed to this kind of thing. My staff read this and they were stunned, they were horrified. They went to the FBI. They reported this to the FBI. Now only to find out about three years later when he was being prosecuted for making some threats against some white politicians, but he got prosecuted for that, what we learned was that he was on the FBI payroll and he was being paid to make those statements against me. That's why there was no recourse when we went to the FBI. So even in a situation like that, I would never say let's go bomb my opponent. It's not the way I think. But these people have decided they want to destroy their country and fill it with the residue, the remains of depleted uranium, and you know what that does genetically, so that they can have their country.

Now I have teamed up with some independent journalist who were among the last to leave and I am hoping that we can have Mahdi Darius Nazemroaya on your show.

CS: Yeah, right. We are trying to work that out.

CM: The last piece that he wrote was extremely instructive because people want to talk about one person. Let's talk about one person but let's talk about the one person who went to Geneva and said that 10,000 I think the number is actually 6,000 that were killed. What Mahdi pierces so carefully is that there is no evidence; there was never any evidence.

CS: And the person that was there said Gadhaffi killed 6,000 people.

CM: There was never any evidence and, in fact, I don't want to tell everything that went into the process of doing. But it is clear that the human rights commissioners also understood that there was no evidence. Mahdi has listed the names of the so-called human rights organizations that signed on to the letter of this particular Libyan person. If you looked through the list and if you were not a questioning person you would say oh my goodness this is authoritative; we have to do something. But anyone of responsibility should've asked, where's the evidence? There was never any evidence.

Now this is eerily similar to the testimony of an Italian who was in the European parliament right after September 11 happened and he has since gone on to do a film, to write a book about his experience. But right after the September 11 attacks happened a ministerial meeting was held of NATO—and of course you know NATO is a collective of security organizations which means that an attack against one can be an attack against all if the relevant articles are evoked—and this ministerial level meeting right after September 11 was to invoke the collective security agreement. What this Italian member of the European Parliament tells me and all of us in his testimony is that the United States said we have been attacked, we've got the evidence, we know who did it but we can't tell you, we can't show it to you, we can't share it with you but we want you to attack Afghanistan. And on the basis of no evidence, once again, NATO is doing what it was doing 10 years later in Afghanistan it spread it now to Pakistan.

CS: Well I was listening to an interview you and Madhi did with KPFK in Los Angeles and they played something that Wesley Clarke—I believe it was Wesley Clarke—who was the former commander of NATO who said that there was a list of countries that the US was going to invade and it was after they were bombing Afghanistan but before the invasion of Iraq. Of course Iraq was on it, Syria and Libya were on that list. So this has all been premeditated many years ago. Not only that, but recently the UN has recognized the transitional government in Libya as the legitimate government while refusing to recognize an independent Palestinian state.

CM: Well you know my undergraduate from the University of California was international relations. I have my bachelor's degree in international relations. My master's degree from the Fletcher school of Law and Diplomacy in Boston, which is a school for study in international affairs. I am an internationalist and of course now a globalist.

CS: But not in a bad way.

CM: Not in a bad way, that's right. But now—and I have honestly, I have believed in the United Nations, but not anymore.

CS: Right.

CM: Not any more. I saw what the United Nations was supposed to do.

Actually my first involvement with what the UN was supposed to do was Rwanda. But prior to Rwanda there was East Timor. So I have seen the failings of the United Nations. Of course now we can list amongst the failings, we can list Haiti as an abject failure and it was the UN that brought in the cholera and no reparations have ever been paid Haitian people for that.

The United Nations peacekeepers go around the world and with them go all the vices known to human kind. So not anymore, not anymore.

The United Nations has become a tool from the aspect of justice. So, apparently, as I have traveled I've noticed there is a kind of apartheid around the world. Now that apartheid even extends into the global economy, administration of justice, culture such that there was a time that the United Nations I really believed that the United Nations was there to protect people, protect cultures—to protect. But not anymore. I don't believe it. So I think that as we look for new structures to promote peace, to promote our values, the United Nations is one of those structures whose time has come and gone.

CS: You know, Cynthia, when the UN first passed the resolution of the no-fly zone in Libya I sent out an email to my supporters and I said, "You all know that a no-fly zone is just code for 'we are going to begin bombing soon.'" And it was just a few days. As a matter of fact, it was the anniversary of the initial invasion of Iraq in 2003, that the Obama administration starting bombing Libya and, of course, there was no congressional approval of that.

This is going to be my last question because we only have a few minutes left. Some people dropped me and people unsubscribed from my email list because they said that I don't care about the people of Libya. What has this UN resolution and the resulting US/NATO bombing of Libya, has it helped the people of Libya in anyway? Was it wrong for me to be concerned if NATO and the US were going to be beginning a bombing campaign in Libya?

CM: You should never be concerned Cindy when human life is at stake and the war machine of the United States and its allies are revving up for action. You should never be sad that you were alert. This matter of the bombing of Libya, the destruction, the total destruction of a country, is not about one man. But it is about one person. It's about each one of us and what it is that we truly value. I am deeply disappointed in the people who call themselves a part of the progressive community and who support what I saw in Libya.

CS: Right. I can't believe that we are already out of time and I have to run over to the lecture hall now and give a talk to the students here at Dominican. Do you have a website that my listeners can read a copy of Mahdi's latest article?

CM: The article is located at wbaix.org I believe. You know, that's really pitiful. I'm sure it's at GlobalResearch.ca also.

CS: I'll also be putting a link on my website to that article. And how can my listeners add to your burden and get a hold of you?

CM: I'm always available at Cynthia@runcynthiarun.org and then of course the relevant Face Book and dignity but there's Facebook and Twitter by my name or Run Cynthia Run so people can find me on the internet.

CS: Cynthia, as always, thank you for your courage and thank you for always being on the right side of issues or at least on the good side of issues.

CM: That's right. I am always on the people's side.

CS: And the Peace and Justice side. We can always count on you to be on that side. Good luck with your studies.

CM: Thank you.

CS: Okay, we love you a lot at Cindy Sheehan's Soapbox. So keep up the good work.

CM: Okay, bye-bye.

Thanks to my sister, Dede Miller, for doing the transcribing.

[The USA is the] most dangerous power the world has ever known - the authentic rogue state, but a rogue state of colossal military and economic might.

Nobel Literature Laureate; Harold Pinter, 2001

As Khujeci Tomai put it, "Dead men tell no tales. They cannot stand trial. They cannot name the people who helped them stay in power. All secrets die with them."

Dictionary.com defines a Rogue State as: "—*n* a state that conducts its policy in a dangerously unpredictable way, disregarding international law or diplomacy." Especially since 9/11, according to this definition, the USA has sunk to the level of Rogue State.

Wow, I thought Bush was bad and that we had sunk about as low as we could go during those insane years, but Obama is excavating new territory.

Just since the Occupy movement began, the Obama regime has (among other things): 1) assassinated several US citizens in Yemen, (without due process) including a 16 year old having dinner with his buddies; 2) Sent "advisors" to Vietnam (oops, I meant Uganda; 3) aided and abetted the assassination of a leader of a sovereign state.

Not a bad month for a Rogue President still in his first term, eh?

After the assassination of Qaddafi, at least two interesting things came to my awareness—the first one was the Rogue Libyan ambassador to the US telling our own Rogue news commentator, Wolf Blitzer, that the "rebels" were so happy that the US paid at least **two billion** dollars for the overthrow of Qaddafi. The second one was a tweet from the OWS movement the day Qaddafi was assassinated that said, "*Congrats Libya! Your struggles against the #Gadhafi regime is (sic) over. Let's hope for a bright future #solidarity.*"

Okay, let's deconstruct and connect these two events.

First of all, Ambassador Ali Aujali was absolutely gloating and so ecstatic that Qaddafi was executed because it was "better" for Aujali that he not be captured and brought to trial—those were unexpected true words from the Robber Class--since dead men can tell no tales. In all his bloodthirsty glory Wolf, who has at last, dropped all pretenses at being a journalist, was also beaming with glee that Qaddafi was slaughtered (also without due process).

During that interview, Wolf did ask Aujali about the chances of the "rebels" paying the US back for the literal blood money taxpayers paid for this criminal regime change. Aujali demurred.

Then the tweet from the OWS movement came to my attention, showing a profound shallowness of comprehension on its part.

The "people" of Libya did not, I repeat, did not, rise up against Qaddafi. While I am sure that there were some well-meaning individuals who wanted to see the end of the Qaddafi regime, it was more like the two billion from the US funny money mint and over 26,000 US/NATO bombing raids that killed unknown thousands of innocent Libyans that actually accomplished that feat.

How can the "struggle" of the people be over if the new government is flying the flag of the deposed and oppressive former monarchy and dividing up the spoils of blood-soaked victory between various foreign oil companies? I really wish the Occupy Wall Street movement would think harder before it parrots the propaganda of the establishment. Even though I am a member of the 99%, that kind of language does not speak for me.

Remember, way back in March when I denounced the UN "no-fly zone," because I said that was code for, "bombing civilians?" Many people accused me of "not caring about the people of Libya," but it appears that I was tragically correct.

Yes, Wall Street is a big problem and Obama is, once again, raking in all the ill-gotten gains from donors from there as he can. But does anyone reading this have any better ideas for ways that the US can spend two billion dollars rather than killing civilians, deposing leaders, and propping up puppet governments that will be friendly to big oil? If the war issues are not addressed in a more meaningful and comprehensive way, then I am afraid the movement has every chance of being neutralized. What happens if Geithner and Bernanke are "indicted," and the crazy-empire train keeps chugging along?

Our Rogue State is clearly out of control and, as I have said many times, economic and social justice just are not possible without complete and unconditional peace.

Monday, November 7, 2011
From OWS to RRC

Recent events at Occupy movements, particularly in Oakland, Denver, Atlanta, Portland and Chicago, where hundreds were arrested and some seriously injured—it's becoming clear that when we in the Robbed Class allow ourselves to be contained in a small, easily attacked geographic location, we open ourselves up for Imperial Abuse and more Police Brutality. As a non-violent movement, we the people do not have the tools or the will to be involved in a war against the Police State. We will lose, especially if we are inclined to confine ourselves to easily surrounded city parks.

Remember the tales we were told in grammar school about our great revolutionary leaders who became almost like guerrilla warriors during the war for independence? How they learned how to break the easily attacked ranks and fight like the "Indians?" Can you imagine the people in the countries occupied by the US gathering in local parks and telling US troops thus making it easy to find them and obliterate them?

Obviously, the United Police States of America knows no constraint on its violence. There is a similar lack of accountability for the goon squads or the people who order them to do attack innocent people. As someone who has watched Occupy Sacramento spend more time fighting with the city to allow its encampment to remain set up in the park than actually confronting the issues I think maybe it's time to move from occupation to solution in smaller, yet connected groups of Robbed Class insurgency?

Since the beginning of 2009, I have been urging people to break their chains of slavery with the Robber Class—that is now happening. The Robbed Class is waking up to the fact that we have been co-dependent with the crimes of the Robber Class for generations now and that cycle must be broken. But what are some of the major institutions or practices that enlarge this vast income and social inequality?

The major problem is that here in the US basic human rights are sold to us as "privileges" that we must either be born into or sell our souls to the corporate devil to obtain—but even that option is disappearing with the outsourcing of jobs and the growth of predatory credit systems. Meaningful work that doesn't make one want to scrub the stench of the regret of selling-out is very hard to come by lately in the "wealthiest" nation on the planet.

What are basic physical human rights as outlined and recognized by the international community?

The right to peace;

The right to health care;

The right to a clean and sustainable environment;

The right to housing;

The right to education;

The right to healthy food free from genetically modified organisms;

The right to clean water;

The right to a meaningful job paying a living wage;

And the right to organize into true democratic systems.

My book, *Myth America, 20 Greatest Myths of the Robber Class and the Case for Revolution* presents an argument against being co-dependent with the Robber Class and offers many do-able solutions to build healthy, healing, peaceful and sustainable communities. Re-Creating Revolution Communities (RRC) begins the hard work of siphoning off the power and resources from the Robber Class and keeping it in our own communities and making civilization work for us.

Another grave, but not insurmountable problem we have here is a vertical, hierarchical power structure—the solution is horizontal, grassroots, decision-making and power sharing.

CINDY NOTE: OWS certainly tanked after MoveOn.org moved in with its "American Spring" action that was actually just a very thinly disguised get the vote out for Democrats!

Tuesday, November 15, 2011
Day One of On the Road to Cuba

In Cuba in 2007

Dear Reader,

How are you doing? I am writing this from an airplane speeding towards Mexico City at about 37,000 feet. I am heading towards my favorite place in the entire world, Cuba.

Few USAians get to visit Cuba since the US blockade began in 1959, and I feel so fortunate to be on my third trip down there. My way is being paid by an NGO in Cuba that I have worked with before.

Cuba is a tropical island that is free of most of the grit, grime and pollution in the States, but also free of most of the crime in other tropical tourist destinations. I have rarely felt more safe than when I am in Cuba and one of my favorite things to do is sit out on a patio in the evening (after a day of meetings and such) sipping on a Mojito or other cold drink and feel the warm, sweet breeze blow over me.

Just a few weeks ago, US President Obama was asked about the possibility of opening up talks with Cuba to help thaw the needless block of ice that has frozen diplomatic relations between our two countries. He answered: "Cuba has to change its society first!" Fidel Castro called him, "stupid," and I agree with Fidel and here's why.

I would like US society to change the way Cuba's society is. Besides providing every resident with a free and outstanding education through university and outstanding health care in a system that trains foreign doctors to work in economically and socially disadvantaged areas (yes, even Americans), the lifestyle is simpler and community is not just a concept, it's a reality.

In 1991 after the collapse of the Soviet Union, Cuba went through what it calls the "Special Period," where its imports and exports were cut by 80% and the Period was defined by a lack of petroleum products. Less emphasis was put on the automobile. Hunger was rampant, and the people of the nation are rightly proud of the fact that everyone worked together to survive and make food security a number one priority. Sustainable farming was instituted by necessity. I was told that the Mothers of Cuba are honored for their commitment during the Special Period to finding enough food to keep her family alive, and ways to prepare it that were not too disgusting to ingest.

I have heard stories from the Revolution and stayed, once, in a hospitality house that are staffed by descendants of men and women who allied with the Revolution in the Sierra Maestras and helped the Castros be victorious. It is a very honored position.

As Fidel said, the US Empire with probably collapse before the Revolution fails in Cuba.

I believe that every American that has the opportunity should travel down to Cuba. We have been propagandized about that country for decades now and Fidel has survived hundreds of CIA assassination attempts. With the profound meddling of the U.S., how has the revolution been able to continue for so long if it is unpopular?

Since my son was killed and I occupied Crawford, Texas, I have been so fortunate to be able to travel around the world and experience things that few Americans have and one of these things has been to go to Cuba and bear witness to the truth.

I will try and post an update everyday, but Cuba is not a frenetic, "we must be hardwired to our technology" kind of place.

Long live the Revolution!

Cuba Libre!

Hasta la victoria, siempre.

Cindy Sheehan

CINDY NOTE: *With this current Ebola "crisis," the US (in characteristic form) sends thousands of troops and Cuba (also in characteristic form) sends hundreds of healthcare workers and doctors to Africa. Fidel is a dignified statesman.*

Part Four
2012

(Afterword to *Myth America II*)
Originally, January 21, 2010

The roses in the window box
Have tilted to one side
Everything about this house
Was born to grow and die
Elton John, *"Funeral for a Friend (Love Lies Bleeding)"*

I hope we shall crush in its birth the aristocracy of our moneyed corporations
which dare already to challenge our government in a trial of strength
and bid defiance to the laws of our country.
Thomas Jefferson

I find it super-ironic that I am writing the very last words to *Myth America II* on the day that any semblance to the US being "by and for the people" died.

The publication of this book has been delayed by so many urgent events—Obama goes on a $50K/week vacation to Martha's Vineyard (August 20009) while war rages on—Obama escalates troop presence in Afghanistan, not once, not twice, but THREE times—Obama approves expanding military and CIA unmanned aerial vehicle bombings—Obama is awarded the Nobel Peace Prize—Senator Kennedy dies and the Dems lose big time in Massachusetts!

I know I am leaving out so many things (***note--especially the many things that happened after Jan 2010)***—like the Obama regime covering up the murder of three detainees in Gitmo and protecting the Bush Administration and following in the footsteps of the Bush regime by fomenting hostilities with Venezuela and Iran.

Then after the people of Haiti suffer a devastating earthquake, Obama appoints George Bush to lead US relief efforts. Obama's first year was quite a busy, busy year that wasn't so much about CHANGE as it was about tying a cement block around HOPE and drowning it in the Potomac River.

I had a busy 2009, too—as Obama climbed to new lows of thuggery—I met him there to challenge him (and you). As one of the only people who, from the beginning, criticized the Dalai Bama, I have been shunned and scorned, but also welcomed to many places where truth, peace, and justice are still valuable commodities.

Today was a landmark day in US history and—even though this book is finished—WE MUST add an addendum about this.

No matter what happens tomorrow—If the Bra Bomber finally materializes, or Obama gets caught in a compromising position with Tiger Woods, or if Michelle is caught growing weed in her organic garden (then, I would think she's cool)—THIS BOOK IS FINISHED, and so might be my country.

We have talked about the scandal of corporate personhood and how two sentences from Supreme Court Chief Justice Waite, before the oral arguments were even heard in the 1886 case of ***The City*** *and County of Santa Clara v. The Southern Pacific Railroad,* changed our history forever:

"The court does not wish to hear arguments on the question whether the provision in the Fourteenth Amendment to the Constitution, which forbids a State to deny to any person within its jurisdiction the equal protection of the laws, applies to these corporations. We are all of the opinion that it does."

No law has ever been passed giving corporations rights, not just privileges—no Supreme Court decision in the past ever gave Goldman Sachs literally millions of more votes than me—it was just a freaking statement before the hearing ever began! We are losing everything because some old dead white guy flapped his jaws and "voila" the Fourteenth Amendment applies to corporations.

Today, in *Citizens United v. The Federal Election's Commission*, the Supreme Court of the United States ruled that any cap put on corporations, and presumably union and other organizations, to spend on campaign ads and other campaign expenses violates a corporation's "Freedom of Speech" which has been illegally protected for 134 years. As I pointed out in "Myth that Elections Matter," our system is already rigged in favor of the Robber Class—corporations HAVE NO MOUTHS. How can the paper entities have free speech?

This expansion (not granting) of "Free Speech" to corporations effectively kills Robbed Class "Free Speech" when it comes to elections.

Money is what buys influence with our government—that's all, nothing else. We ain't got no money, so we ain't got no influence.

The only tool we have left to us is Revolution as JFK said: *"Those who make peaceful revolution impossible, make violent revolution inevitable."*

Peace, Resistance, and Revolution
From NYC
January 21, 2010

Note from Cindy (January 15, 2012): Myth America II: 20 Greatest Myths of the Robber Class and the Case for Revolution, *ended with these words that I wrote from NYC in 2010. Little did I know that in September 2011, the Occupy Wall Street movement would spring up not far from where I wrote those words. I am posting a re-print of this article because I am working on a new piece called:* Occupy Myth, *to analyze the Occupy movement and how we can use that movement and the suggestions of grassroots democracy and community building that I advocated in* Myth America *to actually effect healthy and meaningful change for us.*

CINDY NOTE: (2014) 2012 was actually the year I ran on the Peace and Freedom Party ticket as the vice-presidential nominee with Roseanne Barr at the top, since I love Obama so much, right?

Thursday, February 9, 2012
Republican for President?

When I opposed the wars and oppression of civil rights here at home during the Bush scandal there was a certain segment of the population I knew I could always count on to be in solidarity with me: Liberal Democrats.

While George Bush was president and Congress was primarily of a Republican nature, even organizations like MoveOn.org and blogs like the Daily Kos were on my side. I attended HUGE protests in 2005–2006 before the Democrats took control of Congress in the elections of 2006—but after that, the protests began to weaken or evaporate. In fact, at an event in DC commemorating the 5th Anniversary of the invasion of Iraq in 2008 (Iraq Veterans Against the War's "Winter Soldier"), I was told by the lead organization that it didn't want Cindy Sheehan "anywhere near Washington, DC."

I, and many others, were in favor of a large demo in DC that year, as we always did, but one of the lead antiwar/Bush organizations actually told us, since Democrats were in the majority in the House and they were continuing to fund Bush's wars and not impeach him, that a demo in DC would, "embarrass the Democrats."

Now that we have had two years of a complete Democratic tyranny in DC and almost four years of a Democratic regime in the White House, the antiwar movement has continued its tailspin because "Liberal" Democrats mostly populated it, or other Democratic functionaries like the Communist Party, USA.

A recent poll commissioned by the *Washington Post* shows that by a vast majority "Liberal" Democrats favor (53%) keeping Guantanamo Prison camp and torture facility open and (77%) the drone bombing campaigns that their president has increased by at least 300 percent over the Bush years. Unbelievably, "Liberal" Democrats also are in favor of the Presidential Assassination Program where Obama can have any American executed by his order only. Trials? Like John Yoo's Constitution, these anachronisms will soon be considered "quaint."

What Glenn Greenwald, in his column at *Salon,* recently called: "Repulsive progressive hypocrisy," I called "Faux-gressivism" over three years ago. I began to read the writing on the wall in 2006 when Nancy Pelosi kept saying, "impeachment is off the table" in the election that propelled her to a brief House Speakership—and the consequences of this political perfidy have been dire for tens of thousands of people who would have mattered when Bush was president, but somehow don't seem to matter so much now.

"But, Cindy, John McCain would have been worse." I have heard that tired refrain at least 500 times since 2009, and who knows, maybe he would have been, maybe not. My Republican friends voted for George Bush in 2004 because, even though his lies killed their friend, Casey, they told me that he was going to singlehandedly overturn *Roe v. Wade.* Many people voted for Obama in 2008 because he promised to close Guantanamo. The last time I looked *Roe v. Wade* has not been overturned, and now principled opposition to torture and illegal detention has apparently turned into undying support (until a Republican is back in the Oval Office).

If one of the Republican candidates becomes president in 2012, will the innocent people being slaughtered by US drones matter to these "Faux-gressives" again? Will the antiwar movement be brought back from the dead as, all of a sudden, antiwar feelings are reawakened in people who would have become apoplectic over a Bush invasion of Libya, but were strangely silent or loudly cheerleading the "humanitarian intervention" of Obama's? Will spying, torture, and the sharp erosion of our civil liberties here at home become anathema once again?

Besides being told 500 times that, "McCain would have been worse," I have also heard, or seen myself being called "an extremist" or "ideologue" by some of the very same people that gave me awards and wrote glowing pieces about me just a few years back. If a Republican once again takes up residence at 1600 Pennsylvania Avenue, will I, once again, become smart and courageous?

To me, in the perpetual political hypnosis and hypocrisy that exists in this nation, the most tragic thing is that the dead, too numerous to actually count, were used by the Faux-gressives as convenient weapons to bludgeon Bush and the Republican party, but were so easily discarded as garbage on the dung heap of US electoral politics when victory was declared by the Democratic warniks.

Well, I am going to tell you, for the 500th time, that it really doesn't matter who is in the White

House. The Empire will crush everyone it rolls over without any qualms—and those people and their loves, dreams, struggles and, especially their lives, always, always, always matter. Period.

I now know that to most "Liberal" Democrats, killing by the Imperial Army is only considered wrong if a Republican does it—so, even though it is a false concern, we are at least able to predict that if a Republican is elected, we will see people out in the streets protesting those murders.

CINDY NOTE: Here in the present of October 2014, the names of Hillary Clinton (D) and Jeb Bush (R) are already being bandied about for the 2016 elections. Once again, we will all lose and the oligarchs will be victorious.

Tuesday, February 21, 2012
Surprise, the US Attorney Has Filed a Law Suit Against You!

It's not a secret, and hasn't been one for about 8 years now, that I am a conscientious tax objector. It's also no secret that the IRS has been on my case about it recently.

So, tonight I was having coffee at a local restaurant with an activist/friend and we were chatting about some very sensitive issues when a man wearing a blue long-sleeved shirt and tie approached our table. I thought that it might be the manager of the restaurant but he said, "Hi Cindy, I am Cornell from Channel 10 News in Sacramento."

Sometimes it happens that members of the media recognize me and say "hi" when their presence has nothing to do with me, so I shook his outstretched hand and replied, "Hi, what are you doing here in Vacaville? Just passing through?" He said, "No, actually I am here to talk to you."

I have been pretty quiet lately, working on my radio show and trying to promote my new book, so I was rather shocked by this ambush and said so.

Cornell informed me that he was there to talk to me about "the lawsuit that the US attorney filed against you in Federal Court." Turns out that the lawsuit is on behalf of the IRS, and that was not the first time that I found out something important about my life from the media.

My next question to Cornell was how did he know where I was? Simple, he went to my home and my daughter told him. That is another issue—no one has the address where I live right now, but apparently the IRS told Cornell where to find me. Isn't it nice of the IRS to tell the media where to ambush me before they tell me that the US Attorney is suing me?

I did talk to Cornell on camera but I did not tell him anything that I haven't been publicly and loudly saying since my son was killed in this bloody Empire's illegal and immoral war in Iraq: I made a moral decision to refuse to fund the Empire's crimes, tortures, and wars. I have not been hiding from anybody and am fully accessible and easy to find (obviously).

It's been stated by the perpetrators and proven repeatedly that the Bush regime manufactured and manipulated the "intelligence" to rush this nation and the people of Iraq headlong into disaster. My son and hundreds of thousands of other people should still be among the living. At this moment, I am only talking about the Bush years and Iraq but, this Empire has been out-of-control for generations—ask our indigenous people about that, if you can find any.

Let's cut through all the bullshit.

There is no monetary value large enough that can be placed on a human life or the love of a mother for her child.

I consider that my debt to this country was paid in full when my son Casey was recklessly murdered—with no regard for his safety (remember the rush to war with the "Army you have" which was not properly trained or equipped?)—for the lies of a regime whose members (Bush, Cheney, Rice, Rumsfeld, Yoo, Wolfowitz, Perle, etc.) roam around the world free and unfettered by threatening prosecutions or persecutions after committing war crimes, crimes against humanity, crimes against the peace, and high crimes and misdemeanors against our own Constitution.

After the interview with Cornell was over, he said to me, "You appear so calm. Most people would be freaking out if the US Attorney filed a lawsuit against them." I replied, "Cornell, what are they going to do to me? Kill another one of my children (god forbid)? I had the worst thing happen to me that could happen to any mother and I am still standing."

Obviously there are "Two Americas" especially in the "justice" system. Justice is supposed to be blind to such things as race, religion, or income status, but what she really is blind to are the violent and outrageous crimes committed by the 1%. However, I see nothing but opportunity in this new development. When those papers were filed against me—the Feds did something that I have been trying to do for years—put its evil, illegal, and immoral wars on trial.

The Feds have thrown down the gauntlet against someone who has absolutely not one ounce of fear of them, and when it's over, they'll know they have been in a fight.

I would say, "Bring it on," but I am not about to quote the barely functioning killer that murdered my son and so many more and who is also being protected by the very same agency that is persecuting me—Obama's DOJ.

CINDY NOTE: The resolution of this will be unveiled as the year trudges on.

Sunday, February 26, 2012
The Sound of Collapse

I was invited to jump on a bus called the Green Tortoise this past Friday (Feb 24) to travel down to Vandenberg AFB in central California to protest the test launch of an ICBM missile.

The bus originated in Oakland and we stopped in San Jose and Salinas on the way down to pick up more anti-nuke/pro-humanity activists and met dozens of others who were already near the entry of the base at about 11:30pm. The "launch window" was open from 2am to 8am on the 25th. The missile was destined to come down about 25 minutes after launch in the Marshall Islands.

According to one of the organizers and long-time anti-nuke protester at Vandenberg MacGregor Eddy, the combination of the missile launch and missile cost US taxpayers $28 million dollars. Needless to say, the potential loss of life in a nuclear holocaust is mind numbing. As heroic legend Daniel Ellsberg said at the rally before the launch: "This is only one missile being launched, can you imagine hundreds, or thousands, of missiles being launched and it being the last thing humanity sees?" The US Military Industrial Complex has poisoned the Marshall Islands for generations, and this missile was just another drop in their nuclear slop bucket.

As stated, Daniel Ellsberg was there at the protest, along with long-time launch opponent Fr. Louis Vitale who figured he has been arrested 108 times at Vandenberg (to add to his opposition to the School of Assassins, where he has been arrested and spent significant time in prison). After the short rally, I jumped at the chance to cross the actual line with them that separates real America from Vandenberg AFB where dozens of MPs awaited this "trespassing" by about 17 protesters.

Among the group were also three amazing Bay Area CODEPINK activists and Judy Talaugon, a Chumash woman who, after welcoming the colonizers (we protesters) to her land and giving us approval for being there, she marched over that line with us to inform the US Military that it was "illegally" occupying sacred Chumash land. One of the buzz-headed MPs cracked, "I am an

American; I am here legally." However, he wasn't moved by logical reply that every one of us in the protest line were "Americans" and that meant that we must also be there "legally" and that if he proceeded to place us under arrest, that must logically be deemed "illegal."

After the most invasive search (molestation) that I have ever experienced during a detention from one of the apparently female MPs (only one other activist was as violated as I was), I was handcuffed and put into a van with Dan, Fr. Louis, and four other women, two of whom had never been arrested before. As a matter of fact, many of the 17 who were arrested were "first timers." Except for the usual wonderful camaraderie that occurs in these situations, the rest of our detention was boring processing until we were driven in the same van about five miles away from the base and unceremoniously dumped in the parking lot of Vandenberg Village, a small shopping center, at around 3am. I wondered aloud if we were going to get "ten bucks and a new suit of clothes."

As our cuffs were being cut off (yes, we were cuffed the entire time), the ground began to rumble and a loud noise began to emanate from the direction of the base. The MPs stopped what they were doing to gaze adoringly in the direction of the launch, while we activists paused in horror and sorrow. One of the MPs actually choked out, "That's the sound of freedom."

Speechless.

The sound of a Minute Man 3 missile being launched is the sound of abject tyranny.

It's the sound of the tortured screams of the Japanese being incinerated in their beds or slowly poisoned to death by deadly radiation exposure.

It's the sound of a child whimpering with pain in Basra, Iraq, because she contracted leukemia or another cancerous condition due to the US's use of depleted uranium in her country. It's also the sound of her doctor crying with frustration because he can't treat her properly due to the lack of medicine or other treatments available to him. It's the sound of dirt being shoveled for her grave and the tortured cries of her parents.

The launch of one more missile is the sound of handcuffs being tightened at the back (click, click, click—Ow!) around the wrists of one more peaceful protester. Or worse yet, it's the sound of tear gas canisters being shot into a crowd or students being pepper sprayed while sitting with arms linked in peaceful resistance. This is not in Syria or North Korea and these sounds are becoming more frequent here in the "homeland."

Freedom? What if, instead of hearing the launch, Sergeant MP was hearing the deafening whine of approaching doom? Would his first thought be "freedom?" Or would his last thought be, "Shit, this is it?"

The sound of a Minute Man 3 missile being fired is the sound of silence ringing in the halls of many schools that are forced to close doors because of the absolute fealty this nation pays to the military industrial complex. As one of my contacts said, "It's like firing an elementary school into space."

This absolute fealty to the industry of death and destruction will inevitably lead to the sound of the collapse of Empire. The collapse of Empire will sound like Armageddon to some, but will be music to the ears of others.

The Green Tortoise left Vandenberg at about 4am filled with three-dozen tired, but happy protesters. We napped, we sang, we talked on the seven hour trip home. It was the sound of anger, frustration, and sorrow, but it was also the sound of resolve and success. I firmly believe that our, for lack of a better term, "witness" at the event had a profound impact on at least one of the MPs, and who knows who else?

One of our comrades in the bus stated that he "supported Democrats" because historically, the trends are better when a Democrat is in power. After reminding him that a Democrat dropped not one, but two, bombs and about the "Carter Doctrine" or Presidential Directive 48, a tired, but tranquil Fr. Louie spoke up:

"Obama has said that NO option is off the table in dealing with Iran—so we have to assume that includes nuking a school full of Iranian children."

And people wonder why I don't pay federal income taxes?

We detainees were cited and released, but we will be forced soon to travel down to Santa Barbara to be arraigned. Some will plead "guilty" and pay a fine anywhere from $250 to as high as $5000 —mostly because going to Santa Barbara is a huge inconvenience.

This struggle began a long time ago when physicist Albert Einstein founded the world's first anti-nuke organization and it continues. I know at least for myself and Daniel Ellsberg and a few others, we will plead, "Hell no, not guilty," and fight the higher crime of nuclear weapons.

CINDY NOTE: The resolution of this case will also be unveiled.

Sunday, March 4, 2012
Free the Cuban Five Statement

I will be reading this statement near the US Embassy in Dublin today.

Free the Cuban Five Campaign Ireland

March 5, 2012

Dear President Obama,

As a citizen of the United States of America whose son Casey died in Iraq allegedly protecting his country against terrorism in an invasion that was based on lies and destruction, I call on you to free the Five Cuban anti-terrorists, four of whom are still incarcerated in US prisons.

The fifth, René Gonzalez, was released last October from Marianna prison in Florida after serving his full unjust sentence having been found guilty on charges of conspiracy based on a legally flawed court hearing in Miami. René is also a citizen of the US and was entitled to a fair trial with an unprejudiced jury, a situation that was impossible for him to have in that city.

Roberto González, René's only sibling and an important member of the Cuban Five's legal team, is gravely ill with cancer in a Havana hospital. Although René has served his unjust sentence of more than 13 years in US prison, as a punitive measure he is being forced to serve a further three years' probation in the United States. As a result he is unable to be with his brother at this critical time, unless he receives special permission to do so.

His attorney, Phil Horowitz, has filed an emergency court petition requesting permission for René to return to Cuba for only two weeks to visit his brother in the hospital. The petition states, "Over the past nearly five months since his release from incarceration, the defendant has faithfully complied with each and every condition of his supervised release." Horowitz says, "The motion that is being filed is not unusual; it is common for a defendant to seek court permission on an emergency basis, to travel internationally for health concerns of a family member."

I urge you, President Obama, to immediately allow René to travel to Cuba for two weeks as a humanitarian gesture.

René is also suffering the absence of his wife, Olga, who he hasn't seen since he was imprisoned nearly 14 years ago because US immigration will not give Olga a visa to travel to Miami to see him. This is also a tragic situation that needs to be addressed.

You have the power, Mr. President, to grant permission for the Cuban Five to return home to Cuba where they belong. You have the power, Mr. President, to make sure that Olga gets a visa to enter the US to see her beloved husband, Rene. You have the power, Mr. President, to make sure that René Gonzalez goes to Havana for two weeks to see his dying brother.

For the sake of humanity, Mr. President, exercise that power.

Cindy Lee Sheehan

Tuesday, March 13, 2012
The US Empire is the Bad Apple

This incident is tragic and shocking, and does not represent the exceptional character of our military and the respect that the United States has for the people of Afghanistan.
US President Obama following the slaughter of 16 Afghans
in an unprovoked rampage in Panjwai district of Kandahar

On April 4, 2004, I returned home from walking our two dogs, Buster and Chewy, to find three US Army officers standing in my living room—there to deliver the news that one of my four children had been killed in Iraq.

Life as I knew it was over at that instant, and it has been a steep climb back to what Warren G. Harding called: Normalcy.

On Sunday, I think many of us were shocked at the news of a US soldier who went on a violent, unprovoked rampage against civilians in Panjwai district. Details are slowly emerging that this soldier had a mild brain injury, was on his fourth deployment (three in Iraq, and this one in Afghanistan, which began in December), and was having marital difficulties. There are millions of us who have had health problems and have struggled simultaneously with marital problems, or other stressors in a capitalist society, and who do not subsequently slaughter 16 people, so I am not excusing the soldier's behavior.

This is the part of the story that I find most moving:

The soldier entered the home of Samid Khan and killed 11 of his family members, including four little girls, six years and younger. Samid and one of his children, a son, were spared because they were away from the village at the time.

First of all, what kind of sick monster enters a home and slaughters little girls while they sleep? Eighty-five percent of Samid's family was massacred that night. The US military had given this soldier mental health clearance and a clean bill of physical health to be redeployed for a fourth time to a war zone. Former US Secretary of Defense Donald Rumsfeld famously and arrogantly claimed while visiting troops in Kuwait: "You go to war with the army you have, not the army you want." Well, if this is an example of the "Army we have," then we better get our asses home, and in a just country Rumsfeld would be occupying a cell at Leavenworth.

The four little sisters were not even born on 9/11, when the US rushed to war in the future country of their birth to go after one man that may, or may not, have been involved in that attack. One by one the sisters were born into a war-torn nation that would be home to them for such a short time, in what I am sure was a rough and precarious existence. Yet, the sisters became the latest victims of another "Bad Apple" in the huge cesspool of Bad Apples that rape their fellow female troops, urinate on dead people, burn holy books, torture prisoners, bomb wedding parties, pilot drones carrying hellfire missiles from thousands of miles away, etc., etc., etc.

Secondly, in the tragedy of Samid, my life was destroyed by the news of the death of one of my children. I cannot imagine coming home from a trip to find my entire family massacred by such a barbaric, yet random, act. The floors of Samid's home were covered in blood and the walls covered with the gore of what used to be his family. My heart screams in pain for Samid and my being cries for justice—justice that I have so far been denied; justice that won't bring his family back or give him any kind of recompense, but justice that is demanded in such a case.

The soldier will be tried by the military and the foxes that guard the henhouse will guarantee that this individual madman won't have too harsh a punishment while someone who tried to stop the killing, Pvt. Bradley Manning, has had to endure torturous conditions for allegedly leaking information to Wikileaks.

Even though I do think the soldier who perpetrated these acts of mass murder needs to be held to account, I think the mega Bad Apples who sent him there and refuse to even reconsider the "mission" need to have their heads on the proverbial chopping block, too.

Atrocities have been committed in war since the beginning of time and I think we can stipulate that the US Empire is the global Bad Apple. However, war is barbaric and war encourages barbarism. The only way to stop such barbarism is to finally, once and for all, stop using war as a tool in the repertoire of foreign policy.

This is a note to parents everywhere: The US military, war profiteers, and Empire DO NOT CARE about the children of the world and they DO NOT CARE about your child. If you have a child contemplating going into the service of the banksters and war profiteers, remember the case of this Bad Apple and the people he murdered in cold blood. Remember my son Casey—it's hard enough having to mourn Casey everyday—I can't imagine being Samid, or the mother of the Bad Apple who committed the crimes. Do you want to be me, Samid, or the mother or father of yet another Bad Apple? I hope your answer is an emphatic, "NO!"

Obama's statement that I quoted above should ring hollow to those of us who have been hearing such statements our entire lives in one manifestation of barbarism or the other. In fact, Obama is contemplating other acts of Bad Appleism as we speak and cannot be let off the hook, either.

Afghan President Hamid Karzai has expressed his hollow outrage over this incident, and the people of Afghanistan should insist that this puppet of US imperialism leave with the deadly occupation.

When I awakened on Sunday morning with the news that this tragedy had occurred, one of my first thoughts was, "I am glad that I didn't contribute one thin dime to this cluster f#$k."

As activists who called for complete, total, immediate, and unconditional withdrawal while Bush was president we should be doing the same with a Democrat as Bad Apple in Chief.

How much more evidence do we need that Democratic wars are just as pervasive, wrong, and deadly as Republican wars?

CINDY NOTE: I would hate to see how Obama would treat the world if he didn't have "respect."

Thursday, April 21, 2014
Peace Has a Day in Court

For those of you who know me and have been following my story, you know that part of my resistance to the US Empire is my refusal to pay income taxes.

This morning (April 19th), a new episode unfolded in my ongoing struggle with the IRS and the Empire the agency is nestled in.

I was subpoenaed to appear in the 9th Circuit court of the US Federal Court system in Sacramento, California—my state's capitol.

For background, I have had two meetings with the IRS agent assigned to my case where I expressed to him my unwillingness, due to my principles, to participate in funding a system that commits crimes almost every second of every day. At this point, the IRS is trying to collect 105 grand that it says I owe for the tax years 2005–2006. I first became a war tax refuser in 2005.

My defense is one based on a far superior morality than one practiced by the US government and the fact that my outspokenness against this immorality, and my notoriety in doing so, has put me into a precarious position in a climate where free speech and peaceful protest is being suppressed, sometimes violently, as we have increasingly witnessed.

In the past, after about 15 arrests, I have also had many opportunities to appear in court, federal and otherwise, in front of judges who never showed one bit of compassion or sympathy towards the protesters' first amendment right trumping the government's harsh rules and laws profoundly inhibiting those rights.

I have never once "gotten off" using a defense based on the Bill of Rights of the US Constitution.

In that Bill of Rights, there's an especially pesky little First Amendment that says:

"Congress shall make no law respecting an establishment of religion, or prohibiting the free exercise thereof; or abridging the freedom of speech, or of the press; or the right of the people peaceably to assemble, and to petition the Government for a redress of grievances."

Yet Congress and other legislative bodies routinely pass these laws prohibiting the free exercise of speech and the right to peaceably assemble, and our protests become more and more meaningless as we are pushed farther and farther away from our, for want of a better word, targets. In addition, the police state is increasingly chasing protesters away by tear gas, pepper spray, rubber bullets, sound weaponry, and other supposedly "non-lethal" means.

When I decided to be a conscientious objector to war tax, I knew that the consequence could be harassment and/or punishment, but I decided to do it long before I became well known as a gadfly to Empire. I was willing to accept those consequences because I felt that if I were put on trial, the reasons that I don't fund war crimes would have to also be put on trial, and I think it's the only way that the illegality of the wars can actually get a hearing.

I have an advisor who is an experienced tax attorney and also advises the National War Tax Resister's Coordinating Committee. He feels that the Empire may be targeting me to get publicity and to intimidate others from taking the same course of action that I actually encourage others to do. Although he could inform me as to what usually happens every step of the way, he also said my case could be "special" and contain many surprises, a few of which occurred in court today.

Before I continue, I'd like to say that since I have become an antiwar "criminal," my respect for the legal profession has grown by leaps and bounds. I have always managed to attract some amazing attorneys to help me in my cases and always on a pro bono basis and this case is no exception. My attorney of record in California is San Francisco attorney, Dennis Cunningham, who has been involved in numerous protest cases, and advising us is Peter Goldberger in Pennsylvania. I am so thankful for the help of my attorneys and for the NWRTCC and I honestly don't know what I would do without their legal help and peer support.

There was a pre-hearing rally in Sacramento today and supporters came from Los Angeles, Ventura, San Jose, San Francisco, Nevada City, and Sacramento—we filled the small courtroom after the rally.

After we went through security and had to relinquish cameras and the signs we had pinned to us showing my son's picture and my picture with NO WAR TAXES printed on top, we went to the courtroom where my hearing was the final one on a short docket of four.

133

We were arguing that I had a First Amendment right to the protest and a Fifth Amendment right against self-incrimination. The attorney for the IRS and her buddies that traveled from DC (yes, of course, this is not a political persecution) argued that a "blanket fifth" is not allowed by case law and rulings and she wanted me to be ordered to go to a room in the federal building to answer questions about my "assets." (My lawyer brilliantly argued that the "secret" agencies already had all that information on me, anyway)—but there was no way that I was going to be blindsided by an unwarranted demand like that and this is where some extraordinary things happened.

Dennis was able to expound at length about our fears of political retribution and my moral opposition to the wars, and he was able to iterate that I was against militarism and the huge proportion of our taxes that go towards it. This is what I have always wanted—the position of Peace had its day in court today! I was thrilled beyond belief, but what happened when Dennis finished literally blew me away.

The Magistrate who presided over the hearing, John Moulds, is an older man who my attorney said has been on the bench for years and years, but is known to be "fair" and not too "excitable."

The Magistrate said that he read all of our motions and he looked me right in the eyes from across the room and with great emotion in his voice he said, "It strikes me as a civilized way to protest uncivilized acts." (Reuters) I actually started to cry because it was such a beautiful thing to say in such a loving way and I can't ever recall anyone in the government and/or establishment that has ever genuinely acknowledged my pain and practically admitted that what happened to Casey and my family was disordered. Oh, many democrats pretended that they were sorry for my pain, but they were only doing it for crass political gain—and when the republicans acknowledged it, they were "thanking" me for my son's brave service to the country—I don't know which approach was worse, but I felt no compassion until today.

Then the lady from DC said that she could "sympathize with conscientious objectors" but "losing a son" was no excuse to "break the law with impunity." What's the Empire's excuse for breaking the law with impunity in many ways on every day?

Dennis and I agreed to meet with the IRS at a future date so I could do a line-by-line Fifth Amendment claim to each question, and the lady from DC requested that the magistrate order me to comply and show up for the meeting. He said something like, "I want the parties to talk, this hearing is over and I have 45 days to make a ruling one way or the other on your motion—I may, or I may not." According to Peter, this is also something unprecedented.

I came away feeling very energized and encouraged by today's proceedings, and if the Empire wants to make someone cower before them in fear to intimidate others, they picked the wrong person. Even if the magistrate hadn't been so favorable to our side, I still would feel triumphant.

The fissures of imperial overreach and excess are widening and the Empire is being exposed for the ridiculous bully it really is.

No Empire lasts forever and the terribly destructive nature of ours requires us to help its inevitable collapse. I am doing everything I can in my own small ways with all the courage I can muster and I appreciate all the support and help I get along the way.

CINDY NOTE: *My struggles with the IRS are almost resolved with this hearing, etc.*

Saturday, May 12, 2012
Afghanistan, like Vietnam, Except Nobody Gives a Shit

Dear Friend,

This weekend as we celebrate mothers, it's important to remember that there are mothers all over the world who are in pain because of war and economic oppression. It's also important to remember that Julia Ward suggested this holiday way back in 1870 for peace through her Mother's Day Proclamation.

For me, it's distressing that "liberals" are gleeful over the fact that the president is personally in favor of same-sex marriage (although it doesn't actually change a thing, except he received one million campaign dollars within an hour) while not protesting either in word or deed Obama's drone program and war in Afghanistan.

I am hoping that the NATO protests (remember NATO is just an euphemism for US Imperialism) in Democrat Rahm Emanuel's Chicago next week (I will be there) are large and non-partisan; but, in fact, the largest coalition to protest at the DNC has changed its name so as not to appear it's protesting the Democrats so as not to offend anybody.

I have been blessed with three wonderful surviving children and now four grandbabies and I can be secure that even though a drone overhead may be spying on me, it isn't equipped with hellfire missiles. It's safe to say that every mother in the US will be safe from having their home raided by the US military and having their children slaughtered while they sleep.

I don't know what to do anymore. Why aren't we out in the streets in droves protesting the Drone Bomber and his wars? Why do we worship his words and not protest his deeds? Where are the large war protests during the Vietnam or even Bush eras? Even though Mother's Day is not a happy day for me, I try to put myself in the sandals of a woman in Afghanistan, Gaza, Pakistan, or some other hot zone—and when I look across the miles at the US, I wonder why no one cares about my family and me.

Sunday, June 10, 2012
"Master, please."

Free elections of masters does not abolish the masters or the slaves.
Herbert Marcuse, 1964

It seems that our president is a totally amoral psychopath,
and the revelation of his condition has not hurt his popularity.
Apparently the president governs psychopaths too, because too few of them will say or do anything to oppose his commitment to breaking the law, violating the Constitution, and the word of the god he claims to believe in.
Margaret Kimberley, Black Agenda Report

Emancipate yourselves from mental slavery, none but ourselves can free our minds!
Bob Marley

Ever get the feeling you're living in a nation where the (s)elected officials revel in their megalomania and think we should, too?

Recently, the paper of the status quo, the *New York Times,* gave space to the braggadocio of several members of the current Dictator for the 1%. Some "unnamed sources" boasted with mucho machismo, and not one ounce of shame, about Obama's Hit List (which is called a "Kill List" by the establishment) and the meetings the President with a Grim Reaper Fetish chairs each and every week to put his Imperial Imprimatur on the execution orders.

We also learned that the US, for Israel, has been waging cyber-warfare on Iran for years and, of course, instead of being outraged that the US Constitution, international law, and civil liberties are being severely breeched, the political establishment is outraged at the people who would "leak" such information. Ever the conman, Obama feigned fake hurt at a press conference on Friday, June 8th, that someone would even suggest that "my White House" would intentionally leak such things. I call "B.S." on that one: The arrogance of the Bush regime has been vastly surpassed by the conceit of the Obama scandal, and the only difference is there has been little protest against Obama's Hit List.

I was one of the leading Impeach Bush/Cheney activists for a few years and the only thing that really happened was that the Democrats hastened my political disillusionment and enlightenment by refusing to investigate the Bush crime regime, a policy that Obama's DOJ continues to this day. Before I was arrested in his office with about 49 other people demanding impeachment be put "on the table" in July of 2007, I was a welcomed guest of John Conyers, then Chair of the House Judiciary Committee.

At least two national peace organizations (Voters for Peace and Veterans for Peace) have passed resolutions calling for the impeachment of Barack Obama; and I know the Veteran's resolution has the same language as the one passed calling for the impeachment of Bush, but there is no large national movement on the left (or, as far as I know, the right either) advocating for this Constitutional "remedy."

Now that I have been around the block more times than Carter has pills, I am thinking that the "Founders" of this country set up this whole impeachment thing to fail in the first place. I do not belong to the Cult of the Founders, or the Constitution, because I think the Founders were men who belonged to the 1% of their time and the Constitution was written by them to keep their money and power secure. Of course, the Bill of Rights was a "liberal" addition, but the descendants of the original 1% have made sure that document would be in "paper only."

Even though I believe probably every US administration should be impeached, here is why I have become an impeachment skeptic:

Firstly, our elections have become so compromised by money, cheating, propaganda, and apathy, and the person who ascends to the highest post in our land can only be there with the consent of the elite. The Electoral College effectively took what the Founders considered such an important event out of the hands of the unwashed masses, anyway. If you think your vote counts for anything except giving your consent to be misruled, you're participating in some magical thinking of your own.

Secondly, the process of impeachment has been used only a few times and, as anyone with an average IQ could predict, the process has been motivated by pure political partisanship. The investigation of Nixon and his subsequent resignation came the closest to the impeachment tool actually working, except the criminal removed himself to not destroy the apparent legitimacy of an office he used as his own private crime syndicate (as have every other POTUS—some are just clearly worse than others). In recompense for his resignation, Nixon was pardoned for his crimes and one of his biggest co-conspirators, Henry Kissinger, is still alive and well and prospering.

Finally, We the People should have the power to remove a "leader" from office and advocate for the establishment to police itself for real crimes is unrealistic. We shouldn't have to keep begging "Master" for a few crumbs from his table. We the People were not trusted by the original elitists because they were afraid of our power, so the entire country is set up where only the political establishment and its puppet masters can change anything. The global elite has effectively neutralized the international community, and to be searching for justice and peace in those institutions is a waste of time.

Margaret Kimberley hit the nail squarely on the head with her analysis of psychopathology and we who are sane-o-pathic seem to be on the same reasoned and healthy path.

Had enough? Ready to do something besides vote and bitch/bitch and vote? Non-violent revolution is our only option if we really want the world to be a better place for us—all of us.

Instead of transitioning the righteous and grassroots protest into a failed political campaign to benefit Democrats, activists in Wisconsin could have organized to shut down the state until their demands were met. Similarly from the right, many well-meaning and well-intentioned people fell for the Ron Paul (R) hype machine only to be crushed when his campaign predictably failed and his progeny, Senator from Kentucky, Rand (R-wacko), enthusiastically endorsed the Republiscum candidate, Mitt Romney. US federal politics will always fold, spindle, and mutilate one if you actually have compassion and a brain.

The key is working outside the system to create healthy communities of our own—the 1% own and control the status quo and know how to manipulate it to its own advantage one hundred percent of the time. If the 99% owned and controlled our own systems, we could do the same.

There are many models for this from Transition Towns to the revolution that I propose in *Myth America: 20 Greatest Myths of the Robber Class and the Case for Revolution.*

To close, I recently received an email from a supporter who urges me to throw my support to Democratic politicians and candidates so I can have "hope" again. How cynical is a "hope" that relies on the Democratic Party for existence? Is it not possible to have "hope" if one does not support a violent and greedy institution? Does this person think I wallow in bed all day "hope"-less now that I have seen clearly the problem? And what is "hope" anyway besides a manipulative campaign slogan?

Nope to "hope." Positive action in the direction of Peace and Justice and stopping occasionally to "smell the roses" and avoid the stench of the status quo is what we need in my very humble opinion!

CINDY NOTE: I am adding this piece to this book a few days after the Republicans reclaimed the Senate and added seats in Congress, and Obama has already escalated Imperial hostilities in Iraq, Syria, and Ukraine.

Monday, July 2, 2012
Beware the Electoral Industrial Complex

So, here we are again in the middle of another sham Federal election cycle—it's almost (exactly) like we never left the last one!

The faux-gressive set is in the middle of paroxysms of joy over the sham Supreme Court's recent sham ruling that taxing people because they can't afford to buy health care from private, for profit, companies is somehow Constitutional. I am not a Constitutional scholar, like our president, but somehow forcing poor working-class people to fork over non-existent dollars to private companies for lousy coverage doesn't seem A) Constitutional, or B) Moral.

The re-gressive set is in the middle of paroxysms of angst because of the same Supreme Court ruling. As far as I can tell it's because they very idiotically think that the country is treacherously sliding into Socialism (I wish) and they all want to move to Canada, now (which has national health care).

ObamaCare is neither "Socialism" nor "Progressivism:" it's fascism. Someone who knew the difference, totalitarian Benito Mussolini, purportedly said that fascism should rightly be called, "Corporatism" because it's the union of state and corporate power. Maybe Mussolini didn't say those exact words, but there is a grain of truth in that quote, historically and prophetically. There's a huge difference between having the right to buy health insurance and the human right to health care.

Similarly, the faux-gressive set went bonkers when Barry and Michelle came out of the closet to announce that they were "personally" in favor of same-sex marriage. I say, "So, the crap, what?" I really don't care what toothpaste the president and first lady favor; or what kind of wine they drink; or what they do or don't do in their bedroom; or what god they pray or don't pray to; or if they are in favor of same-sex marriage. What I do care about is that Obama is apparently in favor of bombing wedding parties in foreign countries and his pronouncement to bolster his base of gleeful Democrats did nothing to change policy one iota. Obama said he would "leave it to the states," so he is for oppression of gay rights, only on a smaller scale.

The regressive set also went "bonkers" after this gay marriage pronouncement, but in a different way. The regressive set also thinks that Obama should be bombing more wedding parties, while the faux-gressive set seems to be blocking that grisly little detail out with their blue-tinted Fact Blocker glasses that only work if a (D) infests the White House.

However, the exploitation of this basic human right is not just a wedge issue. After the pronouncement, the Obama campaign sent out a fundraising email and raked in boatloads of money AND there was a fundraiser in Hollywood that netted $15 million for the campaign. I think paying 40 grand for one plate of food to be able to share dinner with a murderer is immoral while so many starve—but, hey, Romney probably raised a lot of money from anti-marriage equality people that day, too.

There are many examples of wedge issues that rile up the electorate that really have nothing to do with profound policy changes that are amenable to the so-called 99%. This entire health care issue is just a great example because the Democratic apologists that are extolling the "virtues" of the recent SCOTUS decision don't even sense the irony (or maybe they do and are part of the propaganda team) that one of their talking points is that ObamaCare is almost exactly like the RomneyCare that was passed while Mitt was governor of Massachusetts. And doesn't it bother the faux that their guy's plan is essentially a Republican one that was written by an industry that contributed $20 million to his 2008 campaign? According to a 2010 story in *Raw Story,* McCain received only $7.7 million from the "health"care industry. The insurance companies clearly got the most bang for their buck out of Obama as the mandate gives them millions of new customers! However, McCain would have found some way to pay back the bribes . . . oops, I mean, "campaign contributions."

The faux-gressive set is so super-duper upset that the Koch brothers are donating to Mitt, while their dude has his own Super Pacs (apparently that's okay) and has publicly declared that he wants to raise one billion dollars for his re-election. One billion: that's a ONE and NINE zeros and fully obscene.

Campaigns are no longer, if they ever were, based on debate over issues that really matter to the ordinary person: Life, liberty, and the pursuit of happiness. Campaigns are now barely disguised extortion where the bribe money goes to enrich Madison Avenue and candidates are packaged and shoved down our throats. We end up "buying" something that isn't either "new and improved" or "innovative" and the product is definitely something the entire world would be better off without.

The "lesser of two evils" meme is also a logical fallacy in this world of prepackaged, processed, product. First of all, to think that Obama is even the "lesser of two evils" is incorrect, as pointed out by Glen Ford of the Black Agenda Report: Obama is "awesomely evil." Secondly, would you choose Product A over Product B because it would poison you just a little more slowly than Product B? No, of course you wouldn't. You would find a way to do without that product.

The Electoral Industrial Complex is intimately connected to DDE's "Military Industrial Complex" which is tied with the "Peace Industrial Complex" and the "Prison Industrial Complex" and the "Big Pharma Industrial Complex" and so on, and our participation in it gives it legitimacy that it does not deserve. Pure and simple, your vote gives your consent to be misgoverned by profiteers.

Voting in a federal election is feeding into the crimes of the 1%. Yet, due to our conditioning as members of an Empire, we are herded like cattle to the slaughterhouse thinking that an essential part of our bodies may fall off if we don't vote. Guess what? That's simply not true.

Vote if some vestigial programming won't allow you to not vote, but don't quit there.

What's the alternative to choosing the most cosmetically appealing oppressor and participating in our own oppression, you ask? Good question!

Planned, local revolution. It takes more effort than walking down the street to vote, but the outcome can be more satisfying and effective.

Saturday, July 28, 2012
Roseanne Barr/Cindy Sheehan 2012 Press Release

ROSEANNE BARR ANNOUNCES RUNNING MATE FOR PRESIDENTIAL CAMPAIGN

Roseanne Barr announced that Cindy Sheehan will be her running mate in her bid for the Peace and Freedom Party's nomination for President. Sheehan is an antiwar activist who first gained national attention for her protest camp outside then-President Bush's Texas ranch.

Barr said, "Cindy and I are the 'Throw the Bums Out' ticket and the 'Ballot Access' ticket. We want people to register in the Peace and Freedom Party so that the party can keep its ballot status in California." After the passage of the "Top Two primary" in 2010, alternative political parties lost one of their ways of staying on the ballot. The Peace and Freedom Party needs approximately 40,000 more registrants to maintain its ballot status beyond 2014. "We also want people to start Peace and Freedom Parties in other states," added Barr.

Former Georgia Congresswoman Cynthia McKinney, who has been working closely with Barr on this campaign, commented, "Access to the ballot is a civil rights issue that needs attention across the country. If voters only have two choices, both of which represent the same interests, then we don't really have a democracy." McKinney went on to describe a higher standard of democracy, "When I was in Congress, I promoted proportional representation for legislatures. This is the only way to make our democracy representative of the people, rather than the corporate donors."

The Peace and Freedom Party nominating convention takes place on Saturday August 4th in Los Angeles. Cat Woods, an officer of the Peace and Freedom Party, echoed Barr on the party's emphasis on ballot access. She said that the party hoped to "draw attention to the ongoing erosion of alternative parties' access to the ballot and how this directly deprives voters of control of their government."

When asked whether she supported the Barr ticket, Woods added, "Our party needs to reach a wider audience with its message of socialist solutions. Roseanne Barr and Cindy Sheehan can bring that."

Responding to charges that she could "steal votes" from Obama or "spoil the election," Barr said, "The American people are sick and tired of this 'lesser evil' garbage they get fed every election year. Both the Democrats and the Republicans do the same evils once they're in office. I'm here to tell the voters: If you want to tell the government and the two domineering parties that you're sick and tired of all their evil, register in the Peace and Freedom Party and vote for me and Cindy."

To contact the Roseanne for President campaign, contact campaign@roseanneforpresident.org

-End-

CINDY NOTE: Thus began a very strange and stressful time for me.

Sunday, August 5, 2012
Barr/Sheehan 2012 vs. The War Party

Just found out today (August 4, 2012) that Roseanne Barr and I were given the confidence and nomination of the Peace and Freedom Party of California at the nominating convention. Even though Roseanne is Roseanne and I have been a member of the party for almost four years, the nomination wasn't in the bag—there were some high hurdles we had to leap first and we did it (with our great, if not small, team) in less than a week!

The Peace and Freedom Party is the only Socialist/Feminist Party with ballot status (for the time being) here in California and many left wing parties or independents vie for the Presidential nomination of our party—so there were originally five tickets seeking the nod: Alexander/Mendoza of SPUSA; Anderson/Rodriguez of the newly formed Justice Party; Durham/Lopez of the Freedom Socialist Party; Lindsay/Osorio of the Party for Socialism and Liberation and Barr/Sheehan of the Peace and Freedom Party (I was added to the ticket just one week ago today).

What made our nomination more and more likely as the week wore on were two things that happened: Though Rocky Anderson had won the PFP primary in June, the primary is non-binding and the nomination occurs at the convention. Well, Anderson did not do the work within the party that needed to be done to consolidate delegates in order to secure the nomination and ballot line AND he is decidedly not a Socialist and didn't even endorse our candidate, Marsha Feinland, for US Senate in June. Anderson discovered that his chances were minimal for getting the nomination and he withdrew the day the convention began. We all wish him well.

However, the most important thing that worked in the favor of Barr/Sheehan was the wonderful act of solidarity that the Party for Socialism and Liberation made on the behalf of our ticket. Peta Lindsay is only 28 and she was leading up the PSL ticket with amazing energy, intelligence, and commitment. Being only 28, though, the California Secretary of State pulled her name off the ballot and she withdrew her candidacy for PFP today at the convention and urged her committed delegates and the undecided delegates to vote for Barr/Sheehan.

I spoke on behalf of the Barr/Sheehan ticket at the candidate forum last night in the president's slot and took questions and gave statements, and then Roseanne (who is being roasted by Comedy Central tonight) blew into the convention today and literally blew everyone away with her humorous, yet deep, analysis of the issues and the way socialism can address them and help lead us to the promised land of: Full employment; Medicare for all; free education from pre-school to university; housing as a right; a sustainable, clean environment; and, most of all, peace!

I had another few minutes to speak today, and I am always introduced as an "antiwar activist," but my resumé has fleshed out a little over the years. I have been traveling the world working with socialist organizations and, especially in Latin America, witnessing socialist revolution at work.

Being a dedicated anti-imperialist, I have seen how the two major parties in this country are both dedicated to war, war, and more war for profit. Looking for peace in the Democratic Party is like looking for integrity in the Corporate Media—it's just not there in a significant way.

All of the socialist-democratic countries I have been to not only recognize, but are committed to the idea of national sovereignty—they rightfully don't want anyone messing in their countries and they return the favor—much to the consternation of the US/British/Israeli military junta.

Because I believe it's the only way to peace and planetary disarmament, I am a convert to, and now an evangelical for, socialist revolution. I have witnessed, before my eyes, the transformation of societies from illiterate, disempowered peasantry to educated and empowered vital members of society.

Socialism has an undeserved stigma in this country because the capitalists surely don't want us to know that there is a better way of doing things and there has been a dedicated smear campaign against socialism since at least WWII. Yet, I have been in the meetings where dry Marxist jargon is bandied about and sometimes I don't even know what the hell they're talking about.

Roseanne and I believe that the only way to stop this Evil Empire from its crimes is to relate to the masses in a way that the jargon can't. Roseanne is from the working-class and I always have been and always will be. Neither one of us are fluent in the jargon, but we can speak the language of the worker: He/she; white/black/brown/yellow/red; Republican/Democrat/Socialist/; Christian/Muslim/Jew/atheist—we all face the same issues and we are all having the life sucked out of us by the Evil Empire that has two heads where one looks strangely like Mitt Romney and the other one is the spitting image of Barack Obama.

Roseanne and I can help form the response that exhibits compassion, intelligence, justice, and peace. Socialism can be defined as "an economic system characterized by social ownership and cooperative management of the means of production, and a political philosophy advocating such a system" but it really is just a system of taking care of each other from cradle to grave and recognizing that we should belong to a community that cares for each other.

There have been a few people who have been appalled by our candidacy thinking that we may "take votes away from Obama" and "cause Romney to win" and there are responses to that one:

Barack Obama does not own your vote.

If you care about peace, justice, and economic equality, he has not earned your vote.

If Obama loses this November it's because he sucks and his presidency has been a failure for the 99% and a windfall for the 1%.

Besides, historically, after the US has constantly bounced from Democrat-Republican-Democrat-Republican-Democrat, etc., haven't you kind of noticed already that it really doesn't matter very much who is president?

It's the cyst-em of control that needs to be overthrown and socialist revolution can do that!

Barr/Sheehan 2012 have two very important people to thank: Cat Woods, a member of the PandFP who worked so hard to get all the ducks in a row, and former Georgia Congresswoman and GPUSA presidential candidate Cynthia McKinney for keeping the dream of Roseanne for President alive.

Go to www.RoseanneforPresident2012.org for more information about the campaign.

CINDY NOTE: As you can tell, I was very excited about the potential of this ticket, which is why the crash for me was so hard!

I believe that a woman's right to reproductive freedom over her own body is an important issue and human right.

I believe that marriage freedom and equality is another important issue and another human right.

At the risk of offending some people (when has that ever stopped me?) I don't think those issues come near to being fundamental key issues. These and other issues aren't called "wedge" for nothing. These issues are designed to drive that proverbial wedge between us down here in the 99%, and instead of the GOP calling for Todd Akin (The Legitimate Rape Dude) to throw in the towel, the 1% should be giving him some kind of medal for pounding that wedge in even more deeply.

And, actually, between the two major parties, the presidential candidates have stated pretty similar positions in the past on abortion rights and gay marriage. It's the things that Obama and Romney agree on that frighten me and should frighten you.

Obama is no "common man" and he may not be worth as much as Romney, but how many of you have $12 million in assets? Also, Obama has protected Goldman Sachs and John Corzine's MF Global (and indeed, Corzine himself) from prosecution. Is it ironic or synchronous that while in Charlotte, NC Obama will "accept the nomination of his party" at Bank of America Stadium? Obama has not been good for jobs, the economy, or workers since he took the helm of this rusty and leaky ship of state. Please, don't tell me about "obstructionist Republicans." Obama had a huge majority of Democrats in the Senate and House in the first two years of his term. It seems THEN would have been the time to fulfill empty campaign rhetoric—if it was anything more than empty campaign rhetoric.

Obama has increased military spending since he became Commander in Chief of US Armed Forces; increased troops to Afghanistan by treble; and he has also increased the use of unmanned aerial vehicles or drones by over 500 percent over his predecessor. I am sure that if Mitt becomes president, those things will continue, but just like under Bush and every Republican before him since *Roe v. Wade, Roe v. Wade* won't be overturned.

Besides Obama bombing Libya, Somalia, Yemen, Iraq, Afghanistan, Pakistan, and etc., his use of a "Kill List" and executing Americans without the due process that's guaranteed to us under the Bill of Rights, the thing that upsets me the most about his regime and the Democrats (in general) is, not only the refusal to hold the Bush regime accountable for war crimes and crimes against the peace and humanity, but how Obama's DOJ protects them while persecuting people like me for being a war-tax resister and alleged whistle blowers like Bradley Manning who are trying to STOP THE WAR CRIMES.

Recently, two significant things happened: Obama's DOJ dropped yet another prosecution against war crimes that happened under the Bush stain, this time for the deaths of detainees in custody due to torture by the CIA. Of course Eric Holder's job is to protect real criminals, not prosecute them.

Then, Nobel Peace Prize winner Bishop Desmond Tutu came out in favor of George Bush and his poodle, Tony Blair, being tried at The Hague for the war in Iraq.

Of course, I have been calling for that for eight years. Accountability is personal to me: I want justice for my son's death and the death of over one million others. However, I am just a Nobel Peace Prize reject, and I wouldn't stop there! However, the Nobel Peace Laureate Obama has carried on the war crimes of the US war machine and his administration should be brought up on charges in The Hague, too.

I am running for Vice Presidency of the US, not because I think Barr/Sheehan 2012 will be victorious and we will "clean house" in DC (but we would); I am running to challenge some very cores of the Mythocracy of this country: That there is a difference between the Democrats and Republicans or that elections "matter" or are even legitimate. Unfortunately, we will not be able to vote our way out of the mess we are in and socialist revolution is the only way out.

I have seen socialist revolution in action in other countries and I know we can do it here—it will just take a little more sacrifice than walking a few doors down on Election Day to cast your vote for more war, more economic oppression, and more environmental devastation.

Vote for life; vote for Socialism, vote for Barr/Sheehan in November and then roll up your sleeves for the hard, but rewarding work ahead!

CINDY NOTE: Soon, I was to figure out that Roseanne Barr was unfortunately not much better than "Robamney."

Tuesday, September 4, 2012
No Longer on Campaign—Formal Announcement

For personal and health reasons, I regret that I have to pull out of active participation in the Barr/Sheehan 2012 campaign. I strongly believe in the Platform as written, and the mission statement of the Peace and Freedom Party, and hope to continue my activism when my health improves. As to the personal reasons, Candidate Barr and I have irreconcilable differences on how best to serve the Peace and Freedom Party. I believe between my health issues and the disparity of our Political approach, the Campaign, Ms. Barr, and the Party would be better served by my resignation. I wish nothing but good things for the Party and campaign.

UPDATE I: APPARENTLY, IT IS TOO LATE ACCORDING TO STATE POLICIES FOR ME TO RESIGN FROM THE TICKET, BUT I AM WITHDRAWING ACTIVE PARTICIPATION IN CAMPAIGNING. SO, I WILL STILL BE THE VP CHOICE ON BALLOTS (CINDY)

CINDY NOTE: By the time I made this announcement, I was seriously ill with infections that were, I am sure, brought on by the stress of having to try to work with Roseanne. People who want more info can check out my book: I Left My Marbles in San Francisco: The Scandal of Federal Electoral Politricks. (Also on Amazon.com)

Tuesday, September 11, 2012
It's Past Time to End the US War *OF* Terror

On this day, Cindy Sheehan's Soapbox wishes to extend heartfelt sympathy to everyone who was killed that day and since, including, but not limited to, Americans killed on 9/11/2001.

Eleven years of US-led terror in the Middle East and Africa has left devastation in its wake and near financial collapse here on the home front.

A new Democrat president has exploited that tragic day to expand the Bush regime's War *OF* Terror and has been able to continue the policies with a "mandate" from a Democratic base that is willing to literally allow Obama to "get away with murder."

I, as always and forever, mourn the loss of my son Casey in Iraq, but understand that the universal pain my country causes is not limited to just me, or my family.

The wars must be ended before they end all of us.

Thursday, October 4, 2012
A Socialist's Response to The Greatest American Scoundrel Show (Debate)

For the record, I wouldn't normally even watch The Greatest American Scoundrel Show, otherwise known as the "Historic Presidential Debates," but, like it or not, I am running for Vice President of the USA on a Socialist (Peace and Freedom) ticket.

There was an "alternative debate" on Democracy, Now! last night, but even though Candidates Rocky Anderson (Justice Party) and Jill Stein (Green Party) are left of the Blue Tie and Red Tie Scoundrels, who are given a national forum, they are still both Capitalists.

I believe that either Anderson or Stein would be better than Red Tie or Blue Tie, but the Socialist solution is the perfect one, in my opinion. Before The Show began, the onomatopoeia pundit, David Gergen (his voice sounds like he is "gerg"-ling), said that, "Style counts in these debates." Of course "style counts," because the idea that a different color tie makes a difference in substance is absurd. The average USAian is all about style and the choice is going to come down to the "lesser of two Scoundrels," and I am not willing to settle for that.

I am not going to do a piece based on "fact checking," because, to me, it doesn't matter if Blue Tie or Red Tie got their facts wrong or correct, because whatever they say is fundamentally flawed to begin with. Similarly, I am not going to judge which Stylist was victorious (but it seems that the consensus from the left-right is that the Red Tie won), because in November no matter whom you vote for and no matter which color tie is inaugurated, the 99% will lose.

So here are my responses to the few questions that the Ties were asked:

The first question, from a strangely black-eyed Lehrer, was: "What are the major differences between you two on how you would create jobs."

Blue Tie went first and went on a long rant on how his presidency has basically been a failure at this, but of course, blaming (with some verity) the Red Tie that went before him. However, give Blue Tie another four years with failed policies and things will get better this time, he swears it on a stack of holy Federal Reserve Notes. ("I really mean it this time, Baby.") Then Red Tie talked a lot about "middle income" people. Both Ties talked a lot about the "Middle Class." Well, the term "Middle Class" is a ruling class diversion from the fact that the USA has the widest (and growing wider) income disparity in the so-called industrial world. That's an inconvenient fact that the Scoundrels don't want us to know, now isn't it?

The platform of the Peace and Freedom Party calls for 40 hours pay for a 30-hour workweek with NO mandatory overtime to approach full employment with Union wages and a Basic Guaranteed Income (BGI) for income security. Also, the Socialist solution would be to put the means of production into the hands of the workers and transform production to "need-based" not "greed-based." Also, end "free" trade agreements that harm workers in all countries and have little protections for workers' rights or the environment. Both Red Tie and Blue Tie are in favor of the disastrous Trans-Pacific Pact (TPP), which would further destroy the working class, yet enrich the ownership class. True and positive change requires big and bold ideas, not reform of the old and corrupt paradigms already in place.

The next question was about "reducing the deficit" and this is also an easy one for me. Trillions of dollars have been spent on the US War *OF* Terror against the world since 9/11/2001 and the Military Industrial Complex is sucking the economy dry with its murderous greed. The wars should come to a speedy end and the bases that the Empire maintains around the world should be closed and our military should be reduced to the size where it can be "drowned in a bathtub." Our platform also calls for the end to the CIA and other alphabet agencies that wreak havoc at home and abroad. And this leads to the next question. There is PLENTY of wealth and resources in this nation but the national priorities are way out of whack. A re-prioritization of programs would render the next question unnecessary.

The Ties were asked about how they feel about "Entitlements." This is also an easy one for we Socialists to handle. What almost everyone, regardless of income status here in the USA, call "entitlements" the rest of the world calls "human rights." Along with our students, our elders are being asked to shoulder an increasingly heavy burden to maximize profits for people like The Ties and their friends. Retiring with dignity at an age young enough to enjoy retirement and where needs are provided by a grateful community is a human right, not an entitlement, and one which is earned not stolen.

Health Care is also an issue that The Ties fundamentally agree on, but one that couldn't be more different in a Socialist planned economy. We call for a National Health Care Plan that means "everyone in, no one out"— Quality health care for everyone with no opt-out for the wealthy. (In our planned economy, the disparity between the rich and the poor would evaporate and the wealth that belongs to all would be more evenly distributed, anyway). Many countries poorer than ours have successful National Health Care systems and we demand no less. A National Health Care system would create jobs, lower health-care costs and would provide Medicare for all. Seniors and veterans would also be equally assured access and the VA system would no longer be needed (and this would also remove one of the problems that motivates many young people to join the service: Lack of access to quality health care).

The penultimate question to The Ties was: "What do you see as the fundamental role of the government?" Blue Tie opened with, "Keeping Americans safe." Boo! The current real role of the US government is being subservient to all the greed of the 1%: Wall Street, the Military Industrial Complex, Banksters, Big Pharma, Big Ag, Big Energy—and Blue Tie has done a great job serving the real Masters; Red Tie would also excel.

In a Socialist system, the essential role of government is to protect Civil Rights and ensure Human Rights. Blue Tie has been the most aggressive presidential abrogator of both Civil and Human Rights, yet he said that the "genius of America is freedom and the free enterprise system." What, freedom for the few and slavery for the many? True freedom is to be free from the government interfering with our prosperity and peace by intervening to protect the interests of the ruling class.

The final question (thank Jeebus) was asking The Ties how they would break government "gridlock." Again, from The Ties I heard a lot of "blah, blah, and blah." Blue Tie was even "gridlocked" when he had a vast majority of other Blue Ties "serving" in his first two years of office.

"Gridlock" is a problem that would not exist in a Socialist system where decisions for OUR lives, OUR workplaces, OUR economy, OUR environment, OUR security, OUR communities belong to ALL OF US, not just an oligarchy that has anointed themselves as our "lords and protectors."

Red Tie and Blue Tie are "by and for" the one-percenters because, after all, they are one-percenters. Trust what I am about to say to you: Neither Red Tie or Blue Tie give a crap about you, your family, or your community—but you know who does? YOU!

It's about 236 years past time to take control of OUR lives into our hands—notice how I don't say, "back into our hands?" We the People have never had control in this putative oligarchy called the USA.

However, make no mistake about it, either Blue Tie or Red Tie will ascend to the thrown of Protector of the One-Percent in November and the rest of us will lose, again. It's a dance as old as this nation, but Election Day is only one day out of the year.

Dr. Benjamin Spock, who ran for president with the Peace and Freedom Party in 1972, once said, "For us, it's not about the next election, but the next generation."

To the barricades of resistance, my brothers and sisters, for the next generation!

Saturday, October 13, 2012
Tweedle-Dumb and Tweedle-Duh—My Response to the VP Debate

Last week, I commented on what I called, "The Greatest American Scoundrel Show," otherwise known as the "Presidential Debates" and I gave the Socialist response to each of the questions that Scoundrel A or Scoundrel B answered—now I would like to present the same for the recent Vice-Scoundrel Debate.

To me, it's amazing that few people seem to really listen to what the Scoundrels say, but *how* they say it. Even though I think the consensus from the presidential debate was that Romney slaughtered Obama, the "winner" of the Vice Scoundrel debate seems to divide along partisan lines, but I know I saw less eye-rolling and heard less sniggering when I coordinated an afterschool program for at-risk middle school students.

Biden and Ryan fought over who was the biggest friend of the War Machine and Wall Street and I believe we need a change—that's why I agreed to run for Vice President. Here are the questions and how I, and my party, the Peace and Freedom Party, would answer:

Wasn't the assassination of the US Ambassador in Libya a massive intelligence failure?
Actually, according to recent testimony on Capitol Hill, it was revealed that State Department personnel in Libya had repeatedly asked and been denied more security forces. So, surprise, the Vice President lied through his teeth when he said that the Obama administration was "unaware." Last time I looked, the State Department, including the Secretary of State, is a cabinet level institution that definitely is part of the administration.

I was against the "humanitarian intervention" in Libya from the beginning and am appalled that in the interest of global resource extraction, tens of thousands of innocent Libyans were killed. The attack that unfortunately killed the ambassador and three other Americans was in reaction to the invasion and corporate occupation of Libya: It's called, Blowback.

Was it appropriate for Romney to criticize president Obama during Libya crisis?
Which Libya crisis? The one where the US collaborated with NATO to murder tens of thousands of innocent Libyans or the one where four Americans were killed? Besides that clarification, I think any criticism of the President of the USA is valid and necessary, unless it is used for purely partisan political posturing as it seems was Romney's intention.

How effective would a military strike against Iran be?
I, and my party, are adamantly opposed to violating the sovereignty of any country and believe that a military strike against Iran would be disastrous and lead to further unnecessary civilian deaths and would obviously lend greatly to further destabilization of the region.

I call for an end to the current wars and closing the approximately 900 bases the US maintains on foreign soil and using the trillions that would be saved on education, health care, infrastructure, clean energy, and housing (among other things).

What's worse: Another war in the Middle East or a nuclear-armed Iran?

The Prime Minister of Israel and politicians in the US are lying when they say that Iran is "months" away from a nuclear weapon. There have been numerous intelligence estimates and independent reports denying these specious claims.

Having said that, the country in that region that actually possesses hundreds of nuclear weapons is Israel, and Israel has demonstrated repeatedly that it is a paranoid state that has no bottom limit to the lengths it will stoop to destabilize the region to protect its colonial project.

This one is a no-brainer to me: Another war in the Middle East would be far worse.

Can you get unemployment below 6% and how long will it take?

The Peace and Freedom Party has a comprehensive program that, if implemented, would bring full-employment for those that seek it and a Basic Guaranteed Income for those who need time off for whatever reason: Childbirth, childcare, disability, age, etc.

We demand:

A socially useful job at union pay levels or a guaranteed dignified income for everyone.

- Support of the establishment of a Universal Basic Income (UBI) to alleviate poverty and homelessness.
- A 30-hour workweek for 40 hours' pay and abolition of forced overtime.
- A legally mandated annual paid vacation of at least four weeks.
- Expansion and enforcement of job health and safety laws. We call for the restoration of all labor rights previously won by women and their extension to men as well.
- Paid parental leaves and time off work for childcare.
- No prison labor for private profit. Living wage and full union rights for any prison labor.
- Workers' rights to organize, form union caucuses, strike, and boycott.
- No replacement of striking workers.
- Federally funded public works programs to rebuild the nation's infrastructure and restore the environment.
- International solidarity of workers against international capitalist schemes such as NAFTA and WTO in defense of jobs, wages, working conditions, and environmental laws.
- International trade agreements that must guarantee the protection of workers and democratic rights in all participating countries.
- A rank and file socialist-oriented labor movement to mobilize working-class people to assume ownership and control of the economy.

I believe if these programs were implemented, full-employment could be reached within the first two years of any administration that did so.

Will benefits for Americans have to change for Medicare and Social Security to survive?

I say that they had better NOT change unless it's to ensure that our seniors and disabled are taken care of in the best way our society is capable.

Of course, if the vast wealth and resources of this Empire were re-prioritized to serve human need instead of the War Machine and corporate greed, there would be enough money for compassionate and fully funded social programs.

If your ticket is elected, who will pay more in taxes, who will pay less?

Since the US has the largest income disparity of any "industrialized" nation, I believe that the tax codes, from taxing real property to taxing unearned income should be eliminated for middle and low income earners, and a greater burden should be placed on corporations that steal from the public good but don't give anything back. Unearned income should be taxed at a rate that would contribute to a more just distribution of wealth.

I also advocate taxing churches and taking the cap off of social security taxes so more of the burden falls on the wealthy.

Why not leave Afghanistan now?

Yes, why not . . . and a better question might be, "Why did we go there in the first place?" Afghanistan did not attack us on 9/11 and that country and its people have paid a high price for the fact that their country is in the way of a gas pipeline and has vast precious metal resources.

The resources of Afghanistan belong to the people, not the US Empire and other multi-national corporations.

What more can the US really accomplish?

What "more" can the US accomplish? What has it accomplished except for further destruction of that country, more violence, the rebirth of the opium industry and increasing tensions with Pakistan?

What conditions could justify US troops staying in Afghanistan?

None.

What was the military reason for bringing surge troops home from Afghanistan?

What was the military reason for sending the surge troops? Besides the uncounted civilian casualties, more US troops have been killed there since Obama has been president for less than four years than the entire time Bush was in office.

The US assisted rebels in Libya; why doesn't the same logic apply to Syria?

Is this question for real? The US has been supplying aid to the Syrian "rebels" since at least August 1st of this year when it was widely reported that: " 'President Barack Obama has signed a secret order authorizing US support for rebels seeking to depose Syrian President Bashar al-Assad and his government,' US sources familiar with the matter said."

Furthermore, there does not seem to be a consensus on the composition of the so-called Free Syrian Army that could have elements of our supposed mega-enemy, Al Qaeda.

What happens if Assad does not fall in Syria?

We respect the sovereignty of Syria.

But, again, is this question for real?

Assad was a major US ally and Syria was a rendition spot for the US until it became inconvenient for the Empire and Israel to have him continue as this ally and torturer. Now, after dutifully performing his lackey duties for the Empire, Assad is called a "tyrant" and "vicious enemy."

Osama bin Laden, Saddam Hussein, Moammar Qaddafy, etc., should have been a big warning to Bashar Assad—the US will use you to commit its dirty work and be your friend until it's more fun or convenient to demonize you and remove you from power.

What is your criteria for intervention in Syria?

No criteria for military intervention or "crippling sanctions."

What role has your religion played on your personal views of Abortion?

None. And I don't think "personal views" are relevant in something that is a right: A woman's full reproductive control over her own body. It doesn't matter what Ryan or Biden, or even I, think. It's up to each individual woman.

If the Romney-Ryan ticket is elected, should those who believe abortion should be legal be worried?

I don't think so since George W. Bush and every Republican president since the *Roe v. Wade* decision has been opposed to abortion and it still stands.

In our administration, abortion would be available on demand and included in a national health care program.

Closing Statement.

The Obama administration has been a disaster for world peace and our economy here at home. I am not willing to give Romney/Ryan a shot at these important matters, either.

True change will not and cannot be achieved in the institutions that created the problems, or with voting for the twin-evils that permeate our lives.

We now live in a dictatorship of the 1% with a seemingly peaceful transition of power every four to eight years. Nothing changes except the face, and continuing to vote for the twin-evils thinking anything will change is Einstein's definition of insanity.

A vote cast for Romney or Obama is a vote for war and economic austerity for us. If you support war, then vote for Romney or Obama.

If you support harsh austerity measures, then, by all means, vote for Romney or Obama.

If you support the rise of Police State America—then—you know what I am going to say.

Send a message to the oligarchy this November—vote Third Party or Independent.

Sunday, October 21, 2012
Talking Flapping Pie Holes and the Damage They Do—War Pundits and Platitudes

Frequently, I watch the Propaganda Media because I want to know of the current propaganda of the Empire.

For example, if the Propaganda Media is telling me that I should focus on one really (but, really not) juicy trial, or that I should be consumed by the autopsy report of the latest celebrity death, or what was in her refrigerator when she died, then I know those are things that I don't need to know and I refuse to be distracted by the shiny keys of the Propaganda Masters.

Lately, I am particularly struck by a rather difficult "shiny key" distraction named Malala Yousufzai, the young female Pakistani who was allegedly shot by the Taliban for being vocal about her rights to an education. Malala is right and whoever shot her is wrong—period.

However, the situation is tricky, because I don't support ANYONE shooting ANYONE—but especially I abhor the shooting of a young lady who is fighting for her rights. However, all of the news coverage she is getting and celebrity support NEVER points out how many children are killed by the US in Pakistan by Obama's abominable aerial assault campaign. According to the very comprehensive and current wiki page: Drone Strikes in Pakistan, these are the statistics of the immoral US policy:

Total strikes: 347

Total reported killed: 2,572 – 3,341

- Civilians reported killed: 474 – 884
- Children reported killed: 176
- Total reported injured: 1,232 – 1,366
- Strikes under the Bush Administration: 52
- Strikes under the Obama Administration: 295

Other reports claim that the percentage of civilians killed in these strikes is 98 percent!

I posted a picture of a Pakistani toddler on the twitter-facebook-osphere the other day and the comments were unconscionably callous, but they all boiled down to this sentiment: "I am glad the president is bombing people who would shoot a young girl for going to school."

I was watching the Propaganda Media show with the letters CNN this morning and the moderator shall remain nameless, but her initials are CC and she is an especial cravenly war supporter on a cable network chock full of them. Anyway, there was a lovely young lady on a panel filled with other perfectly coiffed, suited, tied, and made-up Talking Flapping Pie Holes. The discussion was about the upcoming foreign policy debate between the Red Tie Scoundrel and Blue Tie Scoundrel presidential candidates.

I always notice the mental and logical gymnastics that the panels on these pre-debate discussions have to go through to distinguish and then expand upon the miniscule differences between Blue Tie Scoundrel and Red Tie Scoundrel—but the lovely young Talking Flapping Pie Hole made one egregiously false claim and one dismissive claim.

First, she claimed that Obama "ended the war in Iraq like he promised during the 2008 campaign." Actually, A) It ended because of an agreement that was entered into between the US and the Puppet Government of Iraq before George Bush left office; B) The Obama administration did everything it could to NOT have to leave Iraq; and, C) The occupation continues to this day with tens of thousands of independent contractors and thousands of other civilian employees staffing the enormous embassy and consulates around the country. But, the above are inconvenient facts that we are supposed to forget so we can triumphantly trumpet: "Vote for Obama, he ended the war in Iraq!"

Secondly, Ms. Talking Flapping Pie Hole said that the Obama administration is trying to end the "engagement" in Afghanistan. Excuse me, the Obama regime is doing the same thing in Afghanistan that it tried to do in Iraq—extending its unwelcomed stay—AND "engagement?" That is the most innocuous platitude that I have heard in a long time for an illegal occupation and devastating war!

Obama to Afghanistan: "Baby, I know we have already been engaged for eleven years, but, even though I know you don't want to be engaged to me, I think we should be engaged for at least 10 more years, baby! Oh, come on baby, I promise you it'll be different this time! I can't live without your mineral wealth . . . ahem, baby, I mean I can't live without YOU!"

With "reporters" and "pundits" like these, is it any wonder that on November 6, those Americans who do find the time, energy, or remember to vote, will sludge down to their polling place like The Walking Dead and fill in the bubble for one of the Red Tie or Blue Tie Scoundrels? Good job.

Thursday, October 25, 2012
Stealing Rent Money from a Gold Star Mother

For a brief review, I have been a War Tax Resister since my son was killed in Iraq on April 04, 2004. My only regret was that I ever paid my taxes to this murderous, thieving government in the first place. After almost nine years, the IRS has finally decided to use their powers of thuggery to bring the full force of their illegal aggression upon me, a Gold Star Mother.

Before my son was killed, my family was living the American Nightmare. There were times when I worked two or three jobs just to keep our family covered with health insurance because my husband was an independent contractor. Even back then, our insurance bill was about a grand/month.

Casey joined the military in 2000, in part to help pay for his university education. He had already completed every credit he could at a local community college, but he was feeling the pressure of having a full-time job and going to school and didn't want to burden the family further. Casey paid for his desire for a university education with his life and we buried him on April 13, 2004. I vowed to never, ever again contribute financially or morally to the organization that killed my son.

The US attorney dragged me before a federal magistrate last April who seemed sympathetic to my cause. Then they dragged me back to answer questions to participate in incriminating myself, I refused and took the Fifth Amendment.

Since then, the IRS has been vigorously looking for all my millions of dollars that I must have hidden around in the Caymans or Switzerland, and it has stumbled upon $13 in my PayPal account. Today the IRS mugged $269 from my bank account that was being saved up for my November rent.

I live a hand-to-mouth existence and usually if I receive an online donation or payment for a book I go directly to the bank to remove it and save it in my sock drawer, but I am traveling on a book tour and am in a strange city and my guard was lowered.

It infuriates me that corporations pay very little in Federal taxes and, in fact, at times, get exorbitant refunds paid for by you tax paying citizens.

It saddens me that US war criminals are not only not held accountable, but receive medals, great tax payer funded benefits AND secret service protection.

However, what I don't think these people understand (whether they are "elected" officials or wage-slaves petty thugocrats), is the fact that they can't do anything worse to me than they already have. The tax collectors of the Empire rejoice in taking a "widow's mite," and bringing down enemies of the state with their thugocracy, but my son had his "last measure" stolen from him and I am still standing and resisting with all my might!

My son wanted a university degree and he got a grave and, for me, that's not a movie, TV show, or a one-time 21-gun salute, it's for real and the pain is forever.

I want peace and I want my government to stop killing and oppressing people all over the world and all I get is jail time, fines, persecuted by the IRS, and a precarious life where I am one more stolen bike or stolen bank account away from penury.

I know that I am not the only one in the US who is living such a precarious existence and we have to recognize our enemies aren't in foreign lands or the activists, homeless, single mothers, or immigrants; our enemies sit in the rotten marble halls of power and it's time we made their very existence precarious, and I am not talking about voting for Barack Obama—he's had four years to prove he is not an able servant of the 99% and he has failed. I am also not talking about voting for

Mitt Romney, he sits on the throne of the King of the 1%. I am talking about a revolution of values —what if everyone who feels the same way I do refused to pay taxes or otherwise financially support things that we don't morally support?

I am grateful for my colleagues who give me moral and, at times, financial support to help resist the Behemoth monster of the Empire; and I am grateful that I have a roof over my head and every picture I see of the devastation caused by Hellfire missiles, I am grateful that not one penny of my money goes to help fund it.

We live in a thugocracy where every word, thought, action, and inaction is monitored. We are being folded, spindled, and mutilated in a neo-fascist slow dance of spiraling oppression. Keep smiling; keep singing; keep dancing; keep speaking; keep thinking; and, most importantly of all, keep resisting!

Illegitimi non carborundum. We shall prevail.

CINDY NOTE: Every time the IRS steals money from me, my supporters send me much more than I was robbed of. I include this in this collection because I was never persecuted by the IRS, nor had money stolen from my accounts, when Bush was president. Hmmm…

Monday, November 26, 2012
Peace, How? The Way Forward

I had the strangest dream last night (no, I didn't dream of Joe Hill or that I was eating a giant marshmallow).

It was a vivid dream, you know, one of those that seem too real to be a dream, but too bizarre to be real? I dreamt that the Congressional Democrats (including my old nemesis, Nancy Pelosi) had invited me to speak to a large gathering of the Democratic faithful. Of course, I didn't realize this until I was in the middle of my speech and the details were revealed.

I was giving my regular "It's not about partisan politics, it's about the CYST-em" speech and I was amazed that I was receiving standing ovations from this crowd of raging-Democrats! I was just getting into how the "Fiscal Cliff" could be avoided by ending the occupations and closing the hundreds of US military bases around the world, when I was cut-off by a Congressperson who had apparently had enough of my ranting. After I was cut off, many members of the audience came up to me to hug me and tell me that they had always "loved" me and that I had been correct about Obama and the Dems all along. There was a lot of weeping and hugging and then I woke up! Why do I tell this story?

Well, obviously many, many people who voted for and support Obama don't support drone bombings, targeted assassinations, or kill lists. I am sure that these voters don't go to the polls to give their seal of approval on the Empire's expanding wars abroad and restricting civil liberties here at home; yet, technically that's what Democratic voters do. I have cynically claimed on more than one occasion, that the antiwar movement only has movement during Republican wars because that seems to be the case.

What were Democrat voters afraid of in 2012? That under a Romney regime, their inaction during Obama's wars and attacks on civil rights would seem a tad bit hypocritical and it would now look lame if these things suddenly and magically became wrong again? I can't speak for those people, but if I adhere to the beautiful vision of my dream, peace is possible if we put the safety and prosperity of people outside of the borders of the USA above the uteri of American women.

Is this vision possible? Will the safety of children in Pakistan ever be more important than our children being able to watch a government-funded big, yellow bird? Will families in Afghanistan ever be able to hold a wedding party without fearing it will rain Hellfire missiles? Can the spectacle of "Black Friday" in the US ever be far from the minds of those who are being starved by inhumane US/Israeli led blockades in various parts of the world?

I don't care if a comrade is a Communist or Libertarian, or anything in between. The way forward to peace will be gained only by total unanimity of one point: We must have complete opposition to ALL wars of Empire, even the wars that are waged under the Imperial Seal of "Democrat" and even if the Imperial Spin Doctor attaches the oxymoronic label: Humanitarian War.

Can our former colleagues (D) in the Anti-Bush War Movement be reached? Can we have détente with the so-called wedge issues to courageously, and with the highest regard for peace and the human rights of all, attack the root issues and agree to disagree (we mostly agree, it's just the degree of importance we attach to the issues that differs), for the time being, on those wedgies that are intentionally meant to divide us?

Can we agree with the antiwar right that the Empire is bad but disagree about what a new society built on peace will look like after the collapse? Will we have a planned socialist economy (I hope) or more free market Capitalist chaos? (Ha!)

Apparently, I have many questions, but few answers—not that I haven't tried. Contrary to what the neo-conservative right wants to believe about me, I have NOT retired since Obomber came into being as I have been arrested protesting many times the same things I protested when Bush was there. I tried to stimulate interest in the antiwar message during three camps I held in the proximity of Obomber. I thought the Occupy movement was our chance, but systemic change was not sought and we got status quo on steroids. And contrary to one very angry email I received from a Democrat recently IN ALL CAPITALS: Obama IS NOT the only way to peace. One must have to be on some serious medication to even partially believe that kind of bull crap.

I am just a very tiny operation that consists of me and my computer and a few very dedicated volunteers, but I am going to list contact info for the national organizations (no political parties) that I have partnered well with over the last four lonely years and, hopefully, some momentum will build for peace.

If you want to get involved, contact me, or any of the below organizations!

These organizations have stayed above the two-party scandal and, in my honest opinion, that's the only place true and positive change will ever happen!

World Can't Wait: http://www.worldcantwait.net

A.N.S.W.E.R: http://www.answercoalition.org

The National War Tax Resistance Coordinating Committee: http://www.nwtrcc.org

Coalition Against Nukes: http://www.coalitionagainstnukes.org

ANTIWAR.COM: http://www.antiwar.com

National Lawyer's Guild: http://www.nlg.org

I would also like to recommend these organizations on a local level, if there are chapters near you:

Veterans for Peace: http://www.veteransforpeace.org

CODEPINK: http://www.codepink.org

Iraq Vets Against the War: http://www.IVAW.org

Of course, please stay up to speed at:

Friday, December 7, 2012
Angela's Ash Heap

"It comes from a very ancient democracy, you see . . . ."

"You mean, it comes from a world of lizards?"

"No," said Ford . . . "nothing so simple. Nothing anything like so straightforward. On its world, the people are people. The leaders are lizards. The people hate the lizards and the lizards rule the people."

"Odd," said Arthur, "I thought you said it was a democracy."

"I did," said Ford. "It is."

"So," said Arthur, hoping he wasn't sounding ridiculously obtuse, "why don't people get rid of the lizards?"

"It honestly doesn't occur to them," said Ford. "They've all got the vote, so they all pretty much assume that the government they've voted in more or less approximates to the government they want."

"You mean they actually vote for the lizards?"

"Oh yes," said Ford with a shrug, "of course."

"But," said Arthur, going for the big one again, "why?"

"Because if they didn't vote for a lizard," said Ford, "the wrong lizard might get in. Got any gin?"

"What?"

"I said," said Ford, with an increasing air of urgency creeping into his voice, "have you got any gin?"

"I'll look. Tell me about the lizards."

Ford shrugged again.

"Some people say that the lizards are the best thing that ever happened to them," he said. "They're completely wrong of course, completely and utterly wrong, but someone's got to say it."

— **Douglas Adams, *So Long, and Thanks for All the Fish***

The above excerpt comes from book four of the "Trilogy in Five Parts" of the brilliant series *The Hitchhiker's Guide to the Galaxy,* and this exchange happens between "alien" Ford Prefect and Britisher Arthur Dent after a 30-foot robotic alien alights from a space ship that just smashed Harrods in London and says, "I come in peace. Take me to your Lizard." I post it, because I think the above excerpt describes in less than 250 wonderful words the state of US politics today!

Okay, now no one needs to write to me to remind me that the US is not a democracy and never has been. I know that. The elitist electoral college smashes to hell any talk of democracy (a government by which supreme power is vested in the people) and, even in the mildest state of mis-governance, we live in a representative Republic. However, as in the above Lizard World scenario, we all vote, we all have the right to vote (past age 18) to give us the appearance of having a say. (True to plan) we ALWAYS vote for Lizards.

Why is this? Why have some of us been convinced that at least one of the Lizards that we get to "choose" is the "best thing that ever happened to them?" Could it be because of people like former radical, Professor Angela Davis?

Angela Davis has long been a hero of mine. Even when I was in Junior High in a predominantly white community and not yet of the age of physical dissent, I had heard of Angela's exploits and admired her fiery rhetoric and anti-Vietnam war stance. Today, I think there are few better at working against the Prison Industrial Complex, but (BIG BUT), as a self-described "Revolutionary African-American Woman," I believe she betrays the struggle by supporting the Democratic Party. According to my research, she has long supported the election of Democrats, not just Obama and not just because he is black. Of course, Professor Davis was a long-time member of the Communist Party of the USA (CPUSA), which sold the left in this country down the river decades ago. In 2007, when I first announced that I would run against Ms. Nancy "Impeachment off the table AND war funding on it" Pelosi, of course, the CPUSA was adamantly opposed to me, saying that I was "splitting the antiwar movement" with my "personal agenda." Whatever!

Anyway, it is well known that the CPUSA believes in the Myth of the Greater of Two Lizards, but I felt the need to address a few outright lies that Angela Davis has told at least twice in recent public appearances, because, I believe that enthusiastic (and, worst of all, false) support of one of the Lizard candidates by leaders is profoundly harmful.

In what one of my colleagues calls, "the biggest betrayal of the left by the left in decades," at a pre-election meeting in Detroit that was supposed to be honoring Ms. Davis, but was actually just a big GOTV rally for Obama, Angela early on makes the first claim that actually made my jaw drop while crying out loud, "bullshit."

She is talking about how the black community, at first, supported Hillary Clinton in the 2008 primaries because members of that community didn't think it was possible for a black person to be elected president of the USA. And one of the reasons that Angela claims that the black community believed that Obama's election was "impossible" was because he was a "peace activist." Excuse me, what? I have tried to dispel the myth of "Obama the Peacenik" for years now. Barack Obama is/was not even an "antiwar activist."

How did this lie, as false as George Washington chopping down a cherry tree, get started, anyway? During a speech Obama gave at an anti-Iraq war rally in Chicago in 2002, he says four times that he doesn't not "oppose all wars." He claimed in that speech that he was just opposed to "dumb wars." A true "peace activist" opposes ALL war and especially the expansion of empire that cuts a swath of destruction throughout the world, for profit. With the bombing of about six countries under his "peace activist" watch; support for Israel in its bombardment of Gaza; drone bombing; AND using the scandal of WMD (yet again) in threatening Syria, he doesn't even come within a light-year of being a "peace activist." In a stroke of Lizard genius, however, the Lizards in the Norwegian Parliament awarded Obama the "esteemed" Nobel Peace Prize in 2009, and WE ALL know only "peace activists" receive that award!

Then Angela felt she needed to qualify her support of Obama (to the largely black audience) by saying that he "deeply understands the black struggle for freedom." Apparently, Angela had also made this claim in March of this year (2012) and our friend, Glen Ford, of the *Black Agenda Report,* brilliantly repudiated that claim in an article he wrote called: *Angela Davis has lost her mind over Obama:*

"There was a hush in the room, as if in mourning of the death of brain cells. Angela Davis was saying that Barack Obama is a man who identifies with the Black radical tradition. She said it casually, as if Black radicalism and Obama were not antithetical terms; as if everything he has written, said, and done in national politics has not been a repudiation of the Black radical tradition; as if his rejection of his former minister, Rev. Jeremiah Wright, was not a thorough disavowal of the Black radical tradition. In his famous 2008 campaign speech in Philadelphia,

155

Obama blamed such radicals for compounding the nation's problems. He viewed people like Rev. Wright as having been mentally scarred by battles of long ago, who were unable to see the inherent goodness of America, as he did. This is the man who said he agreed with President Ronald Reagan, that the Sixties were characterized by 'excesses.' Can anyone doubt that Obama considers the historical Angela Davis, herself, to be a part of the political 'excesses' of the Sixties and early Seventies that he so deplores? . . . How, then, did Angela Davis connect Barack Obama to the Black radical tradition? She didn't, because even an icon cannot do the impossible."

I may not have been a leader in the CPUSA or affiliated with the Black Panther Party, but I know for sure that NO ONE, black, white, male, female, or otherwise, becomes POTUS if he/she has not already been chosen for that "honor" by the Military Industrial-Wall Street Complex. Of course, I would be thrilled if someone could achieve the seat of POTUS who did understand struggle and was a peace activist, but that hasn't ever happened, and with great leaders like Angela lying about the Lizards, we may be a long way from it ever happening.

So, after giving people the room and permission to be "disappointed" with Obama, Ms. Davis commences to blame "the people" for his many, many failures. She blames us for not "hitting the streets" the day after his inauguration to "help him" govern the way we wanted to.

I am sorry, but I adamantly refuse to take blame for the actions/non-actions of this able servant of Empire.

I DID hit the streets and was roundly criticized by the Professor's ilk for not giving Obama "a chance." Also, by 2012, I know that I was broke and demoralized by the fact that Obama seemed to be getting away with a whole lot of war and oppression with barely a peep out of the pitiful left of this country. How can a person simultaneously struggle against Empire and Capitalism while campaigning for a major proponent of both? It's not possible. The money and volunteers for those of us who were still trying to dried up after Lizard (D) was inaugurated in 2009.

Off the top of my head, I can think of two great examples of activists doing everything they could to "support Obama" in his first term: The struggle for a National Health Care (Medicare for all) movement and the one against the Keystone XL Pipeline. Both movements had large numbers of people in DC attending hearings and getting arrested in front of the White House, but the Medicare for all activists didn't even have a chance to give one word of input and a fascist health-care-for-profit bill was passed. Almost as soon as the mostly Obama supporting environmental activists left DC, Obama approved at least part of the pipeline and it seems to be going great for the oil companies (not the activists).

Voting for Lizards is certainly a disordered national pastime, so I don't want to seem like I am picking on Angela Davis. Many of my personal heroes have taken similar positions on Democrats in general, and Obama in particular, but her (and their) collaboration with the Team of the Blue Lizards is unequivocally a collaboration with war, murder, environmental devastation and economic oppression, period. Again, how can one claim to oppose any of those issues, yet support the Blue Lizard?

At one point, Angela offers the specious and not provable claim that "McCain would have been worse." Really? We don't know what McCain WOULD HAVE DONE, but we do know what Obama HAS DONE. He's continued Bush's policies, and expanded some. Obama also refuses to hold criminals from the Bush regime accountable.

So, maybe McCain would have been worse, but I can guarantee, Ms. Davis, that McCain, at the very least, would have ALSO been an able servant of Empire. The biggest difference between the Lizard McCain and the Lizard Obama, would be that Angela and her ilk would not be supporting McCain or vehemently justifying his policies and actions.

Instead of encouraging us to vote for Lizard (D), we need our intellectuals, heroes, and leaders to lead us to the Promised Land that is free of all Lizards! The CPUSA and "radicals" like Angela give the Democrats so much badly needed cover! The working class of both parties can look at Obama's support and either be wonderfully, or angrily, vindicated in their perception of him. "Wow, then Obama MUST BE (tragically or happily) a radical Socialist, himself." I think which Lizard one endorses, or doesn't endorse, says more about the endorser than it does about the Lizard!

In this case, Angela is "completely and utterly" wrong, of course—as is anyone who supports either party of the bourgeoisie. I have "said it" before and I will keep on saying it, no matter who wrongly believes that the Lizards are the "best thing that ever happened" to us.

Friday, December 28, 2012
War Control

Full disclosure: I hate guns; I always have—even before my oldest son was killed by a gunshot to the head in a foreign land that the US was/still is occupying. (By the way, Casey had a gun, armor, albeit inadequate, and the First Cavalry, and he was still killed by a gun . . . interesting). I desperately wish we lived in a country, or on a planet, where not one weapon was necessary, but we don't—yet.

After the recent tragedy in Sandy Hook, CT, the predictable blather became the recycled "debate" about "gun control." However, as profoundly devastating that incident, I think the discussion needs to be around "War Control." Besides saving millions of lives, while the Pentagon just received over $600 billion of your tax dollars and needs to be shoved over the Fiscal Cliff, pushing War Control could also save OUR Social Safety Nets that Obama and his buddy, Boehner, are trying to destroy.

I am not opposed to background checks and waiting lists for gun ownership, but why is that restriction only placed on citizens? Here in the US we have an epidemic of Killer Cops and I believe that any new applicant to any police force needs to be first subjected to the most stringent background and psychiatric screening AND, then, the hopeful cop would have to pass the screening of a citizens' personnel review board that is comprised of a diverse cross-section of community members before he/she is allowed to openly carry a weapon in society. Why are our police forces becoming so militarized anyway? Obviously, to protect the 1%, not us.

Gun koo-koos and Second Amendment Advocates have extreme emotional attachments to their guns, and when I say that I "hate guns," one would think I said that I hated babies or kittens, the reaction is so extreme. But putting our love of things that go "boom" aside, what does the Second Amendment to the US Constitution actually say?

"A well regulated Militia, being necessary to the security of a free State, the right of the people to keep and bear Arms, shall not be infringed."

I wonder how many lovers of the Second Amendment actually belong to a "well-regulated Militia?" And what does that even mean? My point is, that if anyone thinks that they own guns to fight the US police/war state in open rebellion, that concept is ridiculous. When the Second Amendment was written, most people died of infection or gangrene than died of the actual musket shot. In the days of gun powder and musket balls, the people may have had a fighting chance against the state—now our weapons are like fleas to an elephant. We are more powerful in concentrated resistance, not rebellion, anyway.

Besides the emotionally charged issue of gun control, why are few people making this point as Martin Luther King, Jr. did so eloquently in his Beyond Vietnam Speech exactly one year before he was assassinated: *"The greatest purveyor of violence in the world today is my own government."*

Why, President Barack Obama even has his very own Kill List and an entire bloated military establishment to do his filthy killing for him. In Sandy Hook we rightfully mourn the deaths of those beautiful children, but in Pakistan, the ones killed in Obama's drone attacks are called, "bug splat" by the drone pilots pulling the trigger thousands of miles away. However, the mentally ill murderer of 20 children in Sandy Hook is correctly vilified and pitied, while the by proxy baby killer, Obama, is enthusiastically welcomed and celebrated almost everywhere he goes. I don't get it.

Presidents of the US are inherently the CEOs of a huge war machine that has momentum on its own, but why does putting one's hand on a bible and swearing an oath confer respectability upon mass murder? Here's an even stickier question? Why, in the eyes of some, is mass murder by, say, someone named George Bush (R) more horrendous than the slaughter by a couple named Barack Obama (D) and Bill Clinton (D)? I obviously think any murderer is a low-life scum and wearing an expensive suit and tie and traveling with one's own squad of heavily armed goons does not give cover to murdering the innocent.

And, guess what, Faux-gressives? The NRA (National Rifle Association) isn't really **THE** problem (I am not saying that I support the NRA, I don't) and making it so is a huge distraction away from the real problem. According to the website, *Open Secrets*, here is the K Street (lobbying firms) Top 20 for government payola:

Lobbying Client	Total
US Chamber of Commerce	$95,660,000.00
National Assn of Realtors	$25,982,290.00
Blue Cross/Blue Shield	$16,238,032.00
General Electric	$15,550,000.00
Google Inc.	$14,390,000.00
Pharmaceutical Rsrch & Mfrs of America	$14,380,000.00
AT&T Inc	$14,030,000.00
American Hospital Assn	$13,275,200.00
National Cable & Telecommunications Assn	$13,010,000.00
American Medical Assn	$12,980,000.00
Northrop Grumman	$12,980,000.00
Comcast Corp.	$12,420,000.00
Boeing Co.	$12,010,000.00
Verizon Communications	$11,670,000.00
Lockheed Martin	$11,518,870.00

Lobbying Client	Total
National Assn of Broadcasters	$11,220,000.00
Royal Dutch Shell	$10,860,000.00
Southern Co.	$10,500,000.00
Edison Electric Institute	$10,130,790.00
Exxon Mobil	$9,870,000.00

Source: http://www.opensecrets.org/ (2012)

I don't see the NRA anywhere on the above list, but I see a lot of war profiteers and oil companies . . . hmm? In 2012, the same site shows that the NRA spent a little over two million lobbying Congress—chump change to GE. And, honestly, I have seen a few NRA spokesmen (I am not practicing gender-exclusive language, they're always men) on the "news" lately and they are not very articulate or well rounded. Their arguments boil down to basically, "ugh, we like guns, ugh."

I was in Los Angeles the past few days where the LAPD was conducting another gun "turn-in." Private citizens bring in guns with no questions asked and then receive a grocery gift card depending on the value of the weapon. That's also a great strategy for War Control and I propose we pay the war machine NOT to produce implements of death and to go away and just leave the world alone.

In conclusion:

If owning a gun is wrong for Joe NRA, then it's wrong for Officer Not-So-Friendly.

If it's wrong to kill children in the US, then it's wrong to kill children EVERYWHERE else.

If killing is wrong for me, then it's wrong for Obama and the Empire.

I dream of (and work really hard for) the day when War Control is a reality and our priorities honor the beating of every heart while we watch our deadly tools of war rust, breakdown, and return to the soil.

CINDY NOTE: Adelante (forward) to 2013!

Part Five

2013

As I, and about a dozen others made the arduous (by today's standards) journey to Guantanamo Bay, Cuba from the states in January of 2007, I was already showing signs of the exhaustion and illness that would lead to my highly publicized "resignation" from being the "face" of the antiwar movement.

Besides me, a mother whose son was killed in Iraq, in our group were also a mother whose son was killed on 9/11 and who was a member of 9/11 Families for a Peaceful Tomorrow, and a mother whose son, Omar Deghayes, was still being illegally detained by the United States at what has come to be known as "Gitmo."

Asif Iqbal, whose story of illegal capture in Afghanistan in 2001 in a "sweep" where many Muslim men were captured, kidnapped, and transported to Guantanamo, was also in our contingent to Guantanamo. Asif and three other friends were born in Great Britain and the British government could prove that they were innocent, but Asif, and his friends, were still detained for over two years and subjected to the most horrible conditions and torture at the hands of the "good guys," the American soldiers and CIA stationed there. The story of the "Tipton 3" (one of their friends was lost and never heard from again), is told in the docudrama, *The Road to Guantanamo.*

On January 11, 2007, our group, many Cubans, and a vast cadre of international media, set up camp outside the barbed wire check point of the prison camp in Guantanamo, Cuba.

That day was a blazing hot one and the sun baked down upon us. As this was my first trip to Cuba, I was amazed at the bucolic nature of the town, and it seemed that I had taken a trip in the Way Back Machine where horses and buggies clip-clopped down the lanes and electricity was a luxury. Guantanamo, and indeed many places in Cuba, are gorgeous in a very romantic and primitive way, but that does not diminish the hardships that the decades-long blockade from the Empire has placed on that undeserving country.

We were all there, of course, to demand that the US shut the prison camp down; free the detainees that had no evidence incriminating them; where it was obvious (as it was with the Tipton 3) that most of the men tortured there were at the wrong place at the wrong time; and, finally, put the ones who may have been guilty of something, on trial: Trials that would be fair and transparent with all due process given to the accused.

January 11th was the 11th dark anniversary of the opening of that torture facility, but despite Obama's empty promises, Gitmo remains open with 166 detainees remaining: Despicable, illegal, immoral, and just plain degrading to the tortured and torturers alike.

I perused the news and there was not one mention of this dark anniversary. However, there are many stories today of the flu and Obama's appointments to fill vacant cabinet posts: Well, played, Empire.

There were a couple of hundred of us protesting in DC today in front of the Supreme Court demanding its immediate closure.

We still care.

We still want it closed!

CINDY NOTE: As of this writing, Gitmo is still open for disgusting business. A continuing, national disgrace!

Thursday, February 21, 2013
Tour de Peace by David Swanson

Between April 4 and July 3, the entire country (and the other 96% of humanity too) is invited to join in a bicycle ride from California to Washington, DC. You can join as a bicycler or as a sponsor.

This won't be a ride to raise awareness about cruelty to animals, but it will raise awareness about war—by many measures the greatest destroyer of the natural environment we have, as well as consisting first and foremost of the mass killing of that peculiar animal we're all rather fond of: The homo sapiens.

This won't be a ride to raise money for cancer research, but it will raise money for the campaign to abolish war—a carcinogen if the people of Fallujah ever saw one.

This paragraph is exclusively for supporters of President Obama. If that's not you, please skip to the following paragraph right now. With Republicans out of the White House and no election this year, there is no need to fund election campaigns or to work against particular wars. This is a moment in which our time and our resources are freed up to support long-term structure building so that the plague of war never returns. Remember all those promises to engage in policy-based activism once the most important election of our lives was over? This is the time to get in better physical shape before phone banking season. Pump up your tires and polish your handlebars! Stop reading and get riding right now.

With presidential war powers expanding rapidly and war gaining widespread acceptance among liberals there is an urgent need for an educational and organizing effort that pedals under, over, and around the barricades of the corporate media. US forces are in more nations than ever before, the military budget is still rising and will still be rising even if the sequester "cuts" go through, the CIA

162

has been handed war-making powers, the president has claimed the power to spy without warrants, imprison without trial, and murder at will. Wars are launched on nations like Libya in defiance of Congress and the United Nations, with blowback spreading rapidly. Pentagon-friendly dictatorships like Saudi Arabia and Bahrain are backed against their people's nonviolent movements for democracy, while violence is encouraged in Syria and Iran. Palestinians are left to their fate, while a new kind of war launched from flying robots slaughters men, women, and children, traumatizes populations, and generates refugee crises, engulfing nations in boiling hatred of the United States of America.

When MSNBC assigns David Axelrod (who refused to deny that President Obama maintains the power to torture anyone as he sees fit) to analyze and punditrify John Brennan's refusal to deny that President Obama maintains the power to murder US citizens within the United States (never mind anyone at all outside the United States or 96% of humanity within it), the triumph of free market journalism will have reached a pinnacle unsurpassed in history, putting the Soviet Union's efforts to shame and finally concluding the Cold War, unless nobody notices.

You know who just might wake some people up to what's staring them in the face?

Cindy Sheehan. Cindy has proposed the Tour de Peace. She's been lining up events and participants along the route. She's ready to ride, and to me she is an inspiration. Cindy's appeal, both before and after the corporate media made her a story in Crawford Texas seven-and-a-half years ago, was the uncensored honesty. She's still got it. I've seen a lot of people dump their heart and soul into the peace movement over the past decade and burn out and quit. I appreciate their efforts. We need sprinters, just as the Tour de Peace needs short-distance riders.

But when I see someone become even more aware of the evil that has swallowed up our government, and continually find new ways to confront it, I see a model others should follow. Cindy's gone at it as hard as anyone. She's taken nasty blows from the right and the so-called left. She's burned out and quit, too, but never for more than a day or so. She just keeps coming. Cindy has quit paying her taxes because of the wars they fund. She's been arrested for nonviolent resistance countless times. She's traveled endlessly, speaking and inspiring. She's written a stack of important books. She's hosted a radio show, blogged, and run for Congress and the Vice Presidency. And in this age in which pundits openly say they'd oppose the president's abuses if he were a Republican, Cindy goes ahead and opposed them anyway, with plenty of opposition left over for the Congress, the courts, the funders, the weapons makers, the lobbyists, and the White House Press Corpse.

Creating a mass of people in the streets for peace or justice usually requires money and staff, bus rentals and legwork, coalition building and compromising. Two moments stand out in my mind when none of that was needed. One was when Cindy went to Crawford. The other was when Occupy went to Wall Street. Both were moments of brilliant principled and courageous activism. Neither would have ever been heard of by most who heard of them if not for the corporate media. I've seen Cindy attempt to recreate Crawford countless times since (not to mention before), without the same success. She does so fully aware of the forces at work. She does so with every effort to create our own media and bypass the corporate censors. And she does so knowing that the only way to guarantee failure is to not try.

What if we were to create a movement capable of thinking of itself as real and national or international even outside of our television sets? One of the side effects would be its inevitable infiltration into our television sets. But the primary effect would be the beginning of hope and change as something more than perverse slogans of stargazing servitude.

When the Tour de Peace leaves Casey Sheehan's grave in Vacaville, Calif., on the ninth anniversary of his death in Iraq and the 45th of Dr. King's in Memphis, it will follow the mother road, Route 66, to Chicago, and other highways and byways from there to DC. The tour will conclude on July 3, 2013, with a ride from Arlington National Cemetery to the White House.

This August will mark eight years since Sheehan began her widely reported protest at then-President George W. Bush's "ranch." She was demanding to know what the "noble cause" was for which Bush claimed Americans were dying in Iraq. Neither Bush nor Obama has yet offered a justification for a global war now in its 12th year. The Tour de Peace will carry with it these demands:

To end wars;

To end immunity for US war crimes;

To end suppression of our civil rights;

To end the use of fossil fuels;

To end persecution of whistleblowers; and

To end partisan apathy and inaction.

Wednesday, February 27, 2013
Cindy Sheehan Leads Coast-to-Coast Bike Ride for Peace

FOR IMMEDIATE RELEASE: PRESS RELEASE FOR TOUR de PEACE

Sheehan and other riders are available for interviews.

WHAT: Gold Star Mother and "peace mom" Cindy Sheehan will lead a Tour de Peace bike ride across the United States from the grave of her son Casey in Vacaville, Calif., to Washington, DC, following the mother road, historic Route 66 to Chicago, and other roads from there on to DC. Bicyclers will join in for all or part of the tour, which will include public events organized by local groups along the way.

WHEN: The tour will begin on April 4, 2013, nine years after Casey Sheehan was killed in Iraq, and 45 years after Dr. Martin Luther King, Jr., was killed in Memphis. It will conclude on July 3, 2013, with a ride from Arlington National Cemetery to the White House.

WHY: This August will mark eight years since Cindy Sheehan began a widely reported protest at then-President George W. Bush's "ranch" in Crawford, Texas, demanding to know what the "noble cause" was for which Bush claimed Americans were dying in Iraq. Neither Bush nor President Obama has yet offered a justification for a global war now in its 12th year. The Tour de Peace will carry with it these demands:

To end wars;

To end immunity for U.S. war crimes;

To end suppression of our civil rights;

To end the use of fossil fuels;

To end persecution of whistleblowers; and

To end partisan apathy and inaction.

CINDY NOTE: We got very, very little national coverage for TdP, but the local coverage turned out to be adequate.

A wonderful human being has passed.

What do I do when I am angry, happy, or sad? I write.

Back in 2004, shortly after my son Casey was killed in Iraq, a grief counselor advised me to write a letter to my son in a journal every night. I filled up three journals in the terrible months after his death. I often wrote at his grave and those journals did help me deal with the unspeakable loss.

Today, I write from a great well of sadness, but not just for me, for the world. My dear friend in peace and justice, President Hugo Chavez of Venezuela, just lost his fierce and valiant battle with cancer.

Many people know about Hugo Chavez, the president, and constant thorn in the side to El Imperio the meddlesome and harmful Empire to the north. But I want to eulogize Chavez the man I knew.

He was my dear friend and comrade in a way where we were united in the struggle for peace and economic justice and equality. It's not like I could text him, or we would chat about current events, but whenever I had the privilege to be with him, warmth radiated from his heart and I was able to connect with him in very real and human ways.

Compared to the palpable realness of Chavez, most of the US politicians I have met with are walking and talking ice sculptures.

The first time I met him in Caracas was in early 2006, at the World Social Forum. I had been invited to sit on the stage while he gave a speech to those gathered there from around the world. He introduced me as, "Señora Esperanza," "Mrs. Hope," in contrast to his nickname for George Bush: "Señor Peligro," "Mr. Danger." However, our brother, Hugo Chavez, was the one who gave us much hope.

I have met and interviewed so many people in Venezuela whose lives were immeasurably improved by the vision and dedication of Hugo Chavez. How can one put a price on going from being illiterate to being able to read? A 65-year-old woman told me her life was transformed by the adult literacy program. It really made me appreciate the fact that I have always known how to read (it seems). What would I have done without my best friends, my books? Wow. I guess Capitalism would tally the cost of educating one student and, of course education here in the US is now just another commodity, but the look of wonder in my Sister's eyes was priceless!

Another woman showed me her perfect teeth in a huge grin. She told me that her teeth used to be so bad, that she would never smile before, but now, due to her new set of false teeth provided by the national dental program, she walks around grinning like a lunatic all day, which made me laugh with joy! Again, Capitalism would say: One set of false teeth equals X amount of dollars. I say being able to smile after years of embarrassing humiliation is worth more than any amount of gold.

Those are just two stories out of millions and my heart breaks with sorrow for the People of the Bolivarian Revolution that must be even more devastated than I, today.

I witnessed Chavez the proud "abuelo" (grandpa) once on a long flight from Caracas to Montevideo that I took with them. We chatted about out "nietos" (grandchildren) and felt a mutual connection there. I hugged my grandbabies a little harder today when I found out that Chavez died, because I know the wonderful connection that he had with his. My heart breaks for his children and his family, and his brother, Adan, who seemed to be constantly at his side. It's just a very hard day.

I was with Chavez in Montevideo, Uruguay, for the presidential inauguration of Felipé Mujica. I was amazed that Chavez could just plunge into the crowds and interact with the people without a phalanx of bodyguards, anti-aircraft missiles, and assault weapons. His security detail was prepared, but not paranoid like up here in the Empire. Someone who is universally loved by the 99% need have no fear. Chavez had no fear.

Chavez's courageous battle against the Empire was more successful than his battle against cancer. Chavez was able to inspire more leftist leaders in Latin America, and my friends in Cuba will always be grateful for the friendship between Venezuela and Cuba. The struggle against neo-liberalism and the Empire has been far advanced under Chavez's inspirational leadership.

This is a sad day and I am angry that the so-called leaders of my own country made Chavez's life a virtual hell, but he survived one coup attempt and the many other attempts through the media and financing of his opposition to undermine the revolution.

When in the hell is this country going to mind its own goddamn business and realize that not every drop of oil belongs to our oil companies and not every democratically elected leader must pledge undying obsequiousness to the Evil Empire?

I am immensely proud of Chavez and I am immensely proud of the people of Venezuela who have worked with him to improve their lives and because they really understand the concept of "national sovereignty."

I know the upper echelons of The Empire think they have won a victory today (if it didn't give Chavez his cancer in the first place—don't even start and say I am a "conspiracy theorist." Everyone knows that the Empire is fully capable of it; they couldn't kill him, or depose him, outright)—and all the oil will now flow back into the hands of our big oil companies; but The Empire underestimates the people of Venezuela and their dedication to the Bolivarian Revolution and love for their leader, Hugo Chavez.

As we sorrowfully say, "Vaya con la paz" to our Brother, Hugo Chavez, let's also say, "Long live the revolution."

Chavez will never die if we honor his vision and continue our struggle against The Empire.

US presidents come and go with destructive, yet boring and predictable regularity and are numbered for history's convenience when they should all have had black and white striped clothing and be behind bars. However, it is my belief that Hugo Chavez Frias will go down in World History as one of the most significant figures of the early 21st century and his passing is a tragic and profound loss to us all, as his life was an inspiration.

A-dios, Señor Esperanza.

Thank you from the bottom of my heart and soul. Your light is far too bright to be extinguished by something as cruel as death, and your light shines in all of us whose hearts burn with revolution and love for all the people.

My life and our world are far better today because of your life and the struggle continues until victory!

CINDY NOTE: *This piece also doesn't mention Obama, but he is one of the US Presidents whose regime worked really hard to overthrow Chavéz and his revolution.*

I have no patience for useless things.

Kevin Spacey as Congressman Frank Underwood in House of Cards

I have come to the conclusion that one useless man is called a disgrace; that two are called a law firm; and that three or more become a congress.

Peter Stone

True story: When I was camping near George Bush's fake ranch in Crawford, TX, I got a message of solidarity and support from KKK Grand Wizard David Duke. I immediately denounced it and refused the support.

Recently, an obvious political stunt was perpetrated by one of the members of the most exclusive group of one-percent jackasses on the planet, the US Senate, and some very shady and harmful thugs are supporting him in it and I would denounce that kind of support if it were me.

Senator Rand Paul filibustered the confirmation of Obama's choice for CIA Director, John Brennan, for 13 hours the other night. Make no mistake, just because I don't #StandWithRand, does not mean that I stand with Obama's "Dick Cheney," Barack Obama, the Democrats, or the use of drones to kill enemy combatants in the US.

Now, the reason I opened this piece with the reminiscence of David Duke, is that I have been thoroughly attacked (again) by the "left" and the "right" because I do not #StandWithRand. I don't support partisan political grandstanding and that's what his stunt was, and that's all. Of course, Rand Paul supports the use of drones to kill brown Arabs in other countries and "enemy combatants" here in the US, and he also hypocritically voted for the National Defense Authorization Act 2013.

I also believe that his father's latest symbolic run for POTUS was used to set Rand up to run for president in 2016, and when Newt Gingrich praised him for his stunt and denounced other old guard GOP who are not supporting The Rand Paul Show, we can tell that the "new GOP" is going to be the younger crop of neocons like Rand Paul and Marco Rubio—the old ones like McCain and Romney are obviously not working out.

Don't get me wrong about this either, I know that both parties support Wall Street and the War Machine and are sucking the life out of working-class and poor America, and I really don't pay that much attention to what goes on out there in the malignant capitol of the USA, but when over a million people around the world #StandWithRand, someone has to set the record straight.

"Purist" is another smear that is swirling around me because I didn't become orgasmic over Rand's "pile driver" the other day in the Senate, because like professional wrestling, his "pile driver" was for show and harmless to the establishment. However, I can stand as a proud purist and not with Rand because here are a few fascist, neocons that do #StandWithRand and if any of these people praised or supported me, I would go to Tibet to find my center and principles again and not come back home until my head was, once again, on straight:

Jennifer Rubin (*Washington Post*, 7 March, 2013) *Sen. Rand Paul (R-Ky.) demonstrated in his filibuster of John Brennan exactly why he is a formidable force and why 2016 contenders and their supporters should be nervous.*

Charles Krauthammer Fox News Mega-Neocon (from *The Blaze* 6 March, 2013): *Syndicated columnist and Fox News contributor Charles Krauthammer on Wednesday called Sen. Rand Paul's (R-Ky.) lengthy filibuster a "stroke of political genius" and said it will prove to be the moment that thrust him onto the national stage.*

"He will be remembered," Krauthammer said of Paul and the filibuster, which (sic) began just before 12 p.m. ET and didn't end until after midnight.

"This raises his image, and he's completely sincere about this," he added.

"This will be a moment that people will say has launched him as a national figure."

Sean Hannity, (Fox News, 7 March, 2013) *Since the election, I've been saying that conservatives now have a few real stars in the Senate: Florida Senator Marco Rubio, Texas Senator Ted Cruz, Utah Senator Mike Lee, and Kentucky Senator Rand Paul. Yesterday, in an incredible display of principled tenacity, Senator Rand Paul proved why he is on that list . . . so that is what led Rand Paul to his epic filibuster. . . .*

Extreme fascist, right wing, neocon radio host, Mark Levin, told his listeners to *"support"* the stunt ("stunt" is my word).

Last, but not least, everybody's favorite prescription drug addict, Rush Limbaugh (Rand Paul was on his show 7 March as reported by Noah Rothman in *MediaIte*):

*In a wide-ranging interview, Paul told Limbaugh that he was (sic) thought it was important to have a debate about President **Barack Obama**'s approach to **American citizens** (author's note: **screw the brown Arabs who are killed by drones**) who are viewed by the administration as being subject to a drone strike. Limbaugh heaped praise on Paul for his ability to "take this president on" and said that many see him as "a hero" today.*

RP: (Obsequiously to Rush): *I was thinking of you when I was in the middle of this 13-hour—I got about five hours into it, and I was like, well, Rush does four hours of this every day. Certainly, I can do four more hours.*

RL: *Nobody in the Republican Party has dared take this president on. You did last night, and you're alive today to talk about it. You are, in certain ways, a hero to a lot of people today. This was, to me, a seminal event last night that could change the direction that we are all heading – particularly in terms of educating and informing the American people about what actually is happening in their country.*

There is an old canard, "the enemy of my enemy is not always my friend," and I highly doubt that any of the above neocons believe that the use of drones is ever wrong, but are using Rand's stunt to attack Obama and the Democrats. I would have been more inclined to take notice if it were a Democrat taking Obama on, but is it news that a Republican opposes the policies of a Democrat? If Romney were president today (a man Rand endorsed) and he was doing the same things Obama is, the above partisan jackals would be thoroughly denouncing anyone who would dare oppose his behavior. I know what of I speak.

Rand Paul supports the "crippling" sanctions against Iran and, obviously, the use of drones on the "battlefield," so I #Stand with the people in Pakistan and Yemen who have been subjected to assassination by drone. Rand Paul went to Israel to pay allegiance to the Zionist-Apartheid state and supports its criminal existence and had a meeting with ultra-Zionist, William Kristol (right before he endorsed neocon, Mitt Romney) to promise that he would also be an obedient neocon.

I #Stand with Anwar al Awlaki, Samir Khan and Abdulramen al Awlaki who were American citizens assassinated in Yemen, without trial or due process. I #Stand with the people of Palestine that are being harmed by the very people Rand Paul is supporting.

However, I will agree that what Rand Paul did was a brilliant political stunt, because all week no one has been having intelligent conversations about how Obama has vastly expanded the use of drones in Af/Pak and how thousands of innocents have been slaughtered. The stunt subject was so narrow that the badly needed conversation of the growing police state and how peace and social justice activists (particularly around Occupy and the Gaza issue) are being targeted and persecuted by the DOJ.

I was in front of the CIA in January of 2010, protesting the CIA's part in the expansion of drone bombings overseas. Brennan could have been put on the hot seat for that, but Rand is the topic, not what should be the real topic.

As Frank Zappa said, "Politics is the entertainment division of industry," but, sadly, not even very entertaining, more like boring predictability!

What happened after the Rand Paul show? Drones are flying all over the world, John Brennan was confirmed anyway, and Rand is "seriously weighing" a presidential bid in 2016? Do tell? What a happy coincidence!

Author's Note: the # (hash tag) is a device used on Twitter to consolidate topics. Over one million people have used the #StandWithRand since his stunt.

CINDY NOTE: *As of this writing (November 25, 2014), it is reported that Senator Rand Paul will submit a bill to "declare war" on ISIS. Many people on the left and right are just now hastily withdrawing their support of this Jr. War Criminal.*

Sunday, March 31, 2013
Literally and Figuratively Spinning our Wheels for Peace

There are millions of mothers mourning the deaths of children today (and every day) ten years after Shocking and Awful.

Some of the mothers on the American "side" take false comfort in the lie that the war was justified and view their sons or daughters as "heroes" who died "keeping America safe" or some crap like that.

However, there are a few of us who know the facts: The war was "justified" by lies and fought for profit and control of resources and our kids are lying in permanent graves for temporary and temporal gain.

So, what's happening now? Obama is president, the wars are over, our troops are home, Iraq is rebuilt and peaceful, and the oceans have stopped rising, George and Dick have been held accountable? Actually, none of these things are true, yet we see few people out protesting anymore.

There has been some good energy around the case of Pvt. Bradley Manning and his persecution by the Obama regime. Of course, Manning is being persecuted for exposing the lies, yet Dick and George are still playing footsies with the 1%, as they are footloose and fancy free. Opposition to drone warfare is up, with little recognition that Obama has increased that program profoundly since he's been in office.

So many lies, so many scandals, so much violence perpetrated by the Obama regime, yet so little protest? And when there is protest, the establishment "opposition" is quick to point out how much in love they are with The Man, but that they would, for example, like him to "pretty please" not sign the pipeline legislation.

Without a doubt, the time has now come for us to get off of our collective asses and hit the streets . . . this past week when Congress passed, and Obama signed, the "Monsanto Protection Act," our government openly declared war upon we the people. We the people must fight back! If you don't fight back now, then what is your line in the sand? Is there ANYTHING that President MonsantObama can do at the behest of his bosses, the 1%, that would finally wake you up to the fact that the US government is rife with war-mongering, greedy scoundrels that don't give a damn about you or your children?

What keeps us, as a nation and a people, so accepting of the wars that our government wages against us here at home and abroad? I believe that it's a combination of a few things, but first is the servile corporate media: The propaganda arm of the US Empire.

For example, on March 27, President MonsantObama signed a spending bill that contains provisions that effectively give the most evil corporation on the planet, Monsanto (and other biotech companies), the green light to continue poisoning the food supply of my grandbabies. While President Congress was approving it and President MonsantObama was signing it into law, the shiny keys of marriage equality were being dangled to distract us from that horrible rider contained in H.R. 933.

Propaganda and misinformation breed apathy and reactionary political analysis. However, I think the number one thing that keeps us bound to the cyst-em is that we continually forge our own chains of partisan political slavery. It's almost impossible to "think outside the box" of the "two" party cyst-em because slavery beats one down and makes a person feel like he/she does not deserve to be free.

For the past three months, a few of us have been hard at work organizing Tour de Peace: A bike ride for Peace and Justice from California to Washington, DC. It has been frustrating to know that President MonsantObama has placed US troops, drone bases, or both, in 35 African countries and he has been responsible for bombing the stuffing out of eight Arab countries while assassinating American citizens and thousands of innocents, checking the dead off one by one from his Kill List.

We organizers of Tour de Peace have been delighted with the energetic, if small, response, but also disheartened with the knowledge that if it were a President Romney or President McCain doing the same things President MonsantObama is doing, we would have an easier time raising money and getting more people to join us in our 90-day protest!

If you voted for Obama, we don't get it, but we forgive you! It's time to break the chains of your slavery to the "two"-party scam and join us to raise a people's movement against our government that does more harm around the world than any other entity.

This is a call to action: Action based on the core principles of each and every one of you who have worked for peace and justice in the past. YOUR principles are the correct ones and I hope that the principles of the US Empire don't match yours.

If I act outside my core beliefs, I become ill. I am impressed with the extraordinary mental acrobatics that it must take for some people to still justify the actions of MonsantObama because those moves must rival those of a Gold Medal Olympic gymnast.

Come home.

The world needs you; we need you!

Hide your daughters.
Hide your wife.
Hide errbody (sic).
2/7 is back in town.

Sign tied to a fence near the front gate of Twentynine Palms Marine Base

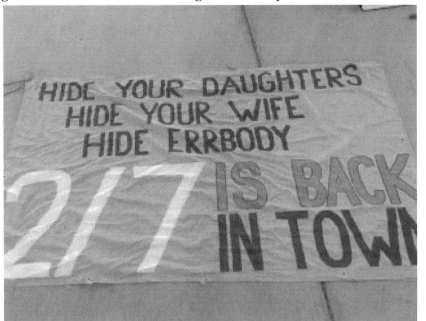

Yesterday, our motley crew of Tour de Peace ended up in Joshua Tree/Twentynine Palms area and one of our stops was to ride to the front gate of the humongous Marine base there in Twentynine Palms.

On the way up to the Marine Base from Yucca Valley, the wind was whipping us from the side with gusts up to 25 mph and the ride was already treacherous, but a few times, Bradleys passed us on the road, giving us an eerie feeling of insecurity.

There were only four of us riding and four following in support vehicles (including one from the National Lawyers Guild). I was chatting with my friend and Biking for Peace companion Ron Toppi (so far, he's ridden all the way, and more, with me) that it seemed like a long hard ride for just a few of us to confront one of the largest military installations in the country, and from the organizer on the ground, we weren't quite sure what the purpose of the "visit" was. By the time we turned left up Adobe Road, there were some really steep inclines AND the side wind had become a fierce headwind to make the ride even more strenuous and awful.

So, about a quarter mile from the main gate, we ran into that sign I posted above. Immediately, I was furious and discouraged. I thought, "If anyone in this country believes that it's okay to post a sign like that anywhere in America, then what in the hell am I doing riding my bike across America?" Then immediately, right after that thought, my second thought was: "That's exactly why I am riding my bike across America." Not just the so-called Blue States, but also through the "heart" of America.

The sign implies so many things: The patriarchal culture of using women and "errbody" as objects of power and pleasure; the glorification of "manly" behavior like war and rape; and the worship of these "heroes" who aren't even ashamed to post terrorist threats against women and "errbody" in their community after they apparently just returned from another Imperial Terrorist mission to another hapless and unfortunate land.

After that sign slapped us in the face with its arrogance and threats of violence, there were dozens of others posted that welcomed home the various sons, daughters, husbands and wives and that also slammed me with the ton of bricks that my own son, and thousands of others, didn't come home to "hero's" welcomes, and I wondered, not for the last time, about all the innocent people of foreign lands that have been slaughtered for Empire.

When we rode up to the visitor's center of the base, we were immediately met by a Marine police officer that asked us if we wanted to go on base. My answer was, "No, I am a daughter and I was a wife; apparently I am on the rape list." I grew angrier at the sign and resolved to rip it down on our way out, which I did.

One man who saw the picture, pointed out to me that perhaps it wasn't anyone in the 2/7 that put the sign up. I don't really care who posted that sign and I don't know how long it was there, but everyone, including the base commander, unit commander, Marine, and just plain regular citizen who passed by the sign gave their implicit approval of the message because it was still there. "Free Speech" does not include hate speech and that sign is most definitely hate speech.

The same person (who served in the 2/7 in Vietnam and claims to be a peace activist) who questioned who placed the sign there then pointed out that it was simply: *"I think the sign is probably meant to portray the unit as handsome manly men who all the women want for lovers rather than rapers or pillagers."*

I tried to debate him, but I will post this reply to him from another Marine, because I could never had said it better: *I'm a former Marine. I know the violent, chauvinistic, sexist propaganda promoted within the Corps. It used to be chants like, "Were gonna rape, kill pillage & burn" and "God damn son of a bitch, I gotta find a whore" and songs about your best girl, "Suzy Rotten Crotch" fucking your best friend. Now it might be subtler but the environment is the same. A society shouldn't have to lock up its women to protect them from its "heroes." If the frequency of rape in the military is any indication, the women of Twentynine Palms might not be safe."*

Then the Marine concluded with: *Explain "skill as a lady's man" and how that "skill" suggests ladies should be locked up. If these "heroes" were such a catch why would we want to prevent the ladies from meeting them? Personally, I'd be irritated to see this banner created by a high school football team also. Suggestion of rape culture debate aside, it is most definitely sexist. It's a glaring example of anti-feminist, patriarchal subjugation of women. And how does this sign include or honor the women who serve in the 2/7? You see, if these young men had real skills or were taught to respect women, they wouldn't dishonor the ladies that serve with them with such statements. I did not enter the Marine Corps as a violent, sexist womanizer, but it took several years after to recognize how I had adopted that mentality. Supporting the troops includes hard rebukes to inappropriate behavior, teaching them how to once again respect others, being patient, but direct, about the degradation of their own human spirit while encouraging them to rejoin society in healthy solidarity.*

We tore the sign down, because we object to its message at the core of our beings AND we are going to carry it to WashedUp, Deceit with us as a reminder of why we pedal, but also to hang up on the fence of the White House. Obama is a man with daughters and a wife and, I assume, he is included in the "errbody" the sign speaks of. Obama calls his troops his "heroes" and, for us, even though "the troops" are called on to do despicable things in the name of Sacred Profit, this behavior is NEVER acceptable and the entire culture of violence against "errbody," not just women, must end from the bottom up to the top and back down again.

Besides all the above, the Tour de Peace is entering into its second week and today we are having our first day off in beautiful and sacred Joshua Tree.

The first day, April 4th, I biked 45 miles to Sacramento and, since Sacramento, our Tour has visited Fresno, Santa Monica, Claremont, Rancho Cucamonga, Palm Springs, Twentynine Palms, and, as mentioned, Joshua Tree.

Everywhere we have been, the energy for our epic adventure has been very high and "errbody" has been very supportive. Our road is Route 66, but we have made deviations to do this incredibly important and successful outreach, as we will soon leave California and our events will be more thinly spread out.

After I spoke to the group in Joshua Tree that gathered to honor we pedalers, a musician named Sequoia sang us a song dedicated to us called: "Bring Heart Back to this Land," because he said that's what we are doing. Until our hearts connect together, this culture of top down and back up again violence will not end!

I pronounce Week One of Tour de Peace a resounding success! If you would like to get more information about our route, supporting the Tour, or anything else, please visit Tour de Peace.

Day off! Hiking and laundry!

Peace out for now!

Friday, April 19, 2013
And Then There Were Three

Cindy, near Flagstaff, AZ

Our bike ride across the country, Tour de Peace, is beginning its third week here in Flagstaff, AZ with an event soon.

We began in Vacaville, CA on April 4 at the grave of my son Casey and are planning on being in WashedUp, DeCeit on July 3 to present our demands for peace and justice in the heart of the Evil Empire.

We began with seven core riders and supporters on that rainy Thursday morning in my hometown, and after tomorrow, we are down to three.

Interestingly enough (as we follow old Route 66) when we stopped in Seligman, AZ a few days ago, we stayed at the Romney Motel and the irony is, we firmly believe that if Romney were the Emperor right now, we would have dozens of people riding with us, considering the State of the Empire and its continuing crimes against humanity.

Starting today, I am the only cyclist in an action that is supporting the reduction of the use of fossil fuels and the expansion of the use of clean, sustainable, and renewable forms of energy. Since we began, the Keystone XL pipeline (FYI to the Environmental Industrial Complex—it's already been approved) has ruptured and spilled in two US states and the BP oil gusher in the Gulf of Mexico is still polluting, AfriComm is expanding into 35 (many of them oil rich) African countries . . . yet, I ride alone.

Hellfire missiles are raining down on the people of Yemen, Afghanistan, and Pakistan, killing hundreds of innocent civilians, and Obama claims that anyone who targets civilians with bombs is a "terrorist" (takes one to know one)—yet, I ride alone.

Bradley Manning and other political prisoners rot in jail only for trying to ameliorate, stop, or prevent the crimes of the US Empire . . . yet, I ride alone.

Obama signed the so-called Monsanto Protection Act that effectively gives the company who gave us Agent Orange, pcbs, bovine growth hormone, and Roundup, 100 percent control of our food supply and prevents any kind of liability against the evil company's poisoning of our present and our future . . . yet, I ride alone.

While your attention has been consumed by the bombings in Boston, top "defense" officials testified in Congress yesterday that US troops were being sent to Jordan to invade Syria . . . yet, I ride alone.

So many crimes perpetrated by the US Empire, but because the leader of the crime syndicate purports to have a (D) behind his name . . . I ride alone.

I know it's not easy to put one's life on hold and strike out on an Epic Adventure of this magnitude —I know because I have done it dozens of times since my son was killed and it's not easy. I left my comfy bed and four grandchildren because I am afraid for their future if I don't.

I sleep in my tent, or a strange bed every night, from 20 degree temps to 97 degrees, because I know the sorrow of burying a child for lies and profit and I can't stand the thought of the terrorism that my own nation is committing on innocent people all over the world. I miss my grandbabies with all my heart, but who is fighting for all the children of the world? Democrats chalk their apathetic inactivity against the wanton murder up to supporting "humanitarian interventions," ignorantly siding with the very same arguments given to support the crimes of the previous Emperor.

Similarly, Republicans currently have little room to criticize the 4th Term of the Bush Regime.

It is difficult to ride 50 miles a day, from town to town, spreading this message, but we also feel like we are hogging all the fun. Biking down historic Route 66 gives one the opportunity to see so many wonderful things that are natural, or the manmade monuments to a failing car culture. We have met and interacted with dozens of interesting characters along the way and, even though we are down to three, we feel someone needs to keep shining the light of peace and justice to a population that is being terrorized by its own government.

I will continue this rolling vigil for peace and justice, whether I ride alone, or not; but it would be much better for me, and the children of the world, if this cause for peace and justice got as much support as the one we held in Crawford, TX received, wouldn't it? It would show our government and the terrorized people of the world that people in the US do oppose what the Empire is about.

Sunday, May 26, 2013
"Just think about it . . . Where would we be?"

As if one could escape the pervasive jingoism of Empire, I am freshly assaulted, as I cycle across the country with Tour de Peace, by every church on every corner that reminded that this weekend is Memorial Weekend.

Since 2004, Memorial Weekend has held special hell for me. My son Casey, who was needlessly murdered in Iraq because of the lies of his government and the greed of corporations, was born on Memorial Day, so I have double sorrow this weekend.

Being here in the Bible Belt of the nation, we cannot pass a church or synagogue that doesn't grossly glorify the horrifically deadly sin of war. There are obviously glaring exceptions like Unitarians, Quakers, Catholic Workers, and Mennonites, but those sects are definitely far outside the pale of extremist US Christianity.

I am never surprised by the warmongering of some purported followers of Christ, but I can still get mad-sad at the "Yea, war!" messages on the garishly lighted signs at these pseudo-religious appendages of the Pentagon. What will these places of mammon worship do when warfare is fully robotic? Will the billboards and the yellow magnetic ribbons of parishioners read: "Support the Drones?"

One such piece of crapaganda in front of a "Christian" church in St. Louis read: "Think about it . . . where would we be without the sacrifices of our troops?"

My first knee-jerk, selfish reaction was: "Well, instead of putting my life on hold for three months and biking across the country for peace and justice, I would be home playing with my grandbabies and Casey would be there, too." Maybe, just maybe, he would be married with children, himself.

Then, of course, I immediately went to the macro-analysis of that wonderful, "Christ-like" statement. MILLIONS of people would still be alive, and that's just from this young century! Just think about it . . . looking back over the life of this war-loving Empire that we live in, the loss of life is practically incalculable, and then there's the loss of limb, sanity, home, security, and reputation that cannot in anyway be quantified. The hearts of millions upon millions of mothers who rarely raise their children to be tools or victims of Empire would still be whole and not broken into a million tiny pieces.

Where would we be? Hmmm . . . the US wouldn't be trillions of dollars in debt and perhaps bridges wouldn't be collapsing and the money we would save on the expansion of Empire could be used to invest in education, infrastructure, health care, and environmental sustainability, among other things. Just think of an economy based on creating art and literature, and manufacturing life affirming and positive products only for consumption and not obscene profit. The war economy the US currently dis-enjoys literally sucks the life out of not just this country, but also the planet.

Just think about it . . . women and girls in other countries wouldn't be raped and female troops would not be sexually assaulted at the rate of about one out of three. Just think about it . . . the snake oil salesmen, oops, I mean military recruiters would thankfully be put out of the Murderers-for-Hire business.

Just think about it . . . the stains of places like Gitmo, Bagram, and Abu Ghraib would have never been opened and countless "terrorists" would have never been illegally detained, tortured, or murdered.

Just think about it . . . a world without the destructive nature of the US Military Empire. Like sociologist Robert Jay Lifton said, "War is an atrocity producing event," and when some smarmy coward of a politician or slimy representative of god on earth starts spewing crap about "freedom," "democracy," "national security threat," "evil dictator," "weapons of mass destruction," "humanitarian intervention," or any number of other lies: RUN THE OTHER WAY.

Just think about it. Think about it carefully. I have, and have come to the only conclusion there can be: This planet would be a vastly different and wonderful place.

SUPPORT THE TROOPS?

HOW ABOUT NO WARS, NO TROOPS?

> *Go ahead and laugh at Detroit. Because you are laughing at yourself.*
> **Charlie LeDuff:** *Detroit, An American Autopsy*

I am naturally an optimistic person, however, after the elections of 2012 when most of the small amount of people who did manage to vote, voted for their oppressors of the Democrat or Republican Parties, I was feeling a little hopeless. There were at least 25 other candidates to choose from and 98.4 percent the people chose War Party A or War Party B.

After decades of propaganda and mass marketing of politics, it seems like the American people have nearly lost the ability to critically think and see through bullshit—and that's discouraging.

One of the goals of Tour de Peace is to encourage others to break free from the chains of partisan politics and re-connect with our own values. Few people that we have met on this tour have the values of war, economic oppression, and environmental destruction, but they keep voting for that. People not only vote for people that grossly deviate from their own principles, but essentially hand their power over to scoundrels, murderers, and crooks. But, on Tour de Peace, I am thrilled to report that we have encountered communities that are beginning to reject any kind of governmental oppression and are turning away from it to each other.

We have been in countless of these fine communities, but I have to think that Detroit is the best example of this. Who would have thought that in Detroit my fountain of hope would be filled—and this is not "hope" based on illusion, but reality-based hope.

Recently (June 7–9), Charles and Sandra Simmons, founders of Detroit's Hush House, hosted the Tour de Peace. The Hush House is a "Black History Museum" and community center in Detroit's District 8. Charles and Sandra have deep roots in the community and, in fact, Charles' grandparents lived in the house that has been set up to be this museum and community center. Our team stayed in two bedrooms upstairs and we were treated to delicious vegan and gluten free community meals that were catered by locally owned black chefs and caterers. As soon as we arrived, we instantly felt like valuable and loved members of the family.

Tour de Peace left Ann Arbor, MI towards Detroit via Seven Mile Road. Until we hit Grand River Blvd, the road was lined with McMansions and white suburbia. Incredibly, we even saw a lawn jockey at the end of one driveway. Seven Mile Road was mostly wide shoulders and clean roads once we hit Grand Mile. However, that all changed.

Cycling down Grand Mile Road was a wonderful experience of life and urban art. We came across a miracle called the African American Bead Museum and I missed Oakland where I used to live.

We spent hours talking to "Baba and Mama" Simmons and other members of the family about the attack against the poor in Detroit that has been ongoing for decades.

I think most people understand that Detroit has "problems," but to sit with our brothers and sisters and hear their stories, that weren't unique, but systemic, was heartbreaking. Mothers with young children and breathing equipment who can't get the Detroit power company to restore electrical and gas power. In the suburbs, gas and electrical are two different bills, but in Detroit they are linked and both shut off with any delinquencies.

We heard of a young mother of three who refused to vacate her home when it was scheduled for demolition. In Detroit, after a home is condemned, it is often burned down and entire neighborhoods are often slashed and burned. This mother's home was endangered by one such plan of urban "renewal." She stood fast and the fire department eventually helped her, but her children had to live with debris and toxicity. She was forced to sleep in the living room with a gun on her lap to ward off hostile invaders demanding that she leave.

Naturally, the much-celebrated "bail-out" of the auto industry was accomplished off the backs of the workers who were forced to make terrible concessions in order for the top tier executives to not have to make any significant ones. With unemployment at 65 percent the corporate unions are also diabolically quick to sell out the workers.

The voters in the city voted down the plan to have an Emergency Manager (EM) who would co-ordinate massive police state collaboration between the FBI, state, local, and private security and police forces called Detroit One. However, Governor Rick Snyder and Detroit Mayor Dave Bing collaborated in some political hanky-panky to foist it on the embattled citizenry, anyway. Along with the EAA (Educational Achievement Authority that has long had this EM concept), Detroit One is bringing the people together to fight it.

We were told horrific tales of elementary school principals walking around with baseball bats and chaining young children into their school cafeterias during lunch in sweatshop conditions—that is inviting trouble, not preventing it.

What gives me hope in the midst of all this blight and oppression generated from above is that through it all the embattled Detroiters refuse to become embittered. The oppressed Detroiters refuse to be oppressed and turn toward each other as they have discovered that the solutions lie in their churches and neighborhoods, not in WashedUp, DeCeit or Lansing.

There are almost no fresh food grocery stores in Detroit, so community gardens are springing up. Children must walk to school past condemned buildings on sidewalks bounded by weeds taller than they are. Elders come out to make sure these youngsters get back and forth to school safely. Women, wonderful women, are running for office to be in city government. Some of the abandoned buildings are being reclaimed for these revolutionary communities of compassion.

I was profoundly honored to be invited to speak at the Historic King Solomon church where Malcolm, Martin, and the mother of Emmet Till have spoken. For the leaders of that community to mention my name in the same breath and sentence was humbling. I never forget that we stand on the shoulders of giants and our work must always strive to recognize and honor that.

Tour de Peace was also welcomed at the Liberty Temple where I spoke during Sunday services and was so sad for a mother there who had recently buried her son. I was able to tell her that she would never "get over" it, but with the help of her community and family, she would get through it. After I spoke, the dynamic pastor told me that I was a "jewel" and a "gift" to this world. The love and support extended to us combined with the tales of thrival (new word I coined in Detroit) are some of the reasons that being in Detroit re-filled my hope tank.

Tour de Peace was also able to share with the family in Detroit about how the "great" experiment of the attack on the poor, privatization, and increased austerity is now being extended into every community we have visited, but now we will also be able to share with each community we've yet to pass through how Detroiters are learning to overcome their problems together, in community.

I am not a huge church person, but when I see believers who are honestly engaged in the work that is the ideal of Jesus of Nazareth, I don't have a problem like I do with the war-loving sects and their hypocrisies.

On Sunday morning, at the Liberty Temple, I was reminded of a song that I sang when I was a youngster in Sunday school that is exemplified in the people we were with in Detroit, but tragically rejected by most:

"Jesus loves the little children, all the children of the world. Red and yellow; black and white; they are precious in his sight, Jesus loves the little children of the world."

When the struggle is long and hard, it's encouraging to be reminded of why we are in it.

Friday, June 21, 2013
Cindy Sheehan to Perform Nude High Wire Stunt in WashedUp, DeCeit
To bring attention to Peace and Justice: For Immediate Release

June 21, 2013

For immediate release:

Cindy Sheehan to perform "stunt" near White House.

Beginning on April 4th from the grave of her son Casey in Vacaville, CA, in an action called Tour de Peace, Peace Mom Cindy Sheehan has recently cycled 3500 miles to the fence of the White House.

Cindy Sheehan and Tour de Peace made numerous stops along the way and were able to reach out to thousands of people to inspire and be inspired by the message of peace and environmental sustainability. Even though Tour de Peace is just one long action in Sheehan's nine-year-long commitment to peace and justice, the Tour got no coverage from the national press or media.

From in front of the White House today in support of her friend, political prisoner, Lynne Stewart, Sheehan had this to say about the news blackout: "I realize that this current president is mired in scandal and up to his elbows in blood and gore, but I have written seven books, run for federal office twice, produce a weekly podcast, am still on the front lines advocating for peace and justice. I find it interesting that these dedicated acts receive very little national attention (even from "left-wing" media like *Democracy, Now*) when the press corps literally followed me to the outhouse when I was camped out in Crawford, TX protesting yet another president mired in scandals and dripping with blood and gore."

To try to do anything to call attention to the Tour de Peace and the thousands of people in solidarity with its demands, Sheehan has announced that she will perform a tightrope ride on her bike while completely nude and noshing on a gluten-free vegan pizza: The high wire will stretch from the tip of the Washington Monument to the statue of Andrew Jackson in Lafayette Park across from the White House.

This Peace Stunt will take place on Junly 34 at Never O'clock.

To schedule an interview with Cindy Sheehan, please contact The White Rabbit at: 1-800-555-5555 or BiteMe@youcowards.com

CINDY NOTE: *Even though the coverage wasn't what we expected, I would love to ride my bike across the US again!*

Monday, July 15, 2013
"Hide Errbody [sic]" Tour de Peace Wrap-up

The cross-country cycling leg of Tour de Peace ended on July 3rd with a very small protest in front of the White House, but I must admit, it is taking me far longer than I expected to recover from the 90-day odyssey in quest of peace and justice.

Cindy is on "first-name basis" with DC police state

I travel a lot and my life has been one protest or long action after the other since my son was killed; I even camped in a ditch in Crawford, TX for one hot August. Why has the end of Tour de Peace caused me so much exhaustion and, let's face it—mild depression? There are a few obvious answers, and some subtle ones.

First of all, I must face the fact that I am not a super-human. I am a middle-aged woman trapped in a rapidly degenerating skin bag, in slightly above average physical condition, who just rode her bike 3000 miles in all kinds of weather and terrain. That feat is one that I will marvel at and admire about myself forever, but one that did take its physical toll. Now, my impulse is to keep going "full-steam ahead," but every fiber of my being is screaming out, "REST!" I am trying to compromise with myself by resting AND continuing to ride my bike—I have to, I have no car—and doing activities that I love, like swimming and walking.

Secondly, I think the mild emotional depression comes from the fact that while the Tour exceeded many of my expectations, it woefully "deceeded" others. Although Tour de Peace was wonderfully hosted in a couple of dozen of communities across this nation with crowds ranging from 10 to 200, I was dismayed to find that there is very little antiwar sentiment out there besides the anti-drone work—which is important, but not comprehensive. By focusing on drones we forget about manned aircraft and there has been very little opposition to the US and its putrid allies arming and training the "rebels" in Syria.

The violence in Iraq, Afghanistan, and Pakistan continues and the use of drones is just one part of the imperial project of world domination.

Most people we encountered are rightfully concerned about what will happen to Pfc. Bradley Manning (in fact, the Tour went to his court martial in Ft. Meade several times to support him), but not up in righteous arms about what he revealed. The Edward Snowden revelation happened at the end of our Tour, but there was no resulting storming (used metaphorically) of the NSA or the White House? How do we get stuck on the cause célèbre, but not the cause?

Also, during the final weeks of the Tour, Obama was in Europe and Africa on his Tour de War—with very little commentary on how AfriComm is digging its vicious hooks into that continent to exploit and steal its vast stores of oil and other precious natural resources. In fact, Obama joined the last undemocratically elected CEO of USA, Inc. in Tanzania and good ol' George W. thinks Obama is doing a fine job. Now, there's an endorsement for the Obama lovers, eh? Anyway, I digress.

I think part of my depression stems from the fact that I am trying to figure out how to be a "peace" activist when there seems so little energy to forcefully and with integrity confront the fact that The Empire grinds on and over people no matter who is the president?

I know that "peace" encompasses so many important issues, such as economic justice, but how can we advocate for that when The Empire spends trillions of dollars per year maintaining said Empire?

I realize that "peace" also encompasses criminal justice, but how can we even begin to address that issue here, when the US wages these racist wars for Empire all over the globe? After the recent Zimmerman verdict in the Trayvon Martin case, the lead Executioner himself, Obama, appealed for "calm" reminding everyone that the US is a "nation of laws." It's so nice to hear Obama say that, since he routinely breaks the law by murdering people abroad with his hellfire missiles and spying on all of us (to name two of his crimes)—now his fan club can look at themselves in the mirror after they hear their abusive father tell them, "Do as I say, not as I do. I know what's best for you." It must all be true because Obama is the smart one and he can pronounce "nuclear."

I cannot say that I am even close to coming to a conclusion in my struggle for a relevant path to be on. I would like to circle my wagons and start growing my own food and producing my own energy, but I have a very deep-seated revulsion to the fact that the Empire I live in is murdering innocent people and stealing their land and natural resources. I want to be involved in a movement of people who fight against the same thing, but dozens does not a movement make.

I said in the beginning that this leg of Tour de Peace ended in front of the White House with a small protest—by "small" I mean less than 20 people. I had hoped that some of the large antiwar orgs would mobilize some people. I realize it was a Wednesday (when the buildings aren't actually empty in DC)—but that "turn out" was obviously a "turn down," and it actually may have demoralized me more than any recent event, or non-event, I guess. The only thing that keeps the hope flickering in me is that people joined us West Coasters from upstate Pennsylvania, New York, Iowa, Florida, and New Jersey to be there.

One of our goals when we reached WashedUp, DeCeit was to hang the banner on the White House fence that we liberated from the fence at Twentynine Palms Marine Base and we did it. I was surprised that we got it back with the mild admonishment of "don't do that again." The sign motivates the title of this peace because it read, "Hide your daughters. Hide your wife. Hide errbody [sic]. The 2/7 is back in town." We on the tour were rightfully outraged and appalled by that banner and that's why we tore it down. Being that the Obama family fits the threat implied in the sign (by the 2/7 Marines), we decided to bring it to DeCeit with us to show Obama what his troops do in the field and at home.

I am going to write a book about the experience (which was absolutely magnificent, no matter how letdown and exhausted I seem right now) called: *2013, A Bike Odyssey: Tales from Tour de Peace,* and I am anxious to get started after I finish *I Left My Marbles in San Francisco,* the book that's been on the back burner (almost finished, by the way). We are also working with the strong core of people that supported the Tour to keep the small, but mighty, energy going. Riding bikes is good for peace because it's good for the environment and our own health. Gotta love that!

I will be traveling back to the DeCeit area for a trial with the rest of the CIA 6. We were arrested on June 29th at the CIA protesting its participation in the US drone program and we decided to fight the charges. More info on that as it becomes available!

Again, a huge THANKS to everyone who supported Tour de Peace along the way! I will be okay and soon, I always am!

> *In the councils of government, we must guard against the acquisition of unwarranted influence, whether sought or unsought, by the military industrial complex. The potential for the disastrous rise of misplaced power exists and will persist.*
>
> **Dwight David Eisenhower, Farewell Address to the Nation, 1961**

Military Industrial Complex: *An informal alliance of the military and related government departments with defense industries that is held to influence government policy.*

As I write this, it is eight years since I marched up Prairie Chapel Road in Crawford, TX on August 6th to demand a meeting with then (p)resident, George W. Bush. I, a Gold Star Mom, who was and is still profoundly against war, had heard Bush say that the US troops who died in Iraq gave their lives for a "noble cause." Not one of the corporate media present at such an absurd pronouncement asked George, "What is that noble cause?" So I resolved to go to Crawford to ask the War Criminal myself.

Eight years later and with tons of blood passing under the bridge of Imperial doom, I am still asking that question. However, I know now as I probably did back then in 2005, that there is no "noble cause" for Empire expansion and the millions of people and trillions of dollars that are sacrificed on the altar of the Military Industrial Complex. The question that I and others repeatedly ask since then is, "Why can't our movements for peace and justice be effective?"

I think one of the reasons that our people- and principle-driven movements are ultimately destined to fizzle or fail, is that any movement that is perceived as powerful by the establishment is immediately channeled into the black hole of US partisan politics. I have written extensively about that, but this political derailment could not be accomplished on the left without the help of the Peace Industrial Complex.

The Peace Industrial Complex (PIC) resembles its counterpart of the Military (MIC) sort by its very alliance with the Democratic wing of the War Party and must bear a great responsibility for the continuing war tactics of the Empire. Language is important, and just because the Democratic wing of the War Party calls its Imperial transgressions "humanitarian interventions" does not make it right, or the lives lost any less tragically unnecessary and sad.

Why do I tie in the idea of the PIC with my experience at Camp Casey? On one of the last days of the nearly month long peace encampment on Prairie Chapel Road, I was overwhelmed that both Reverend Al Sharpton and Martin Sheen came out, we had a wedding, and I was involved in a photo shoot for Oprah's magazine. The wonderful activist Eve Ensler had pitched a story to the magazine and was told that she could do it as long as there was no, "Bush bashing." This is still the problem, when one tells the truth about the pain of burying her oldest child for absolutely no reason, except that he was killed in another war-for-profit based on lies, or actually gives facts, that person is perceived as "bashing." Once the Empire shifted to being "led" by a Democrat, who was also a person of color, my heart truth and facts began to be characterized as "bitterness" by some of the very same people who joined me in "bashing" Bush at Camp Casey.

Oops, I got off the subject. Anyway, on that final Sunday of our first campout in Crawford, I was told by one of the leading members of the PIC, that I was the most "powerful woman on the planet." Then, I was whisked away on a two-year adventure around the world and throughout the US where I believed I was bringing peace, but looking back, what I was really doing was being used by the PIC to deliver the House of Representatives back to the Democrats. After that was accomplished, and a few of us were still trying to hold the Democrats accountable to end the wars (by ending war funding and investigating the Bush regime), we were kicked to the curb like old garbage and the PIC found the language of the right useful in demonizing me and my cause.

In 2008, for example, for the 5th anniversary of the invasion of Iraq, I was even told by United for Peace and Justice (UFPJ) that there would be no mass demo in DC because it would "embarrass" the complicit Democrats, and was told by another organization that we had helped so much Iraq Veterans Against the War, that I was banned from attending its Winter Soldier event in DC in March of that year. Why? Because not all of the vets who would be testifying were "antiwar" and wouldn't want to be seen associating with me. I was hurt, but not defeated, and vowed to always be in the principled struggle for peace, and not on the side where war is only wrong if a Republican regime is waging it.

I look back after nine years of very hard struggle and when I remember the power and serendipity of Camp Casey in 2005, I see that we have very little to show for it with regard to policy, or peace. I recall how naïve I was when I said, "The wars will end and Bush will be impeached." Heck, at the time, I even belonged to a "peace" organization that forbade us members from saying that Afghanistan was wrong because most Americans supported it because we were "attacked on 9/11." We won't end wars or hold USAian War Criminals accountable when we even have to overcome the obstacle of people we think are our comrades who block any kind of relevant action or analysis of Empire.

Another example, by October of 2005, the US was going to surpass the horrid milestone of 2000 troops lost in Iraq. Of course, the US troops killed in the "good war" in Afghanistan didn't count, and the innocent people our troops killed never counted, either. So, an organization that I thought was in favor of peace, but now I know it only wants peace when a Republican is in the Oval Office, MoveOn.org, called for "candlelight vigils" to commemorate that sad number. I was in DC at the time, and I called for civil disobedience in front of the White House. MoveOn.org denounced that action and moved their candlelight vigil so as not to be near the lawlessness of our action. MoveOn.org raised a lot of money and increased its membership dramatically when I was camped in Crawford and my break with MoveOn.org began while I was still camped there.

One hot Crawford day, two MoveOn.org operatives requested a meeting with me at Camp Casey, so we went to my trailer and they informed me that I should back a bill in Congress co-sponsored by two Democrats and two Republicans that was for a slow, phased withdrawal based on "progress reports" and conditions on the ground. One thing the affiliated organizations at Camp Casey did agree on was demanding "troops out, now," and I told MoveOn.org that I could not endorse their "troops out, eventually" bill. That's when MoveOn.org withdrew its support and the "help" of the Fenton P.R. agency, who were only there to try to point our protest only in the direction of the "Rs," anyway.

Subsequently, when the Ds took over control of the House of Reps in 2007, the question of war funding came up and MoveOn.org polled its members with two questions, and the only alternative was to support the Democrats in continuing the supplemental war funding because MoveOn.org knew that PelosiCo would never stop the funding, so the energy of MoveOn.org is to give Democrats cover for any crimes they want to commit. MoveOn.org's very livelihood (profit) derives from covering the crimes of the Democrats and diverting our attention away from those crimes and in blaming only one small part of the problem.

During Camp Casey, I had received some support from director/actor/movie producer, Rob Reiner, and his wife, Michelle. After Camp Casey closed up shop for the summer, I was invited to their home in LA to meet them and chat. In lockstep with MoveOn.org, Rob informed me that I should stop saying "troops home, now" because all of our troops couldn't get "home now" and I sounded "loony" saying that. I was stunned because I can't believe that people would think that the US Commander in Chief was some kind of djinn who could fold his arms and blink his eyes and get all the troops home in a matter of seconds. I presumed, and still do, that it takes planning and logistics, and I reminded Rob that during the insanity of Vietnam, an Admiral was asked how the US could remove troops from Vietnam and he said, "By boat and plane, the same way they got there."

I believe that we always advocate for the greatest good and the highest victory, because the incrementalism of the PIC guarantees failure and more heartbreak, torture, and death. I was booted to the curb by the Reiners when I refused to support warmonger, Hillary Clinton, because they told me she was our "only hope." However, the Reiners did not mean she was our only hope to end Empire, but for the Democrats to regain the "prize" of the Blight House. Even that sell-out didn't work out too well for them, did it?

Where would the MIC be without its wars and, similarly, where would the PIC be under the same circumstance?

I work my ass off to make my activism obsolete. I am not interested in perpetuating wars or political loyalty to make a buck, or gain influence with the very criminals that I loathe and protest. Organizations in the PIC seem to have unlimited resources to hire staff and open offices, where organizations like mine try to do the best we can with the limited resources and volunteers that we do have.

I was very new to activism in 2005, and now I know that there are establishment and revolutionary versions of every movement and that's why movements, by and large, fail. For example, the Environmental Industrial Complex fails when it says, "Democrats, we want you to do X, but if you don't, we'll still vote for you." How about focusing on principles and successful and honest ways to get there? The slimy Democrats deserve your support just about as much as the equally slimy Republicans.

Peace and accountability will not happen unless we guard against the "unwarranted influence" of the Peace Industrial Complex.

CINDY NOTE: Just as we didn't guard against the unwarranted influence of the MIC, the PIC is still inhibiting movements and channeling energy into DNC (Democratic National Committee) politics.

Friday, August 30, 2013
Cindy Sheehan for Reichwing Dummies

Now that the War Party with its leader, Barack Obama, is ratcheting up the rhetoric for another war, the predictable Reichwing attacks against me begin.

Whether written by moronic bloggers, or emailed to me directly, the subject line is always something like this:

"Where are you now?"
I thought to save myself some time, I would write this fact sheet for those Dummies. It always amuses me that they can come to my blog, find the "CONTACT" link, and then write me with misinformed accusations like those below. The Reichwingers can take the time to find my email, but they don't look down the page a little to see that I actually do the opposite of what they want to accuse me of.

"What? You only opposed war when Bush was in office? What a hypocrite!"
I oppose every war of the past and in the present. I oppose every war of the future.

War is a tool of barbarism and it is the opposite of sane and healthy for states to force its young to kill other people in some kind of geo-political game of serial madness and murder.

I don't care what war you want to throw at me, I oppose it and it was/is/will be wrong. People can sit across from one another and solve problems without resorting to murder, plain and simple. Any solution that involves troops, bombing, torture, etc., is evil and fraught with sorrow and destruction. Think about it . . . please . . . if you think about it with a rational mind, you will see yourself how demented war really is.

I can't remember a war that was waged to solve any geo-political problems that weren't created so the war profiteers can get more blood-soaked money. The sane solution would be to dismantle the war machine and mantle a healthy economy based on peace and environmental sustainability. Again, if you take the red, white, and blue cloud out of your brain, I know you will know that I am correct.

Just the wars in Iraq and Afghanistan have cost over three trillion dollars. Where did all that money go? Into the pockets of multi-national corporations from oil companies, to tank builders, to drone manufacturers, and even Burger King and AT&T.

The planned misadventure in Syria will shoot off Tomahawk missiles at 300-million/per missile. Right off the top of my head, I could probably think of 300 ways that money could be spent to contribute to a healthy and sane society and not one that goes around the world killing people to save them from being killed by their own leaders? Again, if that doesn't cause some kind of incongruity in your Limbaugh-esque addelpation, then I am afraid there is very little hope for you.

War is only good for the global elite, and the rest of the billions of us should reject being harmed for the good of the elite.

Again, I can't say this strongly enough—Reichwing Dummies who call me a "hypocrite" should look at their own "values." If you supported Bush and his immoral wars of aggression, then you should support Obama and his. If you opposed Bush and his immoral wars of aggression, then you should oppose Obama and his.

It's just common sense, but when the two violent branches of the War Party come together, we lose our reasonableness and turn into stone-cold killers, or the enablers of stone-cold killers, ourselves.

"What else can I expect from a Democrat."

I left the Democratic Party in 2007—the irony here is that I probably loathe the DP more than you do, because Democrats not only support Empire, but their mission is to demobilize true opposition to the policies of Empire. At the moment, I belong to the Peace and Freedom Party and would NEVER return, or support, the War Party.

"You crawl up the ass of every Democrat out there."

This one is laughable and so easy to fact check.

I ran against Nancy Pelosi (D-CA) in 2008 for Congress.

I ran against Barack Obama (D-MORDER) in 2012 as VP candidate for the Peace and Freedom Party. I have NEVER supported Barack Obama and voted for Cynthia McKinney of the Green Party in 2008 and also supported Ralph Nader (I). I made a vow at Camp Casey in 2005 to NEVER support any politician, or party, that supported war—so that excludes most Democrats and almost every Republican.

Right now, I am challenging Governor Jerry Brown (D) here in California for Governor.

I don't see how anyone with two seconds to devote to a Google search can make that claim with a straight face. I am afraid all of you must really be Dummies, though.

"I haven't seen you crying on the TV every time I turn it on since Obama has been president."

I listed a few things above that I have done electorally, but other than that, I have held three protest camps near Obama: One in Martha's Vineyard and two in Washington, DC—I have been to every antiwar protest (as small as they are) locally and the ones I can get to nationally—I have been arrested several times protesting wars, nukes, drones, and the CIA/NSA—and I just completed a 90-day bike ride across the country trying to gauge the antiwar sentiment of people who should be opposing Obama's wars.

We send out press notifications and we have press events, but NO press ever shows. I haven't been invited on any of the "progressive shows" either, except for once on Mike Malloy and once on *Democracy, Now!* for about 80 seconds in 2010. This lack of coverage doesn't discourage me, obviously, but the idiot box is apparently making idiots out of the Reichwing Dummies.

However, dear Reichwing Dummy, don't make the mistake of thinking that things only happen if they are happening on your magic TV box.

There is a thing called "life" and why don't you turn off your Dummy Box and set up camp in Washington, DC or Martha's Vineyard if you hate Obama so much?

Where are your large marches and rallies? Why don't I see you crying on TV about Obama being a Muslim or Commie (LOL)? I put my money where my mouth is and devote considerable time, energy, and resources to what I believe in—now get off the computer and do the same.

But, Reichwing Dummy, maybe you should quit whining at me and get busy supporting Obama, since he is just carrying on the policies of your heroes, Bush and Cheney?

Saturday, August 31, 2013
"No Boots on the Ground"

The President of the USA, aka, Able Servant of Empire, claims that his planned assault on Syria will be "limited" and he won't order any "boots on the ground" as if he is angling for praise from the almost non-existent antiwar movement and/or to prove that he really earned that Noble Peace Prize!

Besides the fact that the US now has troops on the ground in 35 African countries; destroyed Libya for regime change; is bombing "al Qaeda" in Somalia, Yemen, Afghanistan, and Pakistan; AND is already arming and training "al Qaeda" in Syria, the Able Servant of Empire is chomping at the bit of more mass murder to launch a Tomahawk missile attack on Syria.

My friend Ann Wright, who is a retired Colonel, US Army, and a former diplomat who resigned when the US invaded Iraq in 2003, wrote in this piece about what could be the possible consequences of Obama's "limited" assault on Syria:

Syrian anti-aircraft batteries will fire their rockets at incoming US missiles.

Many Syrians on the ground will die and both the US and Syrian governments will say the deaths are the fault of the other.

The US Embassy in Damascus will be attacked and burned, as may other US Embassies and businesses in the Middle East.

Syria might also launch rockets toward the US ally in the region—Israel.

Israel would launch bombing missions on Syria as it has three times in the past two years and perhaps take the opportunity to launch an attack on Syria's strongest ally in the region Iran.

Iran, a country with a population of 80 million and has the largest military in the region untouched by war in the past 25 years, might retaliate with missiles aimed toward Israel and toward nearby US military bases in Afghanistan, Turkey, Bahrain, and Qatar.

Iran could block the Straits of Hormuz and impede the transport of oil out of the Persian Gulf.

These likely outcomes don't even take into account that the nuclear powers of Russia and China are also very opposed to further intervention in Syria from the Empire.

Besides the fact that there is no evidence that the Syrian regime gassed its "own people," what gives The Able Servant of Empire the right to bomb Syrians with Tomahawk missiles? (At 300 million dollars, each: CHA-CHING, War Machine!)

Today (August 31) the Able Servant of Empire gave a speech in the Rose Garden of the White House and, among other things, he said something that was at once chilling and revealing at the same time: *"We cannot raise our children in a world where we will not follow through on the things we say, the accords we sign, the values that define us."*

What are those "values that define us?" I wonder? I have a strong suspicion that my values and Obama's values (a person can have rotten values) are diametrically opposed. Among the values that "define me" are unconditional peace for all the children in the world. I am afraid the values that define the Empire are the quest for profits over peace and power instead of protecting the lives, homes, and planet where the children live. The Able Servant of Empire has already ordered the murders of thousands of children and if there was a god, Obama would choke on his obvious and repetitive lies taken right out of the Empire's Playbook for World Domination.

How dare the Empire embark on another horrendous war to "save" people by killing them? I always think of my son killed for lies of the previous Able Servant and my surviving children and four grandbabies.

"No boots on the ground" in Syria? I look at the container my daughter has at the front door that holds various sizes and types of shoes for her family and I think of the doomed innocents in Syria.

Maybe there won't be US boots on the ground there, but there are already sandals, bare feet, sneakers, dress shoes, and most importantly of all, baby shoes. Their lives are so precious and they have not done anything to harm, or even threaten the war criminal Obama or America.

The innocents in Syria do not deserve the fate that some dude in an expensive suit and tie thousands of miles away will deal out to them for the benefit of the war profiteers.

No more US intervention in Syria.

Thursday, September 5, 2013
End the Wars; Begin the Healing

*War . . . it paid well and liberated children
from the pernicious influence of their parents.*
Joseph Heller, *Catch-22*

*What message will we send
if a dictator can gas hundreds of children to death
in plain sight and pay no price?*
Barack Obama

We cannot raise our children in a world where

we will not follow through on the things we say, the accords we sign, the values that define us.

Barack Obama

I would much rather spend my time talking about how to make sure every 3- and 4-year-old gets a good education than I would spending time thinking about how can I prevent 3- and 4-year-olds from being subjected to chemical weapons and nerve gas.

Barack Obama

. . . that this action happened, that Assad did it, that hundreds of – hundreds of children were killed. This is behavior outside the circle of civilized human behavior and we must respond.

House Minority Leader, Nancy Pelosi

At this critical juncture, it is essential that we make all Americans – the men and women we represent – fully aware of what the intelligence clearly and unequivocally demonstrates:

that the Assad regime was responsible for chemical weapons attacks against innocent Syrians, resulting in the deaths of more than 1,400 people,

including hundreds of children.

House Minority Leader, "Nanny" Pelosi

If acute hypocrisy suddenly became a fatal disease, I am certain that there would be not one left alive in the federal government. Democrats who opposed Bush's wars are lining up to support Obama's next war crime and vice-versa. However, the sudden concern for the children of the world is a particularly sickening hypocrisy since the Empire doesn't even care about children here in the US.

Here is a partial list of the Empire "caring" about children—historically, and currently.

Native Populations: Massacred by rifle and intentional biological warfare; displaced from their lands. Children were often kidnapped from their families and communities to be raised in "civilization." Today, many of the original people often live in abject poverty and comprise less than one percent of the total population.

Forced human bondage: Mostly stolen from Africa, or descendants of those stolen. Again, many were children and many were separated from their families, tortured, or killed.

Of course, you say, that was back in the "olden days" and nothing like this would happen today. However, according to the National Center of Family Homelessness, one in 45 (1.6 million) children are homeless and this reflects at 37 percent increase over the situation in 2007. Maybe Obama and Pelosi should devote some of those war resources to this emergency?

MonsantObama has appointed many Monsanto executives to his regime and recently signed the "Monsanto Protection Act" into law. This "law" allows Monsanto to continue poisoning the children of this nation with literal impunity.

Obama leaves his crocodile tears for those kids "gassed" in Syria, while at the same time, his use of drones and Hellfire missiles have lovingly slaughtered thousands of innocents in Pakistan, Afghanistan, Somalia, and Yemen, many of those children.

Civilian casualties in "war" (those constitutionally declared, and those not) have risen from practically zilch during the US Civil War to over 95 percent today. Since the US has only not been at war for a few weeks since its inception, more and more children are being slaughtered by our rampant and escalating militarism. Of course, it's for their own good, I guess. Like Robert Gibbs (former White House SpokesSnake) said about Obama assassinating US citizen 16-year-old Abdulrahman al Awlaki in Yemen in 2012: *"I would suggest that you should have a far more responsible father if they are truly concerned about the well being of their children."* Come on kids, if you can make sense of that tragically convoluted and callous sentence, choose better fathers if you don't want Obama to murder you! It's clearly the fault of the children who make the choice to be born to bad fathers, or in areas that unfortunately have vast reserves of oil, or other natural resources.

I know you know that the US massacred tens of thousands of innocent humans when it dropped not one, but two, nuclear devices in Japan. I was at the Peace Memorial in Hiroshima in 2011 on August 6th and I saw the display of a tricycle that belonged to a three-year-old boy who was out riding in front of his home when the US decided to display its deep affection for children by dropping an a-bomb on his sweet little head.

We've all seen the pictures of Vietnamese children burning and running from the Love-Napalm sprayed on them by US forces.

Who can forget the hundreds of thousands of children starved to death in Iraq during the humanitarian Clinton regime in the '90s? Then the Bush regime decided to continue the love by invading the country and killing or displacing millions of children. What was it but concern for children that caused the US to use depleted uranium weapons, white phosphorous and cluster bombs in Iraq? Poisoning future generations of children by these methods and Agent Orange in Vietnam must prove to us all that the US truly adores them, right?

Now, Obama and Pelosi want to kill Syrian children so their government doesn't kill them? I don't want the Syrian government or US supported rebels to kill anyone, but I am sure that dying by a US made and launched missile is much more compassionate than any other way?

Obviously, the "problem" that the US has is not that it loves children so much, but that it's Murder, Inc and wants a global monopoly on carnage.

To me, and many others who really pay attention to needs of children, what is urgent is for the US to stop all its wars that harm families all over the world. Why do you think our economy is tanking and the social safety nets are being greatly reduced or eliminated? Our overwhelming monetary and psycho investment in the military industrial complex!

Another imperial assault on an innocent civilian population will cost many more billions of dollars and while that's good for the bankers and other war profiteers, it sucks for most of the rest of us.

I demand of the hypocrites in DC that claim to be so worried about children, to cease and desist its warmongering and murder everywhere and devote every available resource to solving the nuclear meltdowns and catastrophes in Fukushima.

As a resident and gubernatorial candidate in California, I am afraid that the criminal incompetence and failure in Fukushima will further compromise the health and safety of my children and grandchildren, and it will eventually hurt all the children of the world, even Obama's and Pelosi's.

Containing Fukushima Dai'ichi as soon as possible, if not sooner, is the most urgent global need at this very moment.

End the wars; begin the healing.

Sunday, December 29, 2013
2013 Recap and Looking Forward to 2014 for the Soapbox!

December 29, 2013

Dear Friend,

Twenty-thirteen was quite a year for our Soapbox and me. We accomplished a lot for our cause, and we also had a chance to sit back and watch the Empire crumble from within, and root for its inevitable collapse.

As humans we can rightly decry the violence inflicted on little children in their Kindergarten class in Connecticut, and still be ashamed of the hypocrisy of a president who cries crocodile tears over their loss, but then orders the drone bombing of weddings and funerals in other parts of the world. The citizens of Boston were exposed to what citizens of Iraq and Afghanistan and other colonies see everyday: Tanks and troops infesting their streets.

Who predicted the disaster of ObamaCare? (Me and a lot of other people, by the way). The total cluster-fudge of the "roll-out" combined with the CYA scrambling of the administration would have been amusing if so many people weren't already harmed because of lack of health insurance in this country, and so many people losing the insurance that Obama promised they could keep.

While all that was going on, we took positive action. From April 4 to July 3, Tour de Peace had a successful bike trip for peace and justice from California to WashedUp, DeCeit. The crew and I had many wonderful adventures and, hopefully, in 2014 we are going to put out a "travelogue" called: *2013: A Bike Odyssey*. When the pressures of life and of being an activist overwhelm me, I think, "Hey lady, you rode your bike across the country—that's pretty badass—you can do anything!"

At the end of 2013, I published my seventh book: *I Left My Marbles in San Francisco: The Scandal of Federal Electoral Politricks* about my run for Congress against Nancy Pelosi, with an After(math)word about my run for VP with Roseanne Barr.

Besides throwing my hat in the ring to run for Governor of California in 2014, I will make sure that the Soapbox will continue as a counter-balance to the BS propaganda of not just the "Robber Class" media, but the so-called "liberal" media that seems to be going to the right, right along with the Democratic Party. Cindy Sheehan's Soapbox will celebrate our five-year anniversary with our first show of the year on January 5, which will feature Icelandic Parliamentarian Birgitta Jonsdottir who will tell us about the wonderful things happening in her country—like the jailing of big bankers—and how we can model their fight here in the homeland of the Empire.

On April 4, my family will not just be mourning the 10th year of our dear Casey's death in Iraq, but also the tragic continuation and expansions of the longest "wars" in US history.

Along with campaigning for Governor and continuing the Soapbox, I will be working on a documentary I hope will be released on August 6, 2015, which will be the 10th anniversary since we set up camp in Crawford, TX, at what became known as Camp Casey. The working title is *Prairie Fire: The Camp Casey Story,* and we will let you know more information as it comes along.

We at Team Soapbox are so grateful for your support and would be so happy to get your end of year (tax deductible, if you desire) DONATION.

You can count on me to be persistent in my quest for peace. I won't stop until the Empire does!

Hoping 2014 brings (true) peace, prosperity (for everybody), and environmental healing. Arm in arm, we are going to make some real progress.

Cindy Sheehan

PS: Let's never forget the good people that left us this past year, including, but certainly not limited to, Nelson Mandela and Hugo Chávez (not eulogized by Obama, but loved by his people). Presente! May we all find healing in love and solidarity.

That's all for 2013, folks.

Continuing into 2014, most of my posts will be about my run for governor and less about Obama and his crimes, but let's face it—California is just a microcosm of the US and our current governor, Jerry Brown (D), is nothing but a corporatist like the "big guy" in DC.

2014 is truly the year the Obama becomes the lamest of ducks.

Part Six
2014

CINDY NOTE: *As I write this, we are in the final weeks of 2014; Obama was made a "lame duck" at the midterms when the Republicans surged into the majority of both houses of Congress.*

Of course, as you have seen repeatedly in these pages, it's my opinion that what goes on in WashedUp, DeCeit is as real as professional wrestling entertainment and as relevant to us as what happens on Mars.

As I stated at the end of 2013, the first half of 2014 was focused on my ridiculous run for Governor of California, and I think I will post some articles about that here if I believe they expose the system that we continue to try and fight: Some of them may mention Obama, some may not.

Wednesday, January 1, 2014
Lynne Stewart is Finally Free!

On December 31, we received the most wonderful and surprising news. Our friend Lynne Stewart was being released from prison! Following is Lynne's triumphant return to her friends and family (thanks to Margaret Kimberly of *Black Agenda Report*).

This is Lynne's New Year's Eve message:

January 1, 2014

My Dears:

Well, the impossible takes a little longer!!! We learned this morning that the US Attorney's office has made the motion for my compassionate release and that the Order was on Judge Koeltl's desk. Since on the last go-round he stated in Court that he would treat it "favorably," we are now just waiting expectantly. The wonderful thing is that Ralph is here in Ft. Worth for a visit and will bring me back to NYC with him.

We don't know when, but the rules state that the warden has two days to let me go after he receives the order, so it could be as early as Friday or a few days more. Whatever it is, I can't stop crying tears of Joy!! I can't stop thinking of all the marvelous people worldwide who made this happen . . . you know, because each of you played an integral role.

My daughter Z is already lining up Sloan Kettering and we will have to see if there is a

probation qualification attached to the Order and how it will affect me. After that, Ralph will start making arrangements to rent Yankee Stadium for the Welcome Home . . . . Smile.

So, if this reaches you before midnight tonight raise a glass of bubbly to the joy

of all of us that the old girl is OUT!!

Love Struggle,

Lynne

CINDY NOTE: This piece does not mention Obama, but it's worthy to note that Obama's DOJ has persecuted more whistleblowers and activists than any previous administration, and Lynne's case was reviewed and she received a much harsher sentence under Obama. She was sentenced to 10 years in prison. Personally, this was the best New Year's present ever!

Friday, February 28, 2014
War is Costly (Peace Plan for California)

As someone who is intimately and very painfully acquainted with the personal cost of war, I believe that the carnage and destruction of war is what we need to focus on. We should never give up our struggles for peace and end of Empire as long as one person is being threatened or in harm's way of the US military juggernaut.

However, according to the National Priorities Project, since 2001, the total cost of the US War *OF*

Terror has been over $1.5 trillion dollars and:

*Every **hour**, taxpayers in **United States** are paying **$11.26 million** for **Total Cost of Wars since 2001**.*

Of course, in a 2010 article in *The Washington Post*, economists Joseph Stiglitz and Linda Bilmes compute the "true" cost of just the horror the US perpetrated on Iraq at over "3 trillion."

Not only is the loss of my own treasure, my first born, needlessly relevant in my life, as a candidate for Governor of California, the hemorrhaging of this state's resources to the War *OF* Terror is also needless and significant.

According to the apparently conservative, but verifiable, statistics of the National Priorities Project:

*Every **hour**, taxpayers in **California** are paying **$1.45 million** for **Total Cost of Wars since 2001**.*

Besides the flesh and blood we have had stolen from us, California has ponied up almost $200 billion dollars that could obviously be used for more positive and life-affirming projects here in our own state.

The US Department of War is scaling back its traditional activities, yet expanding black ops and use of drone technology. What we need federally and locally are leaders that know what struggle is and are able to be free of the Military Industrial Complex.

Californians can say "Hell, no" to war and "Hell, yes" to a state that puts the needs of people over the greed of Empire.

Imagine a state as big and powerful as California saying "Hell, no" to Empire?

We will no longer cede any of our tax dollars or our children to the imperial meat-grinder. This is a good plan for our state, our nation, and the world!

Tuesday, March 11, 2014
No Nukes Today and Always!

(Remembering Japan on 3/11)

As most of you already know, three years ago today, the island-nation of Japan suffered a major earthquake and tsunami. The original damage was quite devastating and we mourn and remember everyone who lost their lives that day and their friends, family, and fellow citizens of Japan.

I also stand in solidarity with the demand of millions in Japan and around the world: No More Fukushimas!

That disaster is a continuing worry for us all and demonstrates that nuclear power was never safe or viable.

I also stand in solidarity with millions of people around the world that are demanding an end to the use of nuclear and fossil fuel technology for power and bombs. We demand investment in safe, renewable, and sustainable forms of energy.

I was in Japan just five months after the natural and nuclear disaster in 2010, and I formed many close bonds with my brothers and sisters who are working to hold the Japanese government and TEPCO accountable for the negligence, cover-ups, and other crimes against the people of Japan— and the spreading poison that could potentially affect the entire Western Hemisphere.

A Cindy Sheehan administration in California would work with activists on both sides of the Pacific to make sure all nuclear power plants are shut down and the poisons and radiation emanating from Fukushima be stopped and cleansed for the future!

You are not alone.

Cindy Sheehan

Cindy Sheehan's Soapbox

Cindy Sheehan for Governor, 2014

CINDY NOTE: *Obama is profoundly pro-nuke. After Fukushima, Venezuela stopped plans to build a nuclear power plant as then President Hugo Chavéz said, "It's not worth the risk." After Fukushima, Obama said, "Nuclear power is still safe."*

Tuesday, March 18, 2014
Women and Politics

I think most of us know that in the early days of the US voting was reserved for white-male property owners (WaMPOs as I call them). Even black slaves were counted as "3/5ths" of a person in the Constitution, while women were left completely out. In fact, the Founders didn't even quite trust WaMPOs, hence the institution of the Electoral College.

Former slaves and women fought hard and sacrificed much for their inclusion into this WaMPO paradise (oops, I mean, Republic) of voting. The picture above is of women picketing the White House (something I have done dozens of times and been arrested for many times). The WaMPOs fought back hard and, even now with the passage of the 19th Amendment to the US Constitution some 94 years ago, women—although more than half the population in general—are elected to only about 18 percent of offices in this country.

The WaMPO paradigm was, of course, terrified that the entry of women into the electoral arena would screw things up for their comfort and positions of power. I only wish that this were true. I wish that when we earned our right to vote and entry into higher politics that we would have used OUR power and OUR insights and intelligence to put the breaks on Empire. Jeannette Rankin (first woman in Congress) from Montana should have been our beacon to follow, yet we are left with plastic women who get their minds and pocketbooks filled with Imperial plunder.

When people of color and/or females rise to high prominence in government, a la Barack Obama or Hillary Clinton, they often exhibit more loyalty to the old WaMPO way of doing things than being groundbreaking leaders for their race or gender. I believe it's tragic that many leading female leaders from around the world have been such war-like creatures that we have very little integrity or courage to look up to or strive for.

To most of our fellow consumers (oops, I mean "citizens"), as candidate for office myself, I have a few societal strikes against me: I am a socialist (with a small "s"); I am counter-cultural with regard to what most people feel is the "American Way;" and I am a woman. But I am a woman who thinks that the WaMPO way of doing things has been given free reign to destroy the planet with its form of predatory capitalism and imperial overreach for far too long.

Even women hold these things against me and use some of the basest stereotypes to try to undermine me, or maybe force me to slink back to my home and hearth in shame to lick the claw marks and think about how I can be a better woman.

For example, when I ran for Congress in San Francisco against then Speaker of the House and apparent WaMPO, Nancy Pelosi, MySpace was a big thing. I will never forget this one woman who messaged me on MySpace to tell me that I wasn't "qualified" to run for Congress.

Was I younger than 25? Um, no, I was 51 on Election Day that year.

Did I fail to meet the nine-year state residency requirement? No, I had lived in California for 51 years on Election Day that year.

However, I did fail her requirements: "You aren't qualified to run for Congress because you don't have a car, a job, or a husband." Sadly, she was serious.

Recently, at a protest we were campaigning at, a woman told me that I should wear pantsuits and more makeup because voters want "Stepford Wife" candidates. Wow! That may be true, and probably is, because in this celebrity and excessive worship culture, appearance is far more important than substance. However, the term "Stepford Wife" implies far more than perfect hair, stylish clothes, and clownish makeup. It also implies a woman who will fall into lockstep with the dominant WaMPO culture with a smile on her face, legs ready to spread on demand, and a pan of warm cookies cooling on the stove.

Until we all break free of what an appearance-obsessed culture demands and break out of the DemoPublican political chains, all we are going to continue to get will be wars, economic slavery, and environmental destruction.

I refuse to change myself for a few votes because, win or lose, I know I must be authentic. I was never, and will never be, a "Stepford Wife."

Hopefully, there is a growing contingent of human beings that are sick and tired of the fraudulent images of crass politicians who bend and twist to the winds of Madison Avenue-generated sales campaigns.

NASA just completed a study that said that life on this planet can no longer exist with the crushing weight of demand for shrinking resources. Male or female, we need new and fresh ideas and people that are committed to doing the hard work of pulling humanity from the brink of extinction.

Friday, April 11, 2014
The Tragic Quest for Education

> *S(he) who opens a school door, closes a prison.*
> **Victory Hugo**

Article 26 of the UN Universal Declaration of Human Rights states that *"education is a right."* While public education from K–12 is technically "free" in the United States, access to safe education of an acceptable "well-rounded" quality is essentially disappearing.

Article 26 also declares that: *"Technical and professional education shall be made generally available and higher education shall be equally accessible to all on the basis of merit."*

Of course many elementary, middle, and high schools are being closed due to budgetary concerns and, as I stated before, quality public education is hard to find and College and University in this nation are not even close to being "equally accessible."

Most nations around this world have free, or highly subsidized universities, even in that "evil" Cuba. However, even the public institutions in the USA are becoming increasingly over-priced. With good jobs that have fair wages and decent benefits also disappearing, many of our young people are forced to weigh the cost of education against whether it will be realistically "worth it."

I have a tale of two young Americans from the working-class who dreamed of obtaining a University degree.

The first was a young man who always felt great responsibility to "do the right thing." His parents sent him to Catholic School from K–8 and he was an Eagle Scout. After graduating in the middle of his class in high school he studied Theater Arts at a local community college for three years before he was able to complete his AA degree. He worked fulltime at a local department store and was active in his church whenever he had the time.

In his final semester of courses at the community college, a lying Army Recruiter preyed upon his trusting nature at a college "Job Fair." Long story short, the young man was promised a college education and he enlisted in the Army in 2000 and was murdered in the illegal and immoral war in Iraq in April of 2004.

Our other young working-class American is a woman who did well in high school and on her SATs, but her family couldn't afford to send her straight to university and she did not do well enough for many scholarships. She struggled in community college because she also had to work full-time as a food server to make ends meet. She matriculated to a university after spending about eight years in a community college and within four years of that, she completed not only her B., but obtained an MA as well.

The young lady did not join the military to do this, but she now has a lifelong debt of $50k. After all her hard work, what was her reward? She now works at two bars as a bartender. She jokes wryly, "I needed a Master's degree to tend bar in San Francisco."

Why is it that the children of the "99%" have to go into the military or onerous debt to obtain what most people/governments of the world consider a "human right?" A country that sends all its good jobs with decent pay and benefits overseas, and fails to properly educate all of its young people, cannot sustain itself for long.

The above examples come from my own family: My son Casey and my daughter Carly.

When I graduated from high school here in California in 1975, state colleges and university were free for residents. For an easy solution, this state needs to redirect some of the resources it uses to maintain a vast prison industrial complex and subsidies for big oil and other corporations back into education and other social services like housing, healthcare, healthy food, and clean water.

It's not only possible it's historically accurate and urgently needed.

CINDY NOTE: Obviously, the piece not only applies to California, but the rest of the nation, as well.

Monday, April 14, 2014
Break Co-dependency with Empire

Must the citizen ever for a moment, or in the least degree, resign his conscience to the legislator? Why has every wo(man) a conscience, then? I think that we should be wo(men) first, and subjects afterward. It is not desirable to cultivate a respect for the law, so much as for the right. The only obligation which I have a right to assume is to do at any time what I think right. It is truly enough said that a corporation has no conscience; but a corporation of conscientious wo(men) is a corporation with a conscience.
Law never made wo(men) a whit more just; and, by means of their respect for it, even the well-disposed are daily made the agents of injustice.
Henry David Thoreau, *Civil Disobedience*

When my children were young, my oldest Casey was 10, I transferred from Cerritos Community College in Norwalk to UCLA. Although I was familiar with the work of Henry David Thoreau, I was assigned *On Walden's Pond* and *Civil Disobedience* in one of my classes.

After devouring Thoreau's work, I tried to convince my husband to "cash out" and "check out" of the rat race. This was back in the "good ol' days" of the 80s. I didn't like what I saw of the corruption of government and the growing crass-consumerism and over-consumption of our society. I guess I have always been a starry-eyed idealist, but I cajoled my husband for days about moving to the woods with the children and creating some kind of paradise on earth. He resisted and here we are.

I think many people get trapped into accepting as normal corruption, war, oppression, poverty, pollution, debt/wage slavery, etc., that to try and wrest ourselves away from the disease of living in an Empire seems nigh onto impossible and it's all "fun and games" until your firstborn is killed in another immoral war for profit.

Casey was killed in Iraq on April 4, 2004. I was in a daze of shock, anger, disbelief, and pain when I jointly filed with my husband that year, but after I began to recover from the shock and confront the Empire, I had to first confront the role I had played in my own dear son's murder.

I had to admit to myself that my addiction to driving a car contributed to my son's death and destruction of the environment. I believe one of the primary goals of the US military is to protect and expand the interests of Big Oil. I would eventually dump the car and take to the streets on public transportation, my feet, or biking and come to the conclusion that saving the environment is obviously the most important issue.

To me, my biggest crime was funding the very institution that not only robbed me of Casey, but has murdered, tortured, displaced, or wounded millions of people throughout its bloody history. George Bush and Dick Cheney didn't invent Imperial-Wars-for-Profit-Based-on-Lies and the Bush regime wasn't the first, or the last, to employ those murderous tactics.

197

So, I searched my soul—but I didn't have to do it very long, or too hard, because I had been predisposed to withdrawing my funds and consent from the USG for quite some time—and publicly became a War Tax Resister. First it was about Casey, and next it was about everyone in harm's way of the Empire.

I could not, or would not, kill anyone myself, so I will not and cannot pay anyone else to do it.

I could not and would not torture anyone or anything, so, the same.

I cannot dump most of my budget into feeding the evil and voracious war machine while ignoring human needs of those who struggle to survive under the boot heel of the war economy.

If Barack Obama came up to me and said, "Cindy, can you write me a check for $5k to help me buy another hellfire missile?" I would say, "Hell no, take a hike," so why should I funnel my funds through the IRS to be disbursed to the Military Industrial Complex?

Now, I know the IRS has made it its mission to terrify and persecute the citizens of this country, but I had to do a few things to become a War Tax Resister.

First, I had to divest myself of anything the IRS could steal from me, which were basically my house and car. HD Thoreau convinced me decades ago that, "you don't own your things, your things own you," so that wasn't as hard as many fellow Americans would think.

We are all poor in respect to a thousand savage comforts, though surrounded by luxuries . . . for our houses are such unwieldy property that we are often imprisoned rather than housed in them.

Henry David Thoreau, *Walden*

"Simplify! Simplify! Simplify!" I had to live fully a precept from another Thoreau disciple: Mahatma Gandhi: "Live simply, so others may simply live." It is so liberating to cut the ties between oneself and ones possessions and return to the basics of what is really important: Family, friends, love, and joy. None of those things can be bought, and if they can, I don't want them.

Secondly, I had to come to terms with the fact that if I took this path, there could be a chance that I could go to prison. I don't want to go to prison and have spent enough nights in jail to know this for certainty, but I cannot live with myself free, or not, knowing that I was being financially co-dependent with a murderous entity like the US Government.

According to the National Priorities Project, my state of California sends $65 billion annually to the Feds for the so-called War on Terror since 9/11/2001. We have so many needs in this state that would produce a healthy economy, healthy environment, and healthy humans that we could use that money for, so I also do not pay state taxes.

Instead of supporting The Death State (thanks Arthur Silber), my money goes towards making a society where I would be honored and eager to pay taxes: one where peace, single-payer health care, education, housing, sustainable farming, and energy production, were fully funded, high-quality, and accessible for all.

Many times people will post pictures on social media of little children's mangled bodies that have been torn apart by hellfire missiles dropped from US drones in far off places; or of torture victims; or of police state violence here in the USA and say something like: "Your Tax Dollars at Work." My response is, "not mine." My conscience is clear in that regard, but for years my hands were bathed in blood and the stains are still there.

There are many ways to be a War Tax Resister, all or part. Please go to the War Tax Resistance Coordinating Committee's website for more information.

Stop funding things you oppose while simultaneously working for the things that will improve conditions for everyone on the planet: Peace, justice, environmental sustainability, and income justice and equality.

The US needs to calm the hell down.

Wednesday, May 21, 2014
Walk to Peace through Vacaville

There have been activists from Sacramento, Chico, and the Bay Area, protesting at Beale Air Force Base near Marysville, CA for a few years, now.

Beale AFB is home to the Global Hawk, a surveillance drone.

When Obama was first elected, the antiwar movement gave Obama a very undeserved respite, and although the activist energy against him and his policies is still relatively low, opposition to drone warfare increased in 2010 (probably after Cindy Sheehan's Soapbox held a protest at the CIA in January). Even though I am also adamantly opposed to manned bombing, at least there is concentrated and committed opposition to the escalating use of Unmanned Aerial Vehicles.

Some of the activists from the Beale protests began the Walk to Peace on May 17th at the Golden Gate Bridge and will end up at Beale AFB on May 27th after a 130 mile walk.

On May 20th, the Walk to Peace came through Vacaville, CA, my hometown.

Vacaville is situated amid rolling hills on the Interstate 80 corridor about 35 minutes west of Sacramento and about an hour north east of San Francisco. The Patwin tribal land was "given" to the original Spanish land grant families of the Vacas and Penas. White settlers grew fruit orchards and built Victorian mansions in town on Buck St.

The major industries of Vacaville are retail, prisons, and a nearby Air Force Base of our own: Travis. After I became well known for my antiwar activities, people here in town would honk at me to make sure I could see them flipping me off and, on two occasions, I was verbally assaulted while I was just out shopping. One of the columnists for *The Vacaville Reporter* collaborated on a book in 2005 to lie about me, but to also capitalize on my notoriety for her own profit (*American Mourning by Catherine Moy and Melanie Morgan*).

Imagine my surprise when I joined the Walk to Peace for five miles through town and we were shown nothing but support from passing motorists and pedestrians when we arrived at the picturesque downtown area.

Perhaps after 10 years of war and other devastation, my views aren't so far off-the-wall anymore?

Friday, June 6, 2014
Top Two and Democracy Destroyed

The primaries are over in California and there's good news and bad news.

The good news is that, as of this writing, almost 90,000 Californians voted for left-wing candidates (Luis Rodriguez, GP: 48,000; Me: 39, 000); but the VERY BAD news is that California had less than 20 percent voter turnout and the Top Two vote getters are both corporatist members of the establishment in every way.

The tragic news is that MANY Californians, who voted in the Top Two law in 2010, do not understand it. Top Two is what's called an "Open Primary" where party affiliation doesn't matter and each voter can cast a vote for any candidate, but only the Top Two vote getters in the primary move on to the general election in November. Already, voters are contacting me to tell me that they will be voting for me in November, even though I came in 7th and my campaign is over.

In 2010, Top Two was originally sold to the voters here in California as a way to weed out people that are at the extreme right or extreme left and we know what that means: it means anyone who has a vision for something different from the Corporate establishment and its theft of wealth and resources.

So, again in November EVERY office has either a Democrat or Republican to choose from and not one third party or independent candidate will be on anyone's ballot. This is contributing to the descent into a one-party state where even though the "centrists" are in charge, social services and education have been decimated while Brown's friends in Big Oil, Banks, and Private Prisons are being rewarded.

Neel Kashkari, the Republican who will be facing Brown in November, is an ex-Goldman Sachs executive who managed Obama's TARP (Troubled Assets Relief Program) and is just another member of the parasitic 1% class.

Of course, Democracy USA-style is only a myth, but at the beginning of the last century California led the nation in progressive reforms. The Top Two scam is the nail in the coffin unless we stand up to overturn it and support bills in the state legislature that will at least ameliorate the horrible effects. However, how can we change something that few really understand?

I am excited that I finished 7th in a slate of 15 candidates and the votes are still coming in. So far, I know that 39,085 Californians voted for an unashamed, unapologetic, radical socialist, peacenik and, to me, that's a good base to build upon to organize for the future.

Also, with the co-operation between my campaign and the campaigns of other Peace and Freedom and Green candidates, I believe an infrastructure has been put into place for a relevant Red-Green Alliance of disaffected people to wrest this state and world from the hands of the Corporate Oligarchy.

We the people must demand it because the urgency is now.

Cindy Sheehan for Cal Gov 2014 is deeply grateful to everyone who donated to the campaign, voted for me, or volunteered.

Venceremos! Hasta la victoria, siempre!

CINDY NOTE: I include this piece as a recap of election results and to further expose the "two" party fraud here in the US.

Sunday, June 15, 2014
Intended Consequences: The Imperial Meat Wagon Rolls On

I recently saw an article in the UK *Guardian* about how the global anti-Iraq War movement was correct about predicting that the US-led invasion and bloody occupation would lead to "chaos and instability."

Well, "duh." And, I hate to say this, but, of course, in the place wherever these invasions and bloody occupations are planned, whichever war criminal was in attendance, knew it good and damn well, too. How can a nation's natural resources be stolen and empire be spread if the population of a resource-rich nation is not divided? Ever heard the phrase, "divide and conquer?"

After many years and multiple exposés disproving the "reasons" and "justifications" for going into

Iraq, we know it wasn't because of WMD or 9/11 or anything about defending Americans or spreading freedom, right?

Now, as members of the anti-Iraq War movement "predicted" and the Empire intended, the violence in Iraq is continuing and, by all accounts, unfortunately escalating.

My son and thousands of other US troops were killed in the bloodiest part of the invasion and occupation starting in 2003, but millions of Iraqi have been slaughtered, injured, displaced, and made desperately ill by depleted uranium and other toxins and poisons delivered by the "freedom bringers" of the US military. I just want the US to get out of the war business so there can be peace abroad and peace and economic justice here at home.

No one should have to live under oppressive occupational forces, then to be "ruled" by a so-called elected government that is just a tool of US Imperialism.

No one should have to live in constant fear of being blown-up while doing things we here in the heart of the Empire take for granted (or used to): going to school, shopping, walking down the street.

The USA's allegiance to Empire and absolute devotion to war is hurting everyone, even the jingoists who loudly proclaim "support the troops," while vets are dying waiting to get health services from the VA.

Bottom-line—we should stop stoking the flames of Empire with the fuel of our own flesh and blood.

Recently, I was traveling by air and my next layover was in Las Vegas. A couple dozen youngsters were dressed in desert camouflage waiting to get on my plane with me to head to Las Vegas. They could have been your average American young person, except they were sporting the uniform of carnage. There was probably one reason per soldier for enlisting, but I am sure many of them were economic of nature: our young people have little or no opportunity in the Land of Constant War for the Gross Profit of a Few.

After landing in Las Vegas and taxiing to the gate, it was announced that these "heroes" were coming to the Las Vegas area to train and then "go off to war." The other passengers were asked to show our "appreciation" and the plane went wild with applause and cheers.

Was I the only one who wept?

NO MORE WAR in Iraq!

US troops home from everywhere.

PS: In 2003, in a speech protesting the imminent US invasion of Iraq, then Illinois State Senator Barack Obama called Iraq a "dumb war," a "rash war." My question is when will his Obama-trons finally admit that ALL WARS ARE DUMB, and Obama has been a complete success for the war machine and an able servant of Empire?

Hellory by Anthony Freda

Right after Camp Casey the huge media circus/protest in front of George Bush's ranch in Crawford, Texas in August of 2005, I was invited to the home of Producer/Director/Actor Rob Reiner to meet and have a chat. Also at that meeting was a major philanthropist (although I didn't know it at the time) to all causes Clinton, wealthy Stephen Bing.

I naïvely believed that I was there because Rob Reiner and Steve Bing were against war. HAH! I was there because Rob and Steve were, above all things (even peace and justice), pro-Democrat.

At this meeting, the suggestion was made to me that I should support the potential candidacy of then NY Senator Hillary Clinton for president in 2008. Bing looked me right in the eyes and said, "Senator Clinton is our only hope."

"Our only hope for what? Perpetual war?" I asked. I also reminded Steve and Rob that she not only voted for the war my son and hundreds of thousands of others were needlessly and tragically murdered in, but she proudly did grunt work for the Bush administration in being a chief-Democratic Cheerleader for it. After which, Bing looked me right in the eyes again and said, "Mrs. Clinton is against the war, and she will come out against it when it is politically advantageous to do so."

Well, even though I am not a multi-multi-millionaire with fancy homes and a private jet, I would not sell my soul to the Reiners or Bing to support a person who was/is so thoroughly opposed to everything I believe in.

My suspicions about Hillary Clinton were confirmed in a meeting I had with her on Capitol Hill about a month later where she said— after I told her that I didn't want my son's death honored with more murder and mayhem—that the US had to remain in Iraq to "honor" the sacrifices of those that had died

I suppose since Hillary is potentially running for POTUS in 2016, it has become "politically advantageous" for her to come out with "regret" for her vote, saying in her new book about her pro-war vote: "I wasn't alone in getting it wrong. But I got it wrong. Plain and simple."

Well, also "plain and simple," millions of people are dead, wounded, displaced, lives ruined. That she can be so glib about being a dumb shit while my son, and too many others, are dead forever really pisses me off.

With the Empire beating the drums for more war against Iraq, don't believe a word this shill for Wall Street and the War Machine says about her Iraq vote or anything else—ALL WAR IS WRONG and anyone who votes for it is a murderer, period!

As Secretary of State, Hillary cackled hysterically after a US bombardment of Libya, killing tens of thousands, and Moammar Qadafi was slaughtered in the streets: "We came; we saw; he died." (She's as psychopathic as the male warmongers).

I not only don't believe her "politically advantageous" admission, I don't believe she was fooled into voting the way she did. A lot of us never bought what the Bush administration was selling (SEE, White House Iraq Group) and we weren't in the Cat Bird's Seat in DC as she was. All of these people (Hillary included) should be in prison for life, not out raking in the big dough and running for public office.

Please do not mistake this exposé of Hillary Clinton, Two-Thousand and NEVER, as an endorsement of whatever shill will be nominated by the Republicans that year, it's not.

I am desperately disappointed that out of the ashes of Obama's havoc wreaking on the world, a new and principled antiwar movement has not arisen and that people like Bing and Reiner did not one day say, "Hey, I do care about the world more than I care about Democrats."

Sadly, what the hell will it take?

Tuesday, July 15, 2014
Bill Maher: Soapbox Hypocrite of the Month Award (Instituted specifically for him)

Bill Maher makes us physically ill.

The hypocrite gives Obama's PAC one million dollars in TWO-THOUSAND AND TWELVE and then accuses "liberals" of being "useless Obama hacks."

The saddest part though are the dummies on the right that are lifting Maher up as some kind of god for his "astute" commentary.

I have been almost completely ostracized for about seven years by people like Maher for confronting the Empire, and not just the Republican part of it.

Maher wins the **Soapbox Hypocrite of the Month** award.

Friday, September 19, 2014
World War Forever

A good friend of mine Jon Gold has taken to calling the US wars against the planet, "World War Forever." So, I'd like to thank him for the sadly relevant title of this piece.

Today, a friend of mine named Jacob George killed himself.

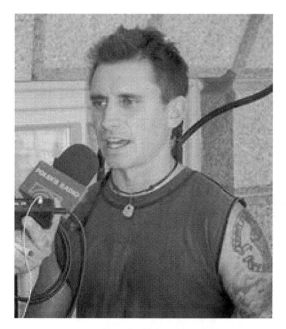

Jacob George

Jacob was a young vet who performed three tours of duty in Afghanistan and I met him last year when I was in the middle of riding my bike from California to Washington DC for Tour de Peace. We met Jacob in the middle of the country: Oklahoma City. I can't begin to say what the death of such a gentle and sweet human means. The loss is horrible and not just for Jacob's friends and family, but for all of us.

Not only is the Empire deadly to the people who live far away in foreign countries, but also to the people it recruits by dangling "benefits" to lure our young people into its bloody maw and then casually tossing them to the garbage pile when they are "lucky" enough to come home from the wars-for-profit.

I know many colleagues and friends, as well as myself, who are beyond frustrated and devastated with World War Forever, but I also used to be friends with and connected to far more people that are now saying they are "disappointed" in Obama. My question to these people is, "Just what the hell did you all expect would happen when you sat on your collective and hypocritical asses for over six years?" Where were these people when Obama sent more troops to Afghanistan, killed people in half a dozen countries with his damned drones, supported neo-Nazis in Ukraine, destroyed Libya, supported violent rebels in Syria (which many analysts say have "blossomed" into ISIS/ISIL), and all the other evil things the Peace Laureate has done during his tenure as Managing War Monger for the One Percent?

I am convinced these same people that are just NOW regaining consciousness will soon go back

204

into an ethics-coma and vigorously support the next Dem warmonger—those who would never have left the streets if a Republican were in the Oval Office.

I don't know which group of people gets under my skin more, the Google-challenged rightwing who constantly accuse ME of being a hypocrite for not "opposing Obama," or the ethically and morally challenged "liberals" who deserted the peace movement like the rats they are because they support Democrats over peace and justice.

I don't know what the solution is because I don't see anything changing as long as We the People keep allowing ourselves to be caught up into this never-ending death-cult spiral of partisan politics, which has led to the death-cult of World War Forever.

While you Republicans and Democrats are waiting for the perfect president (that doesn't exist) or the next Congressional Super Majority (that doesn't help), our young people like Jacob and our brothers and sisters around this planet are suffering.

How can you live with yourselves? ╱

CINDY NOTE: I think this is a good question to end the book with.

There's not much more to be said sliding into the 7th year of the Obama regime.

The next two years will be interesting to see how the 2014 Republican midterm landslide will affect discourse and how many bills Obama will actually veto. Or is this just another ploy in the repertoire of the 1% to get even more of their agenda moved forward?

Then, we will have the 2016 presidential race to face.

I predict it will be more of "Well, do you want Red Tie to win?" There will be no discussion on substance and the US will continue to descend into third world poverty for the many and ostentatious wealth for the few.

The question I ended the book with, obviously doesn't apply to you because you purchased it, but please, share it with a friend.

As I repeatedly point out, nothing will change as long as we on the proverbial left continue to play footsies with the Democratic Party.

About the Author

Cindy Sheehan is an internationally known peace and human rights activist who began her continuing struggle against the US Empire when her oldest child, Casey Sheehan, was killed in Iraq on April 4, 2004.

The Obama Files is Sheehan's 8th book and she is the author of hundreds of articles. She maintains a blog and podcast called *Cindy Sheehan's Soapbox.*

In her spare time Cindy loves being "Gigi" to five wonderful grandchildren who motivate her daily to try and "make the world a better place."